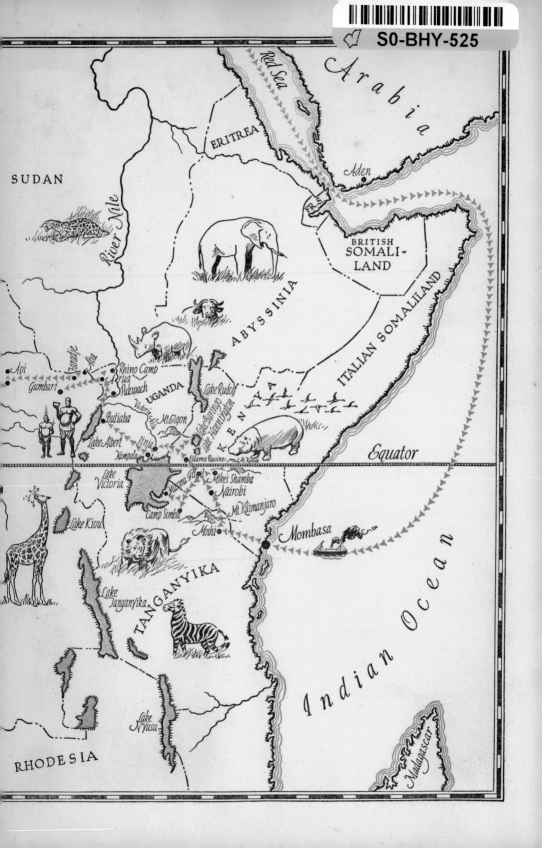

A lion family at home on the Serengetti Plains. From this ant hill a male watches the shifting game herds while his five lionesses patiently wait.

AFRICA SPEAKS

A STORY OF ADVENTURE

THE CHRONICLE OF THE FIRST TRANS-AFRICAN
JOURNEY BY MOTOR TRUCK FROM MOMBASA
ON THE INDIAN OCEAN TO LAGOS ON THE
ATLANTIC, THROUGH CENTRAL EQUATORIAL
AFRICA

BY

PAUL L. HOEFLER, F.R.G.S.

Active member, The Explorers Club, New York; Leader,
Colorado African Expedition, 1928-1929; Cinematographer,
Denver African Expedition, 1925-1926; Producer of the
sensational motion picture AFRICA SPEAKS

ILLUSTRATED
with a map and 143 reproductions from
photographs taken by the author

THE JOHN C. WINSTON COMPANY
Chicago   PHILADELPHIA   Toronto

Africa Speaks

To

MAUDIE B. HOEFLER

MY BELOVED WIFE, WHO, BY STAYING BEHIND
AND BELIEVING IN MY ULTIMATE TRIUMPH,
MADE THE UNDERTAKING POSSIBLE AND GAVE
ME THE COURAGE TO PRESS ONWARD, I DEDI-
CATE THIS BOOK.

EXPLANATORY FOREWORD

THIS is not a story of the picture, "Africa Speaks," but rather a chronicle of events; a record of strange peoples and wild beasts; a history of varied adventures, crowded into fourteen eventful months. The film story depicts life as it has existed in Africa for many centuries and as it still exists today, but it must, of necessity, in order to entertain, move swiftly to its climax. A book can swing along at a more leisurely pace, even allowing the author to pause now and then to paint a picture.

The material for the film, "Africa Speaks," was collected during the expedition's travels in Africa, but in editing a motion picture for the general public, it is essential to take a few liberties in order to construct a smooth-running continuity, and to build dramatic incidents. In the film, the course of the expedition moves from west to east, so that the lions and other exciting scenes woven around them can act as the climax of the production. There are very few lions on the West Coast and no tribesmen comparable to the Masai and Nandi. Otherwise it would have been possible to follow in the picture the actual route of the expedition just as it will be presented in this book; that is, east to west.

PAUL L. HOEFLER
Brown Palace Hotel
Denver, Colorado

TABLE OF CONTENTS

LIST OF ILLUSTRATIONS

PAGE

CHAPTER ONE

TWELVE THOUSAND MILES

ADVENTURE and romance still call from the past to all men and women! Africa offers in this twentieth century a journey backward into the neolithic period; turns back the hands of time, allowing modern man to walk side by side with stone-age men, who wrest their sustenance with bow and arrow or crude spear from the beasts that roam its vast expanse.

By day, from a canopy of azure blue, the fierce African sun sweeps its golden shafts over a stupendous solitude of veldt, penetrates into the deep recesses of mighty forests, glitters on tranquil waters, and burns deep into the sands of endless deserts. By night, the pale moon sails silently through the vault of a star-strewn sky, shedding its mellow beams on a savage world, where the cries of prowling beasts echo through a primal wilderness and primitive man crouches trembling in his grass hut or seeks refuge in tree or cave.

Africa, the oldest known, yet the least known, continent, has been called "the cradle of the human race." It nourished the spark of life when man was amphibious and sprawled, dumb and blind, through the slimy ooze on the edge of a Paleozoic lake. Eons came and fled before he stood upright to tread on the bosom of Mother Africa, where later he inscribed in crude picture language his triumphs and defeats. More eons passed and then glorious Egypt arose along the River

1

Nile, to live her brief day in the infinite cycle of time, recording her history in hieroglyphics for those who might follow.

Africa has also been called "the land of contrasts." In the north lie Morocco, Algeria, and Tunisia, and here once stood the proud mistress of the Mediterranean — ancient Carthage, the titanic, supreme for five hundred years! Here the picturesque people of the Great Desert — Arabs, Douars, Bedouins, and the Touaregs with their dyed flocks, mix in the narrow streets of romantic cities with Hindus and Turks, Marabouts in rags, and Amirs in silks. Tatooed Berber women jostle their way through this kaleidoscopic scene of restless color or stop at street corners to watch snake charmers and fire eaters, or to listen to story tellers. Here is a land of pilgrimage and pageantry, of barbaric splendor, where minarets rise above abandoned Christian ramparts, from which the muezzin calls the faithful to prayer at sunset, his cry of "Allah-hu-il-Allah! Allah Akbar!" echoing through the labyrinths below to mingle with the eerie wail of flutes, the throb of drums, the clinking of silver bangles, and the thump of the tambour.

Southward across the velvety carpet of golden sands, there are today regions practically unknown, and many places now marked on the map as explored remain as primitive to this very hour as they were centuries ago. There live tribes who burrow beneath the ground, arboreal people who share their tree huts with the monkeys, and clans who exist in caves. Beyond the equator and the boundless forest lie snow-capped mountains and reeking jungles side by side, and present flourishing commonwealths where sturdy settlers have hewed a path through the wilderness, building towns around which the virgin country is yielding up its richness.

In South Africa pioneers fought their way through hordes of fighting savages — the mighty Zulu and Matabele — in order to establish themselves in a promising land, there to worship God according to their own beliefs. Now these settlements are up-to-date cities, and the fruitful veldt of the Cape is covered with prosperous farms.

Colossal rivers, the Nile, Congo, Niger, and Zambezi, flow through the heart of the continent on their way to the oceans, and along their banks the villages of uncivilized man echo to the thump of tom-toms and drums, to the shouting of warriors and the chanting of women. Brutish crafts are practiced, bows and arrows are fashioned, spears are beaten from soft metal and decorated with ivory, and cunning witch doctors rule their fellows through superstitious fear.

Into this enchanting country I carried a motion-picture camera and typewriter to picture and record for those who stay at home, some of the fascination and thrill of this alluring but perilous continent. Before my eyes, the gentle antelope came to drink, immense herds of game pounded over the plains, millions of flamingos winged over a remote lake, the prehistoric elephant and rhinoceros ambled through the torrid heat, the strange disk-lipped women passed in parade, the little people of the great forest pranced to the rhythm of their drums, the lion stalked his prey, and the ebon warriors with spear and shield met the king of beasts in hand-to-claw combat!

My dreams in boyhood led me into the far places, and via the book route I traveled the world around.

It was this call to romance that led me into my present occupation. As Africa had always intrigued me more than any other place, it was natural that I should strive to prepare for my heart's desire; so I studied Africa for many years; its animal and bird life; its people and history, believing that some time an opportunity would come to visit this land of mystery.

In July, 1925, I left on my first African expedition, and during that eventful journey discovered that Africa is more fascinating, more colorful, more romantic than I had ever dreamed it could be. After my homecoming, only a few short months elapsed when the urge came over me to visit again that vast continent. The tropical and sleepy coast, against which beats the singing surf; the towering mountains, majestic and silent; the depths of the dark forests, mysterious and compelling, all shouted to me, "Return again." So I set about making plans for my second African journey, during which I was to be successful in accomplishing the first crossing of Central Equatorial Africa by motor truck from the Indian to the Atlantic Ocean.

Since returning from my last expedition I have been asked many thousands of times — what was my most dangerous encounter; if the natives are really savage; how hot it gets; are there many animals left; how I managed to talk to the different tribes, and other similar and different questions seemingly without end. Many people wanted to know the details of the locust swarm, how I got so close to the lions, what made the antelopes fly through the air like birds. Finally, in self-defense, I decided to write this book. I hope you like it. If you do, I may write another— Providence and my publisher permitting.

Paul L. Hoefler

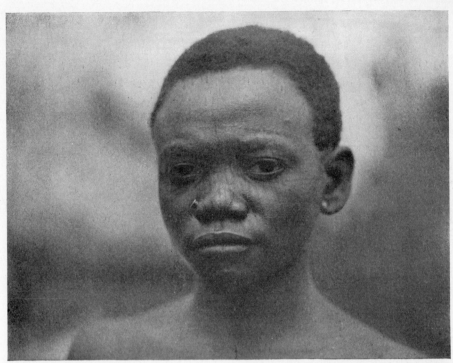

A typical young pygmy woman of the Ifi tribe. Notice the expended .22 shell in her nose and the face markings.

Masai El Moran.

Young Nandi woman.

AFRICAN TYPES

When, on the sunny afternoon of July 18, 1928, a conductor shouted "all aboard" and the "Columbine" glided out of the station at Denver, I was once again returning to this land where the Egyptians, Phœnicians, Sumerians, Cretans, and Romans builded kingdoms which then tumbled into dust, to be swallowed up by the seas of oblivion; I was again returning to hear the roar of the African lion sound through the dismal places where once proud cities stood, to watch the wild elephant follow down the trails over which had rolled thousands of chariot wheels; I was once again leaving a tearful wife and daughter waving farewell.

With my family were many true and loving friends who had come to say good-by. As they all faded into the distance, the realization came that several months would pass before I could see them again, and that during this period many things might happen to them and to me. These were not pleasant thoughts.

With me was a young man who had left Hollywood only five days before. Ahead of us were twelve thousand miles of land and sea, months beneath tropical skies, surrounded by men and beasts who were still beyond the rim of civilization. Austin knew Hollywood and pictures; he knew dogs and wild ducks, but dangerous animals and strange peoples were things only heard about or read of in books.

Days later that veteran of the seas, the "R. M. S. Mauretania," pulled away from her pier, amid the roars of the usual crowd bidding good-bys. Above all this din and commotion, the soprano voice of a large lady from the Bronx could be heard, yelling to "papa," and she continued to shout him instructions as to his conduct while in Europe until the gap be-

2

tween the ship and pier was too great for voice to bridge.
Then "papa" heaved a heavy sigh and made for
the bar.

The sky line of New York passed in parade for those
on deck as the huge ship headed seaward. The boat
sped on, the time flew by, then at about the time
everybody knew the others by sight, and we had
discovered that the two young men at our table were
German salesmen who had just completed a tour of
the United States, the ship nosed into her berth at
Southampton. There was the usual excitement, the
passing of customs, the looking at passports and the
saying of farewells to new-found friends. Our affairs
being in proper order, we were allowed to step on the
soil of Olde England, and shortly the boat train was
puffing and grunting on its way to London.

Most of the baggage was left at Southampton in
bond, as we planned to call at this port again en route
to Africa, and would thus avoid the thing most dreaded
by all travelers — having one's carefully packed lug-
gage flung all over the place by customs men with
prying eyes and large hands.

Upon arrival in London we were transported in one
of those ancient, high-backed taxicabs, which are
always a source of wonder to me — the wonder being
how they hold together. Our short stay was spent in
starting some official machinery into motion, for a
great deal of our work was to be done in British territory and the sooner they knew about it the better.
It rained all the time we were there, but I understand
that the sun does shine upon special occasions.

On a dreary day we were dragged by a sluggish
train over a misty and gloomy landscape from Victoria

station to Dover, at which place, amidst much confusion, we embarked on a Channel boat for the crossing to Ostend. The small boat was packed full to the rails, and I found it my fate to stand up the entire trip, which proved to be a rough one through a choppy sea, with plenty of flying spray and a nice cold wind.

The mad scramble to get off the boat at Ostend could be possible only in Flanders, France, or Italy. Small children in the crowd were nearly trampled under foot. Elbows were jabbed into our ribs and pet corns flattened out while we ran the gauntlet through the customs and raced for our train. Over Flanders fields and through towns made familiar to the world by the World War swayed the little string of cars, taking us to Brussels where I hoped to secure permits for some special work in the Belgian Congo. The Belgians are thrifty and hard-working and for this reason their poverty is hard to see. Well-kept fields of grain, beautiful orchards, small herds, neat looking houses, all bespoke contentment and hid the scars of many battles. Men on the train told of horrors here and battles there, pointing out this place and that. One asked me if I knew Mr. James Smith who lived in Chicago.

A kind old lady in our compartment insisted that we help her eat a box of sandwiches which she had brought along for the trip. Then she offered suggestions for a stopping place in Brussels. I told her we planned on staying at the Metropole, but she protested that the prices there were beyond all reason, telling us of a place where we could stay a week for what one day would cost at this high-priced hotel. We thanked her, but went to the Metropole just the same.

When I received the bill I could not help thinking
of the little old lady and her ideas of high prices, for
the two rooms cost us the enormous sum of two dollars
fifty cents a day!

Sometime in the past the Belgians won and still
hold the world's championship for "red tape," but
after calling on one prince and several ministers, I was
given a letter to the Governor General of the Belgian
Congo. The minister who presented it smiled and
shook hands, so I took for granted that everything was
all right.

At Antwerp we found our home for several weeks
waiting in the form of one ship of eight thousand eight
hundred tons, sailing under the name of "P. D. Adolph
Woermann"; home port, Hamburg; principal cargo,
steel rails and cold beer. We were delayed here one
day while they completed the loading of rails which
were being shipped to Portuguese East Africa. When
a German boat sails, they let the natives and the
entire countryside know that a great event is in progress. So at Antwerp we pulled away with a band
playing at full steam. Streamers were flung about,
and the whistle blew blast after blast until even these
staid old burghers stopped to see what was going on.

The trip down the river Schelde from Antwerp to
the open sea is one of beauty and interest, for as you
leave the city and wind your way down the torturous
channel many different views of the ancient place
present themselves, with the beautiful cathedral dominating the picture. As the river narrows toward
its mouth, it seemed as though the ship were sailing
in the air, for the fields on either side slope downwards—some places at least fifteen feet from the dikes—

Tangier, North Africa. A view looking down on the picturesque city and bay from the old fort.

Messrs. Manning and Hoefler beneath an archway of ivory at the old customs house, Mombasa. The men in uniform are police.

Dhows beneath the bluffs at old Mombasa. The large building is a former sultan's harem.

Many scenes of beauty, such as these, presented themselves as the party cruised around the Island of Mombasa.

and in the very narrow parts, you look down upon the roofs of houses. On the Holland side there are a few windmills as there should be; otherwise, it could not possibly be Holland. People shouted and waved from the shores and, after dark, lights blinked from many village lamps.

Into the English Channel again with the next port Southampton. Nothing of interest until nearing the Isle of Wight where the royal regatta was in progress at Cowes. The ship passed right through the center of things and gave us a fine view of the beautiful yachts striving for glories in this field of sport. There seemed to be thousands of these neat and trim craft all over the place — some standing by, while others with all sails spread were speeding to goal posts and back again. At Southampton I picked up the baggage which had been left in bond. We had a full passenger list, mostly Germans on a holiday who had embarked at Hamburg and were booked to Genoa. They were a fine lot of folk, but could speak very little English, so we were indeed glad when several Britishers came aboard.

Crossing the Bay of Biscay is sometimes a rough job, but this time the weather was perfect. The first night out I beheld one of the most beautiful sunsets which it has ever been my privilege to see. The sun itself was a big ball of golden fire, resting on the horizon and shooting multicolored rays of light through wonderful cloud formations. As I watched, it changed colors through every hue in the spectrum. In the foreground the smooth sea rippled just enough to sparkle with golden tints, mixed with mauve and blue, purple and green. It was truly a marvelous spectacle.

One fine afternoon the ship steamed up the Rio Tejo and made the port of Lisbon. From the sea and river, Lisbon presents an appealing picture. Boats with orange sails were dotted here and there on emerald waters which gently beat against earthen cliffs, back of which were dun-colored, low-rolling hills, topped by white buildings with red roofs. Everywhere golden sunlight, through which slow flying gulls winged their way toward an abandoned fort which stands near the wireless towers. We went ashore, landing at a stone wharf where the smell of fish assailed the nostrils while dazzling uniforms struck the eyes. There was a smell of age about the place as we went up the narrow streets, dodging two-wheeled carts, horses, and donkeys. Men in rags asked us for coins and we asked men in uniforms how to get to the main part of the town. They told us in Portuguese, which, of course, made everything perfectly clear. As we approached the center of things, tramcars and taxicabs, men and women beggars, swords and uniforms, dirty children, white-washed walls, steep hillside passageways, and statues to past glories all increased. When we entered the Esplanade I sat down on a bench for a short rest and had hardly done so when a man dressed like a street-car conductor came up to collect for the privilege of using the seat. This fellow spoke a little English and I found out that there had not been a revolution for several weeks — in fact there was nothing to look forward to in the way of excitement except the opening of the bull-fighting season in a few days.

The next time the anchor struck bottom our floating home was attached to the African continent, and we gazed from the deck on one of the most colorful spots

in the world, the international port of Tangier, North
Africa. A whole book could be written about the
historical past and the romantic present of this most
interesting place. We rode about the town on donkey
back, *à la tourist*, visiting such places as the old fort,
the sultan's palace, and the market place. The walk
back to the pier from atop the hill was a journey never
to be forgotten, for it would be impossible to find a
dirtier place under the sun than this part of Tangier.
Filth and stench both cried for attention, and I am sure
that no one failed to take note. Away from the smell
and dirt, the city presents a beautiful appearance of
white houses with tiled roofs and the people themselves
are of unusual interest, for here many races are mixed,
offering groups and types fit for any artist.

On account of leaving Tangier in the evening, we
passed through the Strait of Gibraltar during the
darkness of night, but went so close to the famous
rock that its outline could be seen plainly. Search-
lights played from the forts, sweeping the water in all
directions and now and then resting for a brief time
on our vessel. I was glad it was not a time of war, and
ours an enemy ship.

Upon awakening next morning and looking out of
the porthole, I discovered that we were anchored in
the harbor at Malaga, an attractive little city in
southern Spain, famous for its wines and cathedral.
A fellow passenger and myself wandered around the
town and tried our best to get into the cathedral, but
found it locked tight and no one about. The many
wine shops were open, however, and so samples were
taken on the spot, both of us pronouncing the product
up to specifications. Inquiries disclosed that the

best quality could be purchased for two dollars fifty
cents a gallon — best quality meaning anything over
twenty-two years old.   The town was being all decked
out in flags and bunting for the opening of the bull-
fighting season, which would commence on the following Sunday.

Once more our floating home went to sea and soon
we were steaming northward along the coast of Spain
between the Balearic Islands and Valencia, past Barce-
lona and into the Ligurian Sea.   We passed so close to
Cannes, Nice, Monte Carlo, Mentone, and San Remo
that they could be seen plainly from the deck, and
through glasses we watched the people on the beaches
and in the water.

Genoa offered the next haven, and we docked late
one afternoon.   From the bay the city is magnificent.
There are many things of beauty in the place.   I went
to gaze on the statue of Christopher Columbus and
while there bumped into a group of American tourists
in tow of a fat and excitable native who was pouring
forth a history of Genoa as the party trotted along at
an estimated speed of eight miles an hour.   I watched
them until they disappeared up a narrow street and
must confess I got a greater kick out of this than anything else in Genoa.

All of the German passengers left the boat here to
travel back to Germany via Switzerland.   We took
on many new voyagers in their places, and among
these was a man who changed the entire course of
my expedition.

I had been on deck making some photographs of
Stromboli, the active volcano, which ancients thought
was the entrance way to hell, when he strolled up to

discuss this marvel of nature with me, and later, while passing through the Strait of Messina, he came over to ask some questions about my equipment, In this way I became acquainted with Baron von Blixen Finecke, a Swedish nobleman who was returning to his farm in Tanganyika after having just completed one of the most thrilling journeys in the history of African adventure. With Sir Charles Markham he had crossed the dread wastes of the Sahara desert from Kano, Nigeria, to Algiers on the Mediterranean Sea.

During our many days on shipboard, after leaving the strait and before our arrival at Mombasa, the Baron and I studied all available maps, and from his vast knowledge of Africa, gained by years of residence on the Dark Continent, he gave me many items of information that afterwards proved priceless. Together we mapped a possible route across central Africa from one ocean to the other.

When I left the United States there were no plans to cross Africa included in the itinerary, and even during these discussions on the voyage to the East Coast, I came to no definite conclusion. Later, however, it seemed the logical thing to do, in order successfully to round out the work of the expedition.

Investigations proved that there was no record of a successful crossing from one ocean to the other. There had been one or two partial crossings, commencing from near the West Coast, and made with very light cars at the most favorable season of the year, but no one had ever attempted the journey from Mombasa westward to the Atlantic.

One bright day we saw far off in the heat haze the white tower of a lighthouse, and I knew that we were

approaching old Port Said, where real romance begins.
When the anchor slid down at the Mediterranean end
of the Suez Canal, I found that progress had even
invaded this place since my last visit. A new pontoon
arrangement was hauled to the ship's side so that we
could walk ashore and did not have to crowd into
little frail boats and argue with dirty boatmen as in
the past. I went uptown to visit the place where I
met the famous "gili-gili" man some years before;
then stopped in at the Simon Artz store.

We started the journey through the canal that same
evening, and when morning broke were in the land of
sand and camels for sure. Many of the barbed-wire
entanglements built during the war were still to be
seen, and the French pilot remarked that there had been
some real engagements fought among the sand dunes
bordering the canal.

The town of Suez may be an interesting place, but,
although I have been in the harbor three times, I have
never been ashore. An officer told me that there was no
logical reason for Suez, except that it held up one end
of the canal, and was the place beyond which, all poets
insisted, lay the lands of romance.

On the first day of the journey through the Red Sea,
we held a mass meeting around many glasses of cold
Pilsener beer and, by unanimous vote, it was rechris-
tened the "Red Hot Sea." Not a breath of air was
stirring, and everybody on shipboard suffered more
or less. It was almost beyond endurance — night
being just as hot as daytime. One of the lady passengers noticed a seaman pulling up a sample of water
and wanted to know the reason. He told her they
had to keep tab on the temperature of the sea as they

feared it would melt the bottom off the ship. This wasn't hard to believe, for the heat was like live steam, and everybody was going around with a cold drink in one hand and a towel in the other.

The Red Sea is hemmed in by deserts, on both the African and Arabian sides. It is only one hundred miles across at the widest part, and during the summer months there is a dead calm, the only movement being the leaping of heat waves from one desert to the other.

During the hottest period of the voyage somebody had a bright idea and, so, one night we had a formal dance. I thought my fat English friend would absolutely melt away, and one of the wits came out with a large mop and began following him about, but even this failed to discourage him. After I had melted my sixth collar I gave up, but he and several others carried on, as befits true lovers of the dance.

Like all things, good and bad, our five-day trip through this inferno of heat came to an official end as we passed through the Strait of Bab el Mandeb. At Aden a hotel with a high-sounding name advertises a "Genuine Mermaid on Show." We were not the first to pay our shilling to view this marvelous creature, and it would really be a shame to give the secret away. This combination hotel and curio shop also advertises itself as being "the oldest established and best European hotel in Aden." I can personally guarantee it to be the oldest, and after sampling one of its meals, decided that as there couldn't possibly be any worse, it must be the best. They handed us a leaflet listing a great variety of articles and calling our special attention to "chemicals, Turkish delight, Mocha coffee, and ostrich feathers."

The steamer's whistle gave the signal for "all aboard" and a short time later we were started on the last leg of the journey to Mombasa. As we rounded Cape Guardafui, called The Sleeping Lion, the breeze turned into a gale and was soon blowing the sea spray clear over the captain's bridge. Now some of those who had been complaining of the heat wished for the calm of that "Red Hot Sea," for they found it absolutely necessary to hide away in bunks down below until either the sea or their stomachs became somewhat settled.

Several interesting days passed as we glided down the eastern coast of Africa—days spent in swapping experiences and listening to unusual tales narrated by men on board who had lived many years on this vast continent. They told of strange people who did strange things; of women with lips as large as saucers; of people who wear iron armor; of naked tribes and dwarfs; of giants and people who look white; of men covered with hair like gorillas; of weird dances and savage methods of hunting. They pointed out districts on my map where game had never been disturbed; places where I would find enormous herds of elephants coming down to drink at unknown rivers; a spot deep in the forest where natives whispered of a mysterious animal called *Nya Gezi*.

At daybreak on September seventh, the ship entered the narrow channel which connects the Indian Ocean with Kilindini Harbor. I was on deck to gaze again on familiar scenes of palm-rimmed banks, with here and there a red-roofed cottage, and over yonder was the palace of Sheik Ali Ben Salim, who was to tell me a strange story.

Rear view of an Arab dhow bringing dates, Persian rugs, and spices into the harbor of old Mombasa.

The statue of Ferdinand de Lesseps, which stands at the Mediterranean end of the Suez Canal.

A bungalow on the Island of Mombasa. The odd-looking tower is supposed to be a watch or signal tower built by the early Portuguese.

Street scene in the old part of Mombasa. Another of the Portuguese towers. Mombasa has a long and exciting history and holds many relics of the past.

CHAPTER TWO

SHEIK ALI BEN SALIM

THE sheik is a kindly old man of about medium size, with gray hair and a large gray beard. He dresses in the spotless white robes and turban of the wealthy Arab. We sat down together in his office, in an old building facing the little square in Mombasa. When we walked up the corridors everyone had greeted and bowed to this genial sheik, for he is loved by all — Mohammedan and pagan, Protestant and Catholic. I do not know his age, but he is old, and for a long time has represented the Sultan of Zanzibar. He has made a study of the history of Mombasa Island and the adjacent mainland, and he spoke of some ruins which had been unearthed a short time ago.

In his very good English, he told me that Mombasa was founded about A.D. 975, was visited in A.D. 1328 by the Arabic geographer, Ibne Batuta, who described it as being "a large town, abounding with the banana, the lemon, and the citron . . . the people are religious, chaste, and honest and of peaceful habits." The old gentleman chuckled, saying that the people who lived here at the time might have been of peaceful habits, but that Mombasa had certainly had its share of war. It was originally known as Mvita — that being the Swahili word for *war* — because of the many battles waged here between rival nations which were trying to establish themselves along the coast.

The history of Mombasa is interwoven with that of
the entire East Coast and reaches far back into the
dim past. Somewhere about three thousand years ago
the mighty Bantu race was filtering into the unknown
interior of the continent, and at about that time the
ancient Phœnicians landed along the north coast,
founding Carthage. Before the Romans razed Carthage in 146 B.C. and later destroyed or absorbed the
Phœnicians into the Roman race, these ancient people,
or a kindred Semitic people, had left their mark in
northern Africa and in Egypt, and to this day their
descendants are the dominant race in Abyssinia.

The old Portuguese Fort of Jesus dominates Mombasa town and harbor, and from it still flies the red
flag of Seyyid Khalifa Bin Harub, Sultan of Zanzibar,
for a strip of land ten miles in width, from the sea
inland, is still under the suzerainty of the sultan. The
fort now serves as a prison and signal station, and it
is from here at midday that a cannon is fired to set the
correct time. Old Portuguese inscriptions and a
colored bas-relief of the Virgin and Child can still be
seen on the crumbling walls. Many of the ancient
guns still point silently seaward, never to speak again.

The Arabs practically controlled all of East Africa
until, in the fifteenth century, the Portuguese rounded
the Cape of Good Hope and Vasco de Gama anchored
at Mombasa in April of 1498. This gallant navigator
lost no time in securing a foothold for his countrymen.
Seven years later Sofala and Mombasa were captured.
Another four years found the Portuguese building a
capital at Malindi to rule over the new Province of
Ethiopia, which extended from near the present bound-
ary of Italian Somaliland to Sofala, south of Beira.

For some three hundred years thereafter, the Portuguese had a constant struggle, with fluctuating fortunes, to hold their possessions against attacks from the sea by Arab pirates and Turkish corsairs and from the interior by fierce native tribes. The Turks were successful in capturing the Portuguese settlements in 1585, only to be driven out again four years afterwards at about the period when flags of the English and Dutch appeared for the first time in the Indian Ocean.

In 1696 the Arabs under the Imaum of Muscat beseiged the fort at Mombasa, the Portuguese managing, however, to repel all assaults for over eighteen months of continuous warfare, at which time reinforcements arrived. These gave them only a brief respite, for the Arabs redoubled their efforts and, after a further blockade of fifteen months, the Portuguese, being unable to renew their supplies, were compelled by famine and disease to surrender, and the remaining members of this heroic garrison were put to the sword by the conquerors.

For over half a century after the final expulsion of the Portuguese, most of the East Coast came under the control of the Imaums of Muscat, whose viceroys reigned in Zanzibar. The slave trade was now ravaging the continent of Africa and the terrible cruelties committed under the rule of the viceroys attracted attention in Europe.

During the early part of the year 1824, the Arabs voluntarily placed Mombasa Island, the Island of Pemba, and the country reaching from Malindi to Pagani under the protection of the British flag, and later, in the year 1887, Sheik Sayyid Bargash, then Sultan of Zanzibar, granted to what the following year became the Imperial British East African Company, a fifty-year concession of his mainland possessions between the Umba River and Kipini.

After the sheik had finished relating this brief history of Mombasa, I inquired if it would be possible to stage some shark-fishing scenes with the natives in their Arab dhows. He was afraid it was the wrong time of the year and intimated that the best place to get this material would be around Zanzibar.

He was there twelve years ago when an enormous flatfish was caught, of a species never before known. Upon its sides were patterned Arabic characters, and the fishermen in reverent awe had brought it to the wise men of the town, who interpreted the message as a direct command from Heaven, for upon the stranger from the deep was written "You must trust in Allah."

I had often heard the natives speak of mermaids, while the fishermen around Mombasa assured me that they had seen beautiful women who lived in the water along the coast. Ali Ben Salim now confirmed my opinion that these comely ladies belonged to the same class of sea nymphs as the mermaid at Aden, which was nothing else but a dugong, an aquatic herbivorous mammal of the order Sirenia and allied to the manatee. They are found in the Red Sea, Indian Ocean, around the East Indies, and about Australia, and are considered a great table delicacy by some peoples. We talked some more of present and ancient things, and then, after a handshake, I went to take up my post at the shop of Ramji Thakershi.

Upon the recommendation of my good friend Mr. J. Doherty, Government Coastal Agent, I hired this Ramji Thakershi, an Indian fundi, or workman, to

The old Portuguese Fort of Jesus, Mombasa, from the harbor. The Sultan's flag flies over the prison. This fort has been the scene of many battles for the control of the East Coast.

There are only a few camels on Mombasa. These are used for the grinding of grain and for the extraction of oil.

Looking across Kilindini Harbor to the palm-fringed mainland of Africa, from the Mombasa fish market.

Mombasa. The unloading and loading of ships is carried on in primitive fashion at the old port.

build the bodies on my two Rugby chassis. After much dickering over the price and much explaining of what I wanted, the deal had been set and operations were supposed to start the next morning. The next day I was busy and did not get around to the shop, which in this case was the shade furnished by a large pepper tree. On the following morning when I arrived on the scene and found that nothing had been started, I was plenty mad. Ramji was not a bit perturbed; he simply smiled and shrugging his shoulders said, "It is the will of Allah" that the beams for the chassis had not been delivered.

After two or three days of dilly-dallying by Ramji, I had my boy bring a comfortable chair and took up a station near the shop, where I spent most of my time supervising the job. It was well that I did, for by insisting upon large nails where they intended to put small ones and upon angle irons where they were needed, I was able to save myself a lot of grief later on. As it was, the finished product was anything but beautiful; however, the bodies did hold together during our trying journey, which is more than they would have done otherwise.

Ramji was always finding new reasons to add on a few shillings, but I made him stick to the original agreement, in spite of his constant crying that he was losing money. He had four carpenters working on these bodies whom he paid two dollars a day for ten hours of work. Then there was the toto who did the odd jobs for the magnificent sum of twenty-five cents a day. I'm afraid that Ramji was like a lot of others in East Africa. He thought that every American was fit game with no closed seasons.

3

A great deal of the native life of Mombasa passed before my observation post. Off to my left was the main crossing of the town, where stood the native traffic policeman in his neat uniform and bare feet. By his gestures and mighty blowing of the whistle, I gathered that he felt himself as important as any officer of the traffic squad wherever found. Negroes from the mainland, naked except for a loin cloth, would stop to gaze, while the city boys who sported around in the familiar kanzu, which looks like a nightshirt, would simply take a glance, tip their red fez to me and pass on. Others with white skullcaps would not even stop because they had attained to a high plane, being servants in the houses of white men. Smart police boys, trim soldiers, Arabs, Indians, Goanese, native women, both fat and slim, tall and short, little naked boys, and girls not quite so naked, all passed before me through the bright sunlight, like actors on a brilliantly lighted stage. It was sometimes hard to realize that this was all fact and not fancy, but when I looked at the slowly moving Indian workmen who were eating up my time, I realized it was not a dream but a horrible fact!

Meanwhile Baron von Blixen had been looking forward to the day when his imaginary safari car would become a reality. He had given its design long thought and study, and upon arrival at Mombasa had purchased a Chevrolet chassis which he drove to the shop of an Indian fundi, to whom he gave instructions for the building of his brain child. Now he came to me and quite proudly described this marvelous body which was being constructed. I had my doubts about the result but thought maybe he had found a better fundi than mine. As he was taking his wife and nephew to Moshi the next day, I promised to accept delivery on the car, hire a native driver, and bring this revolutionary contraption along to Moshi as part of my motor caravan.

Mr. A. C. Manning, who might be termed Chief of the Revenue Cutter Service of East Africa, took us on a marvelous ride around the tropical island of Mombasa. We made the trip in the thirty-six foot launch which Manning uses to patrol the coast for some two hundred miles north and seventy miles south during the dhow season, when the Arabs and Persians run down on the northeast monsoon from the Persian Gulf to trade along the coast, bringing pottery, dried fish, carpets, rock salt, and dates. In this small boat he visits many subports and keeps a lookout for smuggling.

One of his subports was the ancient town of Kilwa, which he told us was, at one time, a Persian settlement of some importance, and it would be well worth our while to visit this place and also Lamu, where it was still possible to pick up many relics; also remnants of Chinese ware called *Lamu china*. He explained that during the twelfth century there was quite an extensive trade between this coast, China, and Malabar.

Manning took us down to the old fish market, a colorful but smelly place where I found a great variety displayed on the long tables. There were sharks, swordfish, rays, angel fish, sardines, bonito, crayfish, mullets, barracuda, crabs, and a large fish looking like a red snapper.

A little below the market they were selling dried shark and barracuda, Lamu baskets, and old hides by auction. We found these things and big baskets of dates piled up together, with an old black hen and several chickens making the most of the opportunity. The hen was quite excited; she couldn't decide which she liked best, the shark or the dates, while she seemed to be fascinated by the eyes of the barracuda. While she stood there clucking, scratching, and picking, an old Arab rushed up and with much spluttering and waving of arms shooed her away.

At the edge of the water several native dhows were resting in the mud while a string of husky porters carried large blocks of coral ashore. Each load weighed from eighty to one hundred pounds. With these on top of their heads they would stalk through the mud and make their way up the steep embankment where the coral was loaded on donkeys to be distributed throughout the island. Most of the building on Mombasa Island is done with coral blocks.

As a guest of Mr. Doherty and his good wife, we were driven about the island in their Austin; down through the native bazaar where Hindu and Arab owners sat cross-legged in long rows of little stalls, surrounded by their wares. Ready to their hands was one of those ancient balancing scales, pictured being held by Justice. They sold a penny's worth of ground corn, of betel nuts, salt, tea, rice, shredded coconut, sugar, tobacco, and dried shark. Small bottles contained lion oil and ghee. Hucksters mingled with the crowds crying their wares — fried fish, African doughnuts, greasy looking cakes of all sizes and descriptions.

Boys in flowing kanzus; turbaned Arabs; hawk-faced Persians in silken robes carrying jeweled daggers; seamen from the dhows, cruel, rough-looking men who might have stepped out of the Arabian Nights;

tall, graceful Somalis; squat, thick Negroes; semicivilized blacks from the mainland; young women with babies strapped on their backs; old women carrying wood on their backs; men balancing five-gallon petrol tins full of water on two ends of a stick, all mingled together in a colorful pageantry through the narrow streets of the bazaar. Parrots and monkeys mixed their squawks and cries with the jabbering of the multitude, and close to the statue erected in memory of those who had fallen in the World War was being held a n'goma m'kuba, or big dance.

I took a picture of this monument and found that the inscription was by Kipling and written in four languages: English, Arabic, Hindustan, and Swahili. The mother of an Arab rifleman had raised an awful rumpus when she saw the statue, accusing the white man of killing her son and turning him into stone.

On the opposite side of the island from the town are beautiful coconut groves, thousands of marvelously straight trees bearing abundant fruit. They use the same system of ownership here as in Zanzibar where the land belongs to no one, but rather the individual trees, each of which is branded with the owner's mark, and the wealth of a man is reckoned by the number of coconut trees he owns.

It is a pleasure to motor over these wide coral roads through the dark green groves of graceful trees, for there is a lure about the palm which is hard to define. We found the natives husking coconuts and, when we stopped, they would offer us delicious coconut pulp and cool drinks of coconut water. On one tip of the island we found some thatched huts with several old camels tethered near by. These are used for motive power just as they were by the ancient Egyptians. They walk all day in a circle around a center pole, the power thus developed being used for the grinding of grain and expressing of oil.

The town of Mombasa itself is a curious mixture of Arab, Portuguese, and modern English buildings, churches, mosques, and cathedrals. On a Sunday those riding home from the impressive ceremony of the Church of England or from Mass in the Catholic cathedral must pass where the faithful of Mohammed are kneeling, row upon row, in the dim interior of a mosque, bowing and praying to Allah.

Narrow, crooked streets with high, iron-barred stone houses, overhead passageways across narrow alleys, mysterious balconies, and quaint, towering observation shafts built by the Portuguese are found in the older quarters, while in the new part of town are wide roads, with fresh, airy bungalows set in open gardens, elaborate houses built by the government for its officials, cricket and bowling greens, golf links, and a country club.

We stopped at the club toward evening for a sundowner, which was served to us at little tables set under the sky, by white-gowned black boys who silently stole about in their bare feet. As it grew dusk, a gentle and cooling breeze came in from the sea, and at this best time of all the day we strolled over to the lighthouse near the point to look out over the heaving expanse of the Indian Ocean. We watched as the last rays of the sun played in constantly changing colors on the face of the rippling waters, then turned to look upon the waving coconut groves and beyond to the distant hills of Shimba.

Several days later I met Jaffer Dewjee, called Jaffer
the Ancient, and he kindly showed me through his
most unique museum.   Here I looked upon a marvelous Persian rug over four hundred years old which
had belonged to King Shah Abas.   There was a hawk
of ancient carving which represented the god Horus
of Egypt. It had lain buried for three thousand two
hundred twenty-eight years in the tomb of Pharaoh
Seti I, King of Upper and Lower Egypt.   There were
rubies, emeralds, and turquoise over five hundred years
old; and here was an ornament of gold, inlaid with
over one thousand precious stones, that had belonged
to a prince of India.

Wonderful china, brass work, porcelain, hammered
copper, ivory, Oriental rugs, vases, cut-metal designs,
old Lamu chairs inlaid with ivory and native wood,
silver nails, and ancient coins were displayed around
the room.   Jaffer showed me amber which he said was
over two thousand years old.   It was full of bugs, and
he explained that amber was tree gum which had been
buried underground for long periods of time.   He had
twelve pieces of porcelain from the door of a Persian
tomb, and when I marveled at its still brilliant coloring, he told me that the Lamu people had built porcelain into their walls and arches, and although it had
been exposed to the elements for centuries, it had
never lost its brilliance.   There were wonders without
end in this museum of Jaffer's.

Now he shouted to his servants, and soon a boy
fetched me an old book while another came in bearing
a tray with tea. We sat down on a divan among all
these rare curios, and while we sipped the cup that
cheers, I glanced out of the open window across Kilin-

dini Harbor to the mainland. The sun was intensely bright, and it was a rest for my eyes to gaze on the long line of swaying palms which fringed the farther banks. I was looking westward, visualizing familiar scenes on the highlands of Kenya, on the vast expanse of veldt in Tanganyika where roamed immense herds of graceful antelope. I could see, as on a screen, the galloping herds of zebra and wildebeest raising clouds of dust into the air; the gentle giraffe looking down from his great height on the passing caravan. I was in memory crossing the Stony Athi and experiencing my first rhino encounter. Beyond this I again could see the beautiful hills around Sienna and wondered if the lions still roared there each night. Now that I had made up my mind to push on to the West Coast through the very heart of this continent, I pondered what the deep forests and the unfamiliar trails held for me in the way of adventure. These thoughts made me impatient to get started, but there were many things yet to do in Mombasa.

I had received a telegram from Mike Cottar, my friend and companion on a previous safari, and had wired him to join me at Mombasa. Now on the morning of September twenty-third, he stepped off the train with a smile on his face, a bright red shirt on his back, a rifle over his shoulder, and a five-gallon hat on his head. He was the same Mike I had left in Nairobi two and one half years before. We were undertaking a hazardous adventure. The coming months would be filled with hardships and dangers, among wild animals and wild men, but, because of Mike's knowledge and promised assistance, I felt assured of success and looked into the future with anticipation and confidence.

CHAPTER THREE

HORNS AND THORNS

AN old book presented me by Jaffer contained many interesting, and some amusing, experiences connected with the early history of the East Coast. A description was given of the elaborate preparations made by a German captain who hoped to cross Africa from east to west by motor car. The time was about 1904, and he started with great ado from Dar es Salam. The report then goes on to say that he traveled "some forty miles westward, overcoming great difficulties" until "all four cylinders on the motor broke down." It seems that this major calamity put an end to the expedition, nor could I find any record of further attempts to cross from east to west.

Early on the morning of September 26, 1928, the members of the Colorado African Expedition met in the little dining room of the Palace Hotel, Mombasa, for an early breakfast. On this day we planned at last to push off "into the blue," this being a phrase commonly used in East Africa to signify "the remote and wild places." There had been many last-minute preparations, including the hiring of two black boys. Mike had insisted that none of the boys from the coast were worth having on safari, so we were managing with these two until reaching Nairobi.

We had also hired a driver for the Baron's new truck and had given him instructions to bring it to the court-

yard back of the hotel this morning. Now we stepped
out through the rear door to where our two trucks were
parked. They looked quite neat and trim, but maybe
that was because we had nothing to compare them to.
As we gazed upon them, with a certain amount of
pride, we heard the roar of another motor, and amid a
blinding cloud of dust, up sped the new driver in
Blixen's dream child.

There it stood like a grotesque cartoon; out of joint,
out of plumb, with no resemblance to the marvelous
veldt cruiser so proudly described to me by the Baron.
Mike strolled up to the thing as I have often seen him
do when approaching a rhino. After one long look he
said seriously, "Don't think it will hold together as
far as Moshi, but we'll put a few more nails into it
before we start and hope for the best." Then he sent
a boy after the man responsible for this dream which
turned out to be a nightmare, with instructions to
bring back nails, hammer, and wire.

We completed loading our two trucks with all the
miscellaneous equipment, films, and cameras, then
drove around to a garage where the Vacuum Oil Company had arranged for us to load up with gasoline and
Mobiloil. This company had undertaken the tremendous task of supplying these necessary items
throughout the course of the expedition. To lay down
supplies across central Africa from one coast to the
other, it would be necessary to send gasoline and oil
to predetermined points, some up the Congo River
and then into the interior by dugout canoes, some by
camelback into the sand country near the Sahara,
and some on the heads of porters into the swamp and
bush country. The difficulties were even greater than

we apprehended and how well they succeeded will be disclosed as the story of the expedition progresses.

We were joined at the garage by Blixen's body builder who didn't seem a bit upset upon finding out what we thought of his ability. Under Mike's direction, he drove a few dozen nails here and there and twisted a few yards of wire at other points. Then with a parting benediction, which just fell a little bit short although he does have long legs, Mike sent this particular fundi back to his spreading mango tree.

Now we were joined by our good friends Mr. and Mrs. Doherty and Mr. Manning who accompanied us to the ferry which was to carry us across to the mainland. From there my first objective was Moshi, which lies in the shadow of Africa's majestic mountain, the mighty Kilimanjaro that towers nineteen thousand eight hundred nineteen feet into the ever blue heavens of Tanganyika.

A steep road runs down to this crude native affair, which, however, is powered by one of those "put-put" motors. There was considerable excitement while the trucks were being eased aboard, and several dozen natives, assorted as to degrees of color and nakedness, clambered on to the rickety contraption and draped themselves around, wherever they could find a place. I gave the signal to go ahead, but nothing happened. Excessive weight had us anchored fast to the shore. It was necessary to cut down our passenger list, and we accomplished this by getting all the huskies behind the ferry to give a big shove. We then got under way in a hurry and only half a dozen of the most agile were able to scramble aboard; the disappointed passengers joining our three white friends in waving us good-by.

In due course of time we crossed Kilindini channel;
Kilindini being a Swahili word meaning "deep water."
When we ran off the ferry, the rear wheels dipped into
the warm waters of the Indian Ocean, then the front
ones touched the dusty road and headed westward
toward the distant Atlantic, where it rolls in white-
capped surges across the Gulf of Guinea, to break
against the silent palm-lined shores of the Slave Coast.

On the first day we climbed from sea level up to the
high plateau, leaving behind the damp heat of the
tropical coastal region, and entered into a vast plain
where still roam immense herds of game.　Here in a
landscape of flat-topped mimosa trees and huge ant
hills, with distant mountains just visible through the
heat haze, live the great and small animals of Africa,
the graceful antelopes and those queer beasts left over
from past ages.　This is a country of heart's desire to
all those men who love God's great wild places.

Many giraffes raced with us along the road, or stood
at what they thought a safe distance and gazed in
popeyed wonder as we passed.　Herds of wildebeest,
kongoni, zebra, and tommies kicked dust into our faces
or stood at attention to see us by, while thousands of
small animals and game birds were continually scat-
tering away from the roaring trucks.

In the mountains that rimmed the horizon lived
herds of elephants, while in the thorn thickets at the
mountain bases the black rhinoceros browsed on the
tender leaves or stood dozing in the shade.　Here the
days are dry and hot from a sun that burns in a clear
sky, and the nights are cold under bright stars that
wink just over your head.　When the first stars appear,
a strange hush comes over the veldt, then an uneasy

stirring, and when the gentle breezes have brushed away the lingering waves of heat, the lords of the night come forth from their cool lairs in the dongas to hunt and kill.

Eyes that come and go in the camp fire's glare, the smell of coffee, of frying buck liver and bacon, the deep-throated roar of the lion, the coughing of leopards, the yapping of jackals, and the mournful laughing cry of the hyena — these are the things that spell the romance of an African night.

On the second day we stopped for lunch at Voi, where quite a good meal was served by the Indian station master. When we returned to our trucks we found that one of our two boys was missing, and inquiry disclosed that he had gone off to a native village near by. We made a search, but after wasting nearly two hours proceeded without him. When you hire a native in East Africa it is necessary to sign his kipande, or certificate, which gives his name, his father's name, his tribe, his thumb print, and his registration number. A record of all these boys is kept by the Labour Section, Department of Native Affairs, in Nairobi. When a boy who has not been signed off by his last employer, is picked up by the police, he is held in jail until they get in touch with his last master and find out the reason. Any boy leaving his master while in good standing is signed off, and when a boy's kipande does not show this, it indicates that he may have committed a crime. About three months later I received this telegram from the police at Moshi: "Have one boy named Titos in jail. Says he is your boy and was deserted at Voi. Please advise." To which I replied, "Boy Titos left safari without permission to visit

village near Voi and could not be located.   Advise
keeping him in jail."

After rounding the Teita Hills we bore toward Kilimanjaro.   Toward evening, after we had passed Ta-
veta, a small herd of the rare gerenuk stood like stone
images as we approached and then fled panic-stricken
into thick bush.   A stationary bull giraffe was mistaken
in the gloaming for a dead tree by the tenderfoot of
the party until it suddenly came to life as he almost
drove the truck under its arched neck.

This same young man had the first thrilling experience of the safari.   It happened this night as we were
motoring toward Moshi.   The country was fairly pop-
ulated with lions and this was the time for them be to
getting about, but as Mike and I had been through
here before, we never gave lions a thought and were
pushing on ahead in order to reach an old camping
place near a small stream.

The headlights of the second truck told that the
tenderfoot was following all right until we got into a
stony country covered with bunches of wild sisal and
thorn thickets.   Here it was necessary to twist and
turn a great deal, and we could not see his lights for
any distance but felt that he would be right behind the
dust cloud, so continued on until a long straight place
was reached, when we found that the second truck
was missing.

As he was a poor driver and was in a strange country
we thought he was just a little bit slow, so waited half
an hour, putting in the time watching a small herd of
antelope which could be seen in the moonlight around a
tiny water hole.   When he failed to show up, we
became a little bit uneasy and decided to return and

find out what was delaying him.   About three miles back we found him standing in the middle of the road with a rifle in his hands and the following story to tell:

He had been driving serenely along when suddenly the only other occupant of the truck, our surviving black boy from Mombasa, shouted in Swahili, "Simba, bwana, Simba!" The words meant nothing to this embryonic explorer but the boy's actions did, so he slowed down to see what the excitement was about, and glancing down beside the truck beheld a big male lion crouched almost within arm's reach.   He stepped heavily on the gas, choking the carburetor, and, after going about three hundred yards, the truck stopped. The boy immediately shoved a rifle into his hands, put down the side curtains of the cab, and pulled out his knife, shouting all the time for the master to shoot.   He had never before held a heavy rifle, had no idea of how it worked or if it was loaded, so he sat there wondering what would happen, while the boy bounced about in a panic, finally climbing on top of the cab.   The tenderfoot had then climbed out and stood in the glare of the headlights, where we found him, all hot and bothered!

On the next day we arrived at Moshi about ten o'clock in the morning.   As we drove up to the little hotel we beheld the Baron and his nephew coming out to greet us, while the Baroness stood on the porch waving a welcome.   As, with a smile on his face, he came up to our trucks, I noticed that he was anxiously gazing about and knew he was wondering about his truck.   We jumped out and, after greetings and handshakes, I told him not to worry, that his safari cruiser was bringing up the rear and was due most any

moment. While we were speaking we heard the unmis-
takable roar and rattle that had become an integral
part of this remarkable outfit. The Baron gazed
toward it and, when it drew up alongside and stopped,
he took a quick glance and then turning to me queried
hopefully, "This is not it?" For a few seconds no one
spoke, then fixing my gaze on the radiator cap I broke
the sad news: "Baron, I take great pleasure in presenting the result of your marvelous plans as interpreted and carried into being by the Indian fundi in
Mombasa." He took another look, gulped a couple
of times, and then turning around to us, said, "Boys,
let's have a drink."

After luncheon and good-bys we took the route between the two peaks of Meru and Kilimanjaro and
made our evening camp at Longido. Some of the most
marvelous scenery in the world was ours to enjoy this
day, for from our camp of the morning until that of
the night, we were always close under the snow-capped
peak of Africa's greatest mountain.

This giant that sleeps under the equator is quite
different from any other of the world's great mountains. Its snowy peak is no sharp point, but rather a
long, bare ridge, over which the white mantle is draped,
extending downwards many thousands of feet toward
the timber line. Many of the rare African animals
live on its slopes, and it is still a favorite haunt of
the elephant. From its eternal snows many cool, clear
streams rush into the thirsty lands below.

Longido's hills saw some of the hottest fighting
during the East African campaign of the World War,
but the crack of rifle fire has long ago died away and
the hills again belong to their ancient inhabitants, the

Official start of the Colorado African Expedition from Mombasa.   This native ferry carried it to the mainland.

Mr. and Mrs. J. Doherty and Hoefler beneath a giant baobab on the Island of Mombasa.

En route from Voi to Moshi. Giraffes on the slopes of Mount Kilimanjaro. Notice the large ant hill in the center of the picture.

lions and leopards. These rocky outcroppings are isolated in a plain upon which thousands of animals roam, and, being covered with densely grown dongas, offer an ideal retreat to the great yellow cats and their spotted cousins.

The camp was located in a delightful spot close to good water. We had killed a buck during the day and after feasting on some of the meat, canned beans, crackers, and tea, had put our blankets on the ground in preparation for a night's rest. Our black boy was not experienced in safari life, never having before been far from Mombasa Island, which meant that he knew little about the dangerous game. So when some leopards began to cough close at hand he insisted on moving his bed as close to ours as possible, whereupon Mike told him to carry the rest of the antelope a hundred yards or so away from camp, that the leopards might feed on it and not bother us. The boy stood petrified for a moment, then wanted to know if the leopards would attack him while he was carrying the meat out. Mike told him not to worry, that they preferred good antelope meat any time to a tough punda (donkey) like him.

During the night we heard many lions about, while the leopards seemed to be all over the place, coming close to the fire in order to have a good look at us. Their peculiar coughing got on my nerves, for I have no liking for these savage little brutes, and would much rather have lions prowling around. Just before going to sleep I noticed the boy from Mombasa huddled over the fire, but when we awoke next morning we found him sleeping in one of the cabs with all the side curtains fastened up.

4

Shortly after leaving camp we came to the customs
station on the border between Tanganyika and Kenya
Colony.   There were many huts clustered about a
large cattle boma and, of course, there were a few
score idle natives hanging about; also many sheep
and goats.   The station was in charge of an Indian
customs officer who was very courteous and passed
us through with little ceremony.   We now headed
toward Kajiado, and during the day encountered many
herds of giraffe, being fortunate in securing some
excellent still photographs at very close range; in fact
the best that I obtained on the entire expedition.
Giraffe must be increasing in numbers for never have
I noticed so many.   No sportsman ever shoots them,
and their worst enemy, the lion, is becoming scarce in
this district, so it looks as if the meek shall, in truth,
inherit the earth, at least this small section of it.

The fourth day carried us into the southern game
reserve, the country of the Masai, and about noon we
stopped near a small swamp hoping to find some
drinking water.   We had hardly done so, when three
Masai warriors and an old chief came up to the trucks.
One of them understood a little Swahili and informed
us that there was a spring about a quarter of a mile
away.   I told the faithful servant to fill the water bag
at this spring and hurry back.   He stood there shaking
like a leaf until Mike, a little bit peeved, asked him
what was the matter now.   He was afraid of the
Masai; he had heard that they were very bad men
who speared any other black man on sight and felt
sure that as soon as he got away from our protection
one of the warriors would step out from behind a bush
and put a spear through him.   Mike's reply was that

if we could be certain of this he would make him walk back and forth to the water hole all afternoon, or until some El Moran obliged. After some strong persuasion, the boy fearfully made his way toward the spring, taking a wide circle around all possible hiding places.

The Masai are a nomadic people, inhabiting the high plateau steppe of Kenya and Tanganyika. Their historical beginnings are lost in the dim past. A theory was once put forth that their ancestors immigrated from Arabia by way of Egypt into tropical Africa; that they were descendants from the same Semitic stock of nomads as the ancestors of the Hebrew nation of herdsmen. However, they are a purely pastoral Hamitic people, speaking a Nilotic language. Closely allied and speaking the same language are the Samburu. Other East African tribes classed as Hamitic negroid are the Nandi, the Suk, and the Turkana. It now appears that this strain originated in the steppe country of the Abyssinian Highlands by the intermixture of Galla and Somali with Nilotic Negroes.

The pure blooded Masai is considerably lighter in color than the Negro, has clear-cut features, well formed hands and feet, and is of magnificent physique, seldom under six feet in height. The stalwart, bronze-colored El Moran with his spear and shield is the very embodiment of physical courage and force. He is still the proudest of men, fearing no danger and looking down on all who are not so warlike as himself. Since time immemorial, the Masai El Moran or warriors have roamed over this vast steppe, keeping the other tribes in subjection and incidentally enriching their own cattle herds by raids, for these men made of cattle rustling a fine art.

They still maintain tremendous herds of cattle, and up until the time they were brought under the control of the white man, continued their raids. Whenever the chiefs desired new pastures, they would send forth their warriors to conquer, and they seldom failed in their mission. No wonder they were feared far and wide by all the other tribes!

All of their wealth is figured in terms of cattle. A man pays so many steers for a wife or is fined a number of head for some offense against tribal law. The herds supply them with practically everything needed in their Spartanlike life. They milk the cattle and bleed the steers, these two fluids being mixed and allowed to curdle. The resultant product constitutes their principal diet. It is an interesting fact that the Masai disdain all vegetable food, living on meat, blood, and milk exclusively, while members of surrounding tribes prefer a mixed diet. When an animal dies they use the skin for clothing and the meat for food. The cow dung is used as a building material; also for medicine, fuel, and chairs. This material has the redeeming quality of being antiseptic, killing germs which would otherwise take full possession of the village where, of course, there are no sanitary arrangements.

Essentially a pastoral people, they have no central settlement and their home comforts are few, because they are always shifting about taking advantage of the best pastures. They have no pottery, basketry, no blacksmiths or grain fields; nor in fact any sort of agriculture or industry. A stoical race, they have reduced their needs to the very necessities of life.

This magnificent tribe is undoubtedly dying out, due to changed conditions brought about by the white

This old chief and three El Moran who were with him were the first Masai encountered.

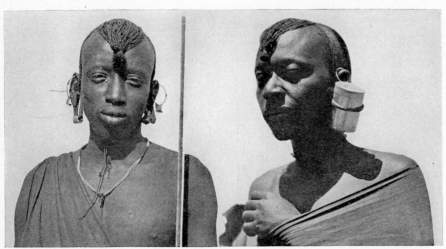

Two Masai El Moran. The warrior at the right wears a small milk can in his ear.

Masai El Moran outside their club.   The boulderlike background is a hut.

Government road in Nairobi.   Main street of the capital of East Africa.

man's domination, and also, in no small measure, to their own customs and the moral laxity of the last few decades. When tribal warfare and raids were almost continuous, the El Moran had plenty to occupy his mind and time, but now that these outlets for his energy have been curtailed, sexual excesses are bringing about a decadence of the race.

The warriors have always been quartered by themselves, where they lived in a state of free love with the young women of the tribe. Girls were not allowed to remain true to any one man, but were considered community property within the kraals of the El Moran. This custom, and the fact that the young men are not allowed to marry until after their term of service as warriors, has brought about an unusual condition, unique even among the tribes of Africa.

When the boy returned with the water we bade good-by to the old chief and the three El Moran, then continued on our journey which we found interesting every mile of the way. We got into some mud which made things a little more difficult, but the constantly changing views of mountain and plain, with herds of zebra, wildebeest, kongoni, and the smaller gazelles always in sight made it a memorable journey. We arrived in Nairobi after dark, tired, dusty, and happy.

The next day we were again on the road en route to our base camp in the Aberdare Mountains. Upon arrival there we had traveled six hundred thirty-six miles since leaving Mombasa and had risen from sea level to an altitude of eight thousand eight hundred feet. Mike was growing wheat on these high slopes and had constructed a very comfortable house where we were welcomed by Mona and Pat.

CHAPTER FOUR

PROWLERS OF THE PLAINS

SEVERAL days were spent at Mike's shamba, or farm, making final preparations for our trek into Tanganyika. Mike's wife, Mona, served us many enjoyable meals at her table. It was much more comfortable here than camping.

Just before leaving Nairobi we had noticed the town was being decorated and learned that they were expecting the Prince of Wales. His visit so upset the regular routine of life in the capital that it was no use trying to do anything until after the official welcome was over. So we all decided we might as well be in the receiving line ourselves. We found that most of the Europeans, Indians, and blacks who were able to motor, ride a bicycle, or walk into Nairobi had the same idea.

He arrived on a dull and windy day with the dust blowing in clouds all over the town, and it is reported that the Prince's first remark was, "What a damn dusty place!" If he did say that, he surely hit the nail on the head.

There was a great gathering at Government House, and to this shauri came chiefs and warriors from many tribes to honor the Prince. The show was arranged by local officials, not only for the Prince, but to impress the natives with the importance and power of the white man. Savage psychology, however, has some peculiar twists. They love pomp and ceremony; it is part of their lives, so that failed to impress them. Airplanes, radio, telephones, elevators, and automobiles are all part of the white man's sorcery. He is capable of most anything in their estimation, so no matter what the miracle, it is taken more or less for granted. On going to the fair grounds, however, we found the chiefs and the warriors gathered around the water faucets, where they stood by the hour gazing in wonder and amazement. They seemed almost awe-stricken whenever anyone walked up and turned on the tap. Here was a real achievement of magic! Their women had to walk for miles and fetch water in little jars on their heads, while the white man simply went to a stick in the ground, turned the little spigot and the water ran out clear and cool in an endless stream. Some of the chiefs asked me where they could get these charmed sticks. I couldn't tell them!

Early on the morning of October seventh, I stood shivering in a heavy sheepskin coat watching the sun rise from behind the slopes of Mount Kenya. Here on one of the highest points in the Aberdare Mountains it had frozen ice that night, and between me and snow-capped Mount Kenya lay the equator. It was hard to reconcile this to my earlier conceptions of equatorial regions. Now Mona, who had been busily supervising our farewell breakfast, came to the door and shouted "Chakula tiari," which, for the benefit of those who haven't yet mastered the Swahili tongue, means "food is ready." As I turned my back on the sunrise, Bud came up saying that the trucks were all loaded, that everything was ready for the start.

We gathered around the breakfast table, Mike, Bud and Ted Cottar, Mona, Austin, and myself. Patricia, Mike's little daughter, more familiarly known as Pat, was still asleep. Young Ted was sadly disappointed, for he had to stay behind and this didn't fit in with his ideas of adventure at all. Although only seventeen years old, he had already seen more of adventure than most men do in an entire lifetime and plenty more was in store for him.

Down the slopes of the Aberdares on this cool morning, we bumped over the worst road in the whole wide world, until we reached Gilgil. Here we loaded up with all the gasoline and oil it was possible to carry, for our camp would be several hundred miles from a filling station. Then down the main road toward Nairobi, across the cut-off to the old quarantine station in the Kedong Valley, up the Mau Escarpment, and toward Narok, at which point we entered the Masai Reserve. Now passed many scenes made familiar by my previous expedition. The game increased in numbers and the first herd of graceful impalla leaped across our road. Toward evening as we were approaching Sienna, five big spotted cats jumped out just ahead of us. For a moment I thought they were leopards, but upon second look discovered them to be cheetah. We all had a prejudice against the leopard for several good reasons, so were a little bit quick on the trigger, and it was necessary for me to kill one of the cheetahs which had been wounded. Shortly afterwards we made camp at a place where I had spent many thrilling nights before, and while the cook busied himself with the evening meal, faithful old Maniki was preparing the cheetah skin.

This aged Wakamba was a real character, who had been on some of the most notable safaris of the last twenty-five years and was rated among the very best of skinners. His age was now against him, but although somewhat blind, he was a much better man in most respects than many of the younger ones. I was glad to overlook his infirmities because of his practical knowledge and likable disposition. He was one of those who accompanied me later on the journey across Africa.

Although we had already heard many hyenas, I knew that in this section they would be plentiful. Now, just as we were preparing to eat, several of these gruesome beasts took up the mournful refrain which was to continue throughout the night. One of them approached within the circle of firelight and as he stood there his large eyes burned like two bright red coals. It was the first one seen so far, the scout, so to speak, for the thousands of others which were to parade before us in the weeks to come.

The next day's journey carried us through what to me was virgin territory. The farther we penetrated into Tanganyika, the more numerous became the game herds, while a greater variety of animals was seen. We pulled up to Klein's Camp at Gurmeti, finding no one there except a native boy in charge, and an assorted lot of shenzis or bush savages. This boy wanted us to stay and shoot a rhino which had been making life miserable around the vicinity, but in spite of his entreaties, we proceeded on our way to Kilimafeza. This is the official name given to a gold-mining camp here on the edge of nothing. It is more popularly known as Kill-a-man-ezy, because of the great number

of deaths among the white people who have been connected with the mine. It is not only a bad fever
district but also a sleeping-sickness region.

Before reaching the mine we felt the first stings of
the tsetse fly. Austin was riding with me when one
of these insects bit him. He jumped and said something had "bit his leg off!" Some people may get
used to its bite, but each one that I received felt as if
somebody had stuck me with a red-hot needle, and it
left a white blister which itched for hours. There are
many species of tsetse flies, but the two which are most
feared, because of their fatal results to man and beast,
are the *Glossina morsitans*, which carries the parasite
Trypanosoma brucei to many animals, such as cattle
and horses, causing the disease known as nagana, and
the closely related species *Glossina palpalis*, which was
introduced into Tanganyika from Uganda and the
Congo. The latter carries the sleeping sickness to
man. This scourge of Africa is little larger than the
common house fly, but is capable of penetrating through
the tough hides of such animals as antelopes and
zebras, in order to reach the blood stream. This
insect is only found in certain areas known as fly
belts, having definite boundaries, and after we had
passed beyond the mine a few miles they ceased to
bother us. Subsequent experiences proved that they
were not only restricted to definite areas, but that they
were active only during the daytime, remaining dor-
mant throughout the hours of darkness. For this
reason we often went after our drinking water after
night had fallen, because it was necessary to pass
through this fly belt on the outgoing and return
journeys.

Our first night on the plains of the Serengetti was spent at a hastily constructed camp near the Serra Nyiro. This river bed, dry most of the time, was to play an important part in our future operations, and by way of introduction, that very night we heard the lions roaring along its banks.

We had arrived after dark and things were, of course, in much confusion, to which was added a little excitement, when one of our boys shouted that a big snake was crawling through the center of the dining room. There was a mad scramble to attack the intruder with sticks, and in the semidarkness a thorough job was done; but before we could congratulate ourselves, it was discovered that our victim was a small python, nonpoisonous, worth five dollars a foot alive and nothing dead.

We didn't quite relish the idea of being so close to the bushy grass-filled ravines, or dongas, for there was a good possibility of finding lions prowling around in camp, which, of course, would get quite wearisome after awhile.

Next day Mike and I went in search of a better camp site, being successful in finding a marvelous location on the slope of a small hill four miles away. Here in the shade of some beautiful, flat-topped mimosa trees we pitched our tents. Thus was born Camp Simba or "camp of the lions" which was to become world-known. Next we built a dining banda, or hut, by placing over a framework of small limbs a thick covering of grass. This made a cool and comfortable retreat, which was used as an assembling place; also for a dining room. The cook, or as he will be called hereafter, pishi, which is Swahili for cook, preferred to

keep his kitchen out in the open, so selecting a place
beneath one of the trees about thirty feet from the
dining shack, he set up his establishment, hanging his
pots and pans from convenient limbs. Afterwards he
took some empty cases and had a regular system of
shelves. With a can opener he evolved from an empty
five-gallon gasoline tin a very good oven. From this
kitchen, spread beneath the Tanganyika skies, Ali
Ramazan produced as occasion required, not only
breakfast, lunch, and dinner, but banquets. This
was really and truly a house of mystery, for no matter
what the form of the supplies turned over to pishi,
it was impossible to foretell the finished product.

I do distinctly remember, however, that the most
important commission given to Bud when he went
for the first load of supplies was to bring back a meat
grinder. We obtained enough physical exertion ram-
bling over this tremendous country without wasting a
lot of energy chewing up shoe-leather steaks. I doubt
if the animals were really that tough, but when Ali
got through with them, they not only all tasted alike
but had the same rubberlike consistency. After the
arrival of this important item, we had a deluge of
hash, lasting over an extended period of time, until
one day while Mike and I were in a boma photographing six lions, he suddenly gave a little start and said,
"Wonder if we're going to have hash again tonight!"
This brought on a discussion which ended in an agreement to take forcible means, if necessary, to bring
about a change of diet. The pishi was so enamored
with this marvelous machine that we had to hide it
away until such time as we were able to withstand
another epidemic of ground meat.

This wise looking bird is a marabou stork.

Tanganyika territory. Baby bat-eared foxes.

61

Camp Simba, Tanganyika Territory. This camp was in the center of the finest game country in the world.

From our camp we could look across a wide sweep of plain which ran into a low range of hills whose tops peeked over the horizon. As we gazed over this rolling veldt, which was hemmed in on the left by large hills and on the right by trees which melted into the sky line, we could always see many thousands of animals. Here in our front yard the tommies, Grant's gazelles, topi, kongoni, wildebeest, and zebra kicked up their heels in play, or stampeded in fright from a real or fancied danger. On the farther plains were eland and giraffe, while the wooded hills sheltered many mountain reedbuck, water buck, duiker, stine-buck, dik-dik, and impalla. In the dongas lurked not only the big cats, the lion, leopard, and cheetahs, but many lesser Carnivora. Scattered all over this tre-mendous area were troops of ostrich, thousands upon thousands of hyenas, jackals, bat-eared foxes, and wart hogs. Once in a while a black rhino, a herd of buffaloes, or a few roan antelope would pay our front yard a visit. At no time, night or day, were we out of sight or hearing of animals.

"Just got back from being lost," heads an entry in my journal dated October twenty-fourth. This is not a pleasant experience in Africa, where sign posts and traffic cops are very scarce. Bud and I, with three boys, left camp early in the morning to fetch water from the spring some twenty miles away. As we had made the trip several times, we went without taking food or blankets, expecting to be back in time for lunch. The cameras were carried, however, because I made it a practice never to go anywhere without them, for as sure as I did, something unusual would present itself and I would not be able to film it. About halfway to the spring we came upon a large herd of giraffe, and after chasing them around for a while to get pictures, returned to the road. After another mile or so we beheld a great number of vultures circling low in the sky and turned off into the bush for a look. Gathering vultures always indicate a dead animal, and as often you will find lions on the carcass, it gives you quite a thrill to stalk the kill and see what's there.

On this occasion we found a dead zebra without any marks on it to tell what had caused its death. We filmed some vulture pictures, then starting back to the road encountered a second dead zebra with more vultures and marabou storks standing in a large circle. As the tails of both these animals were missing, we now concluded they had been killed by some Ikoma hunters, as this was the method employed by them for marking their property, in order to prevent other wandering natives from taking the meat. It is an unwritten law among these savages never to take meat so marked. When a third kill was signaled by the vultures on the slope of a small hill, we made our way through the thorn bushes to investigate, finding two dead zebras, both of which had their tails. Still another vulture and marabou convention attracting our attention, we sallied over to find that the punda milia were indeed having a hard day, for here was the fifth defunct zebra, this one also having its tail in the right place. The score now stood three with tails and two without, which seemed to indicate that the zebra deaths were not due to native hunters. The short rains had set in and these were probably immature animals who were not able to survive the first wet season with tsetse-fly poison in their veins.

Those without tails were animals which had first
been found by natives who had availed themselves of
this gift of Providence, by staking out their claims.
The savages hereabouts know little concerning white
men and try to avoid them whenever possible, so that
our appearance on the scene had caused them to hide
in the bush.   As soon as we left they would drive the
vultures away and start cutting the meat into long
strips to be hung in the sun to dry.   Fresh zebra meat
and meat dried in this form seem to be the principal
food of the Ikoma, and I got so I could tell them
from other natives by their peculiar odor, due, no
doubt, to this constant diet.   Zebra flesh has a sick-
ening sweet smell.

All of this time we had been making pictures and
nobody was paying much attention to our directions.
In fact we had twisted and turned so many times that
it was hard to tell where we were.   All of this country
looks more or less alike, and once you lose your way,
the thing is hopeless.   After wandering around for
about thirty miles, we came to a spring of clear, sweet
water hidden away in a small, rocky donga.   We had
discovered it from far off in the distance, for although
it was on the side of a barren hill, many green trees
and several beautiful ivory palms surrounded the refreshing pool.

Upon arrival there we found it to be a favorite
drinking place for lions.   Their tracks were thick on
the trails leading to the water.   It is very probable
that no white man had ever been to this donga before,
although we did find an old camp which had been
abandoned long since by natives.   Possibly they
couldn't hold their own against the many lions and

leopards which came nightly to quench their thirst.
Maniki became quite excited and called me over to a
game path where he pointed to the largest lion spoor
I had ever seen. If the rest of this *Felis leo* was built
in proportion to his feet, he would be the world's
largest lion!

We were all hungry and it was time to eat lunch,
but as no food had been brought along, we decided
against it, taking a good drink of water instead. It
now began to cloud up, the sky darkening as distant
thunder warned of rain. To be lost was bad enough,
but to be far from the path with miles of soft earth
between, where every foot would be an effort in case
of rain, was still another thing; so we went about the
serious business of looking for the road, stopping only
once to shoot a reedbuck in case we had to dine out.
The sound of the shot had hardly died away when a
miserable hyena appeared and only our presence prevented him from attacking the meat. He must have
been very hungry because he certainly was bold. However, this was a case where boldness didn't pay, for
with a carefully placed bullet from my Remington 30
he went down in the dust and into history as my
fourth hyena.

I might explain that a road in this country is nothing
more than tracks left by a motor car, and sometimes
it is not an easy thing to find. After about four hours
of following a donga which we couldn't cross, we came
into an open plain which seemed a wee bit familiar.
While crossing this open space we came upon three
large herds of eland, and a solitary old bull gave us
an awful scare. As we were passing a small clump of
bushes, he sprang out with a mighty snort and for a

Masai manyatta, or thorn-inclosed village, showing cattle within the protecting wall. Note the inward-facing huts.

Masai women, Tanganyika. Copper and iron wire form the principal adornment of these primitive women. The more they carry on their arms and legs, the higher their social standing.

second we thought a rhino had charged us. The eland is the largest of all African antelope, a full-grown bull probably weighing as much as eighteen hundred pounds, while he stands about six feet at the withers. The cows are somewhat smaller, but in spite of their great size they are among the most graceful of all animals. I have often watched them kicking up their heels in play, leaping over each other without apparent effort.

An hour or so after crossing the plain we found the road and started toward camp, which was reached after several hours of fighting the mud and rain that now broke upon us in full force. Upon arrival there we found that Mike had returned with supplies and some mail, which, of course, was exceedingly welcome. The balance of the evening was spent in reading letters and discussing plans for securing some film of a Masai manyatta.

We had been making a film story around the Masai, for which we needed pictures of their cattle within the protective boma. These people build an oblong inclosure of thorn walls about eight feet high, inside of which the huts are placed with their entrances facing toward the center. The framework of these rude shelters is built from small limbs, the whole being plastered over with cow dung. It is necessary to stoop in order to crawl through the four-foot-high opening, and the inside is as crude as the outside. Within there is a small wall separating the young calves from the young Masais, with two built-in bedsteads covered with skins. Between them is a space for the fire, with barely room enough for the family to gather about. These shelters are usually four-

teen feet long, eight feet in breadth, and six feet
in height, but most of this space is taken up by the
calves, their comfort being considered above that of
the humans. This circling wall and ring of huts is
collectively called a village or manyatta and varies in
size according to the number of individuals living
under one chief.

These inclosures are built to protect their cattle
during the night from the prowlers of the plains, but
in spite of all precautions, lions often gain an entrance
and make a kill.

The Masai has many noble qualities, but no one has
ever accused him of the virtue of cleanliness. After a
manyatta has attained to a certain age, it is almost
impossible for a white man to approach it, but the
terrible odor seems to be perfume to him. It was
necessary for me to go inside in order to secure pictures and while doing this work I made one of the
greatest scientific discoveries of the age. Probably
you have wondered, as I had, where all the flies go
in the wintertime. The answer is to a Masai manyatta! These pestiferous insects are here in endless
swarms, and it was all I could do to endure two hours
of their constant attentions. I had my boys standing
by, trying to brush them away with wildebeeste-tail fly
swatters, but it was not possible to keep back the endless tide. How human beings can live in such filth is
beyond the white man's knowing.

The large village where we hoped to secure our
pictures was situated eight miles directly east of our
camp among a large outcropping of rocks. Here we
went the next morning before daylight expecting to
find the cattle inside the boma, but were disappointed.

The chief could speak Swahili, and after greetings he registered a few complaints, one of them which I particularly remember being concerned with the price of wives. It seems the market on new wives was all shot to pieces while secondhand ones were not in demand at all. He had quite a few young ladies for sale, the price of each being two steers, two cows, and one drum of honey beer. I think the old codger was making this sales talk for our benefit, but we diplomatically evaded the point.

We made a deal with the chief to hold the cattle within the inclosure until after sunrise, but upon our arrival next morning found the boma empty. We had another pow-wow with the chief during which he raised the ante. He was now to receive fifty shillings, a bag of posho, and some sugar. The sun arose again on the same story, the cattle were gone. We were quite peeved by this time and told the chief in no uncertain terms that another disappointment might cause him plenty of trouble. He was very sorry but some of the lesser chiefs had told him he should have more shillings, more posho, and more sugar. We asked him how much of each he wanted, whereupon he named an enormous amount to which we agreed outwardly but not inwardly.

On the morning after this arrangement, we were up long before dawn, headed across the moonlit veldt toward the weird hill of rocks that hid the manyatta. En route we almost ran over five hyenas solemnly walking in a row. The leading one was dragging a large piece of meat and the others were following in the hope he would drop it. Outside of these and a few jackals we saw nothing and arrived at the village just

at the first peep of dawn. As soon as the sun arose
we found that the entire sky was filled with dark
clouds making photography impossible, so walked
around the manyatta saying "good morning" to
several young ladies who were repairing huts with
fresh cow dung.

Later in the morning we went to our lion donga.
En route I shot a kongoni which was placed in the
truck and afterwards at the end of our tow rope. We
dragged this around the donga in an attempt to entice
the lions out, but without results. As we neared their
favorite spot, Bud came up in Mike's touring car with
the information that he had just seen six lions about
one mile away. I transferred to the fast car with my
graflex in hopes of securing a few still negatives. Within
ten minutes we came upon five of the lot and managed
to get up to within twenty feet of them. The light
was very bad and I could not get much heart into the
work until later when the sun broke through for a
short time, and then we drove to within ten feet
of a big male who with a growl sank back on his
haunches for a jump. The top was down and I stood
up in the back seat to get the picture; Bud looked
around and seeing the lion just about ready to spring
stepped on the gas; the car gave a sudden leap forward
and I nearly pitched into the lion's mouth. I managed
to catch hold of the folded top and, after tetering back
and forth for awhile, fell inside the car. We got a
good laugh out of this, but it came very close to
being a tragedy.

Next morning, according to instructions, my boy
Kahindi awakened me before dawn, but when I found
it was raining, I went back to bed until later. It rained

most of the day, but we did manage to get out long
enough to shoot a few birds for the pot.

There are great quantities of guinea fowl in this
district and they not only offer fine sport, but are
very good food. I should hate to state how many
millions of guinea fowl there are in Africa, for on my
previous expedition into Southwest Africa and Angola
I found them in untold thousands, while here they
were in clouds. Later I was to find that all these were
just a few that had left the main flock living in the
French Congo.

It got dark as we went back to camp, so we took
a short cut through some small trees. Here we saw
large red eyes hopping and bobbing all over the place.
It was both thrilling and mystifying to watch these
twin balls of red fire as they darted hither and thither
through the air. Mike cleared the mystery when he
told me they were lemurs, a small night animal living
in trees. As they make excellent pets we tried our
luck at catching one. After climbing many trees,
cutting off branches, and running like mad through
the thorn thickets for a couple of hours we were successful in capturing one little lemur which we took
home and put in a box. About the time this was
taking place Austin and a boy had captured seven baby
bat-eared foxes, so the next morning we awoke to find
that we had quite a zoo. Although the lemur is a
very small animal it has a very large hop and
the way it can cover distance is most remarkable, not
only on the ground but by jumping from one tree to
another. Their eyes are Van Dyke brown in color
and the largest I have ever seen in proportion to the
size of the animal.

We decided to get a few bomas ready for photographing purposes, so taking one of the trucks, we loaded in several boys and proceeded to our lion donga. Upon arrival there we found four lionesses watching us. I shot a topi which we dragged inside an old Masai manyatta that had been abandoned for several years, and everybody got to work on the building of the blinds. While this was going on the lions came to the edge of the thicket to watch us more closely. As it was not wise to keep them waiting too long, just as soon as the rough work on the boma was finished we motored away leaving them to enjoy the topi.

Now we went several miles northwest of the camp to explore the country. The rains had caused the grass to spring up almost like magic and where yesterday all was brown and covered with dust, today beautiful hills of green rolled before us. The moisture had brought the grass and the grass in turn had attracted the game, so that now the whole veldt teemed with thousands upon thousands of wild animals; the big migration was on.

Placing two kills for lions in likely spots, we were just starting for home when a terrific storm broke, making it necessary to put on the chains, but even then the soft ground seemed to slip from under the truck. In the midst of this rain I spied a hyena watching us, and as he seemed to be laughing at our plight, I made him number five in my list.

While passing near a herd of wildebeest I noticed one unfortunate fellow who could hardly run. He had been bitten and torn by hyenas. His rump and belly were badly swollen and covered with matted blood. How he had managed to escape was a mystery.

With a well-placed bullet I put the poor beast out of his misery.

I hate hyenas; they are not only ugly, evil-smelling brutes but the cruelest of all the killers. They have been seen to tear open live animals and start feasting on them while the poor victim cried in agony. They also are eaters of corpses, hanging around the native villages in order to dig up the buried dead. For this reason most Negroes hate them as devils and whenever I would shoot one they would laugh and shout, "Muzuri sana, bwana!" very good, master!

Upon revisiting the baits we found no lions but plenty of hyenas. As we rounded a small hill and came toward the first kill, we discovered hyenas scattered all over the landscape. I counted fourteen on the carcass and there were more standing here and there, around the veldt, so I added number six to my score card with one shot. At the next bait we found little left. The entire zebra had been eaten, while the rain had washed out all the spoor, making it hard to tell if lions had been there or not. The hyenas made our work of attracting lions very difficult, the country being absolutely alive with these brutes of the large spotted variety (*Hyena crocuta*) and a bait could hardly be placed before they would flock there from every direction, devouring the carcass long before it was possible for a lion to scent the kill.

It was necessary to visit our lion donga at frequent intervals, as we had to feed them in order to keep them around. Once, with a dead zebra on board, we approached their favorite lair, where I espied a lioness in the grass about two hundred yards from cover. I shouted to the driver to head that way. As the truck neared the spot, she stood up and growled, showing her teeth and slowly whipping her tail to and fro. This is a sign that all African hunters know. It means "keep your distance." As we were wondering at her temper, Bud discovered that she had cubs with her, which, of course, explained everything. As nobody offered to go out and bring in the little fellows, we proceeded on our way to one of the blinds.

With the cameras and one boy I crawled into the boma, which was simply a circular wall of thorn branches with no roof. We had taken a section of side wall from one of the old huts in the manyatta and propped it up to make the blind look more aged. Through this wall I had cut a hole two feet square facing the bait which was exactly eighteen feet from the opening. Nothing happened for a long time and while waiting I watched, through my binoculars, two distant lionesses as they stalked a herd of Masai cattle. For some reason I hoped they would be successful, for, after all, this was the lion's own country, wherein the Masai were intruders.

After a few hours I heard the truck chugging toward me so got ready for what might happen. Soon it came through the gate we had made in the manyatta wall, dragging a dead wildebeest behind. Mike was at the wheel and brought the fresh bait up to our anchor. Stopping the truck he fastened the animal, then joined me in the boma, saying that there were some lions following the scented trail. Less than five minutes later a lioness came around one of the huts and strode swiftly toward the kill. She walked right up until only twelve feet away and then, hearing the hum of the camera, hesitated and slunk to one side.

Shortly two more lionesses joined her. Then a huge male came stalking through the entrance and with long strides came up to the bait and crouching low peered into the lens opening. For a second or two our eyes met, during which time funny little sensations ran up and down my spine. Then he joined the group in the grass. For a tense hour we waited while the lions prowled around the boma.

Finally they all laid down about fifteen feet from us and went to sleep. I could see them very plainly from my position by simply turning my head. After awhile Mike and I began to talk about the coming wheat crop and other important things concerning the shamba. This seemed to annoy our feline visitors, for suddenly one of them gave a loud growl and springing to its feet faced us with an expression which seemed to say, "Shut up in there! Can't you see we're trying to get a little rest?" As there was no roof on this boma, and it was an easy jump for a lion, we decided to keep quiet. The light was getting bad and we wanted to go home, but four hungry lions within a few feet was sufficient reason for delaying our departure.

At last there came a clear morning and long before dawn we were on our way to the Masai manyatta. This time there would be no mistake; we would complete the work. After arriving at the village we placed a truck across each of the two gates so that the cattle could not get out. On top of each cab sat a white man with a rifle over his knees. The camera crew and myself proceeded to the top of the enormous rock which rose about a thousand feet back of the village. On its summit I assembled the equipment ready for the picture taking, while Mike pow-wowed with the chiefs below. It seems there was a superstitition connected with the opening and closing of the thorn gates to the boma, that no one was permitted to touch them out of time for fear the spirits of the tribal forefathers would be offended, but Mike dropped a few remarks now and then about the men on top of the cabs, about the sugar, the posho, and the shillings. In this way he managed to keep the cattle where we wanted them until it was light enough to photograph. After about two hours work, during which time we secured all the scenes we needed, including the driving of the cattle in and out of the inclosure several times, we turned them back to their herders.

While I was putting my cameras away several El Moran surrounded the truck and nonchalantly leaned against their spears. I wasn't sure whether they meant harm or were only curious until the old chief came up with a smile upon his leathery face, and spitting on his hands as a sign of friendship, told me how glad he was of the opportunity to coöperate!

CHAPTER FIVE

THE LIONS OF TANGANYIKA

OF all animals the lion is the most interesting in its natural haunts, and because they are so fascinating we can find no end of reasons to write about them. Not only has *Felis leo* always intrigued the imagination of mankind, but in spite of the popular beliefs to the contrary, he has always been a gentleman. The lion is brave, and, like a brave man, he is never treacherous nor trouble seeking. He goes his own way and only asks to be left alone. When danger threatens he will seek to avoid it if possible, but when pressed too much, his oppressor is courting swift punishment, for the lion will not allow his dignity to be assailed, nor will he allow a hurt to go unchallenged.

When the early Egyptians became acquainted with the king of beasts, they started a line of argument about his habits that has persisted to this day. Even these ancients, however, were aware of his nobler qualities and blunted many a chisel carving his image in stone.

From that time to this, the lion has received more space in print than any other animal. He has been written about and sung about. He has been painted and sketched often enough to make his face and general shape well known to everybody in every land.

Since the time when the Nile was the Broadway of the world, and later when the Greeks and Romans made the lion an unwilling adjunct of their sports and the executioner of innocents, good people have been led to believe that lions were all that was cruel and bloodthirsty. Of course, it was admitted that he made a fine appearance and some nations even adopted him as the symbol of greatness, of strength, and of character. The general opinion still prevails that lions are cruel, bloodthirsty, killers for the love of killing, man-eaters whenever possible, and yet, noble, majestic and strong.

I have had unusual opportunities to study wild, full-grown African lions in their native haunts, but no matter what I write about them, someone is sure to disagree with my conclusions. The fact remains, however, that I spent many weeks with a troop of lions, right out in the open, under the blue sky of Tanganyika, and watched them do all the things that go to make up a lion's life.

Most men go out to kill a lion on sight, and if he resents this treatment and fights back, they call him evil names, and thus add a score to his already bad reputation. These men never give a thought to the fact that the lion was only trying to mind his own business, whereas they came looking for trouble. Then, of course, there are a few lions that have gone wrong, and as in the case of humans who do the same thing, they stir up more interest and attract more attention than a whole generation of lions who have been home-loving and peaceful.

On my first African journey, which took my party into the Kalahari Desert and into the mysterious Kaoko Veldt of Southwest Africa, I had few chances to study this animal, for he was scarce in these parts and very shy. We saw spoor and other signs, but no lions to write about. On this trip I lived with lions day and night; the fact is that the whole country was full of them.

Shooting lions with a camera is much more difficult than doing so with a gun and brings the shooter into more intimate contact, for to secure motion pictures of wild lions near enough so that they will really look like close-ups on the screen, the cameraman must get right under their noses. Lions in their native element are not to be played with, and no matter how often you approach them and get away with it, the very next time may bring plenty of trouble. The public has become accustomed to seeing tame lions on the silver screen, animals that must have their meat chopped up for them, and that could not exist one week in the wilderness. They expect to see the wild ones just as near, so I made up my mind to film them close, and did, succeeding almost too well!

While making scenes at a native village, the chief came to us and asked if we would shoot some bad lions that were killing his cattle. When we agreed to remove these brutes, he sent a guide to show us where they were to be found. After our arrival at the donga, or ravine, we discovered a lioness crouching behind a small tree, but did not shoot her as we expected to find others about and wanted to get our bearings first. I then noticed in the tall grass near the donga a dead topi, which investigation proved had just been killed by her, we having arrived on the scene before she could start her meal.

Now we did a very impolite thing. We put a cable to the topi and hitched the other end to the truck, then went off with the kill, leaving the angry lioness watching us from the grass. About half a mile from the starting point I looked back through the glasses and saw her following us, which gave me an idea, so we pulled the carcass to a lone tree away out on the veldt and there anchored it.

Early the next morning we neared the spot and, although we hoped to find the lioness there, what we did see more than surprised the lot of us, for there, in the tree's shade, were not one but six lions. Approaching to within about a hundred yards, I began to grind out film as if these were the only lions left in Africa, while Mike and Bud stood with their rifles ready for action. The lions looked as big as horses to me and the first scenes were taken with a telephoto lens. As we approached closer I don't mind admitting I was somewhat nervous and kept glancing toward the two riflemen to see what effect it was having on them. They didn't seem to think any more about it than if they were waiting for a flock of ducks, and I couldn't understand how they could be so callous. After a while we got closer, then still closer until within thirty yards, but the lions were none too friendly, often growling toward us which made it necessary to keep close watch with rifles ready. We spent the whole day with them and went back to camp well satisfied.

Next day found us back, and from that time on, with the exception of a few days when weather prevented, we visited with these lions for several weeks. Each day we thought that nothing else of interest could be found for the camera to take, but always during the next visit they would put on something new for us, something we never knew lions could do.

So I photographed them day after day, living their natural lives, and in doing so we all became friends.

Our regular group consisted of four females and two males, and these were soon named George, Jim, Lizzie, Betty, Hazel and Flossie. Then there were two others, one a lioness with cubs whom we called Cleo and a strange "lady" who never became very friendly, and so was named Madam X.

Each had individuality. George was the strong man of the troop and leader in all things. Jim got along all right when George was not there, but he did not seem to be so popular with the lionesses as George. Jim was light in color with a white collar around his neck, and when he looked at me I could not help thinking of a big, kindly Newfoundland dog. George was much darker in color, with a fine head and a face full of expression. They were both lions just the same and staged many a fight for our benefit, mostly at meal time.

Lizzie was our dearest friend, for it was always she that led the way and by her example got the others interested in the work. Betty was second lead in the troop, with the others helping all they could. They did many queer things and often had us laughing at their antics. Sometimes there was a great temptation to go and pat them on the head for some cute action, but nobody ever did!

The lion is by nature a shy animal as is proven by the fact that many people have spent years in Africa in lion country without a single sight of these tawny cats. They are by nature nocturnal or seminocturnal, and in those districts where often molested hide away during the daytime. Here we had found "daylight lions," due perhaps to the remoteness of the country from white habitation and to the vast expanses without even a native village. That we only saw a fraction of the lion population however, the incident here related will in a measure explain.

One hot afternoon after having spent weeks with our lions until, as far as we were concerned, they had no fear, we were making some scenes near a water hole with six of them. Everything was going along smoothly when suddenly they began to stand at rigid attention, gazing the while toward the hill back of us. After a short time they walked into the tall grass one by one and hid themselves away. We were nonplussed as to the reason for this, and remained without an answer until two Masai spearmen appeared almost at our feet. The lions had spotted them as they topped the hill and their natural suspicion of man asserted itself. They had long looked upon us as friends but were not sure of strangers. After the Masai were out of sight they came back to us again.

This explained to me why so many hunters never see a lion. The lion sees them first and from then on keeps well out of the way. As to hiding ability, I have seen lions conceal themselves in places that a rabbit would scorn, and do it so well that the inexperienced eye could never detect them.

They did not fear us because we had repeatedly shown that our intentions were peaceful. We had lost most of our fear of them because we now believed that a lion would not molest man under ordinary conditions. There is a saying in Africa, however, which has time and again been proven absolutely true: "The only certainty about a lion is his uncertainty." We

Two lionesses near their own donga.   The females are more uncertain in
their dispositions than the males.

Tanganyika. Lion and lioness on top of an ant hill near a water hole. The row of trees in the middle distance marks the donga where the lions lived.

always went about our work with this saying in mind, for it would, of course, be courting sudden death to throw every precaution to the winds and believe that all lions were friendly and that their friendship could be depended upon.

After our first few days with them we became convinced that it would be possible to win their confidence and by so doing obtain motion pictures that would be hard for anyone else ever to surpass. With this idea in mind we fed them every day or so. Our method was to take the meat to that part of the donga where we knew they lived and so place it that the smell would be wafted to them. Later, as we became better acquainted, they would come out at the approach of the truck and meet us half way.

If we desired that they perform somewhere else we would drag the meat away with the truck, and they would follow behind until the spot selected was reached. Then it was a matter of man's wit against theirs if anything worth while was to be filmed. To them the all important thing was the meat and Mike Cottar, who knows the ways of the lion, was able to arrange things so that to get the meat they would have to do certain feats and then we would get our pictures. Why, we even had them climbing trees!

People who have never seen a wild lion will scoff at such a thing and say it is impossible, but I have all the evidence in the world, both in motion pictures and in regular photographs. We had a lot of fun with our boys, for these Negroes depend on climbing trees to escape lions. When they saw one after another of our troop jumping into and climbing a tree, they shuddered to think of what might have happened

6

in the days gone past, and each saw before him a dark future.

Never had our actors been in higher spirits and each seemed to vie with the others to show us what it could do. One lioness proved to be an expert at jumping and whenever another one started to climb the tree she would jump into it first. They had a few spills, with once a lion falling smack into the bunch grouped under the tree. All were up in a flash and the fur flew for a second until they discovered that it was an accident.

A most exciting time for me was when for the first time I filmed them from a boma. Six lions grouped themselves within twelve feet and one lioness, not being satisfied with such a long distance view of me, came up to the peep hole and stuck her head in to smell me at not more than six feet from nose to nose. It took some time for my heart to slow down after she backed away, and then I resumed the work in hand, which was that of filming the troop of them as they fought over pieces of meat. After the meal was over, to show that no harm was meant, they would rub against one another or lick one another's faces, purring the while like big house cats.

After we had left the boma and were in the truck ready to start for our camp, we watched the lions as one by one they filed past the lens opening in the blind, stood on their tiptoes and peeked in. They knew we had left and were probably curious to see what the place looked like inside, or maybe they were giving it the once over, with an idea of moving in.

A shooting party from England, another from America and then some old-time Africans from the

Tanganyika gold mines were our guests at different times and were taken to watch our lion troop perform. The English party did not see them at their best, for they came before the lions were our friends. The Americans, however, got a real thrill as well as a rare treat, and when the gold mine folks came along, they beheld the sight of six lions coming out to meet us and then sitting around within a few feet waiting for us to explain the day's business. The Englishmen thought it was "topping," the Americans "wonderful," while the gold miners said it did not seem possible, but since they had seen it with their own eyes it must be true. One of them had shot a lion that morning and now talked of it in an apologetic way.

Next day we motored to Kilimafeza to secure a few supplies of flour, jam, milk, and other items. I had made arrangements at the mine whereby they would let us have anything they could spare, provided we replaced things when our supply truck came back from Nairobi. Between our camp and the mine it was necessary to cross three dry river beds; the first being the Serra Nyiro, and the second the same stream after it had taken a bend. This second ford was called the "Baboon Crossing," because we never approached it without coming upon a troop of noisy baboons. Between here and the Benogi rolled a beautiful veldt, surrounded on three sides by hills through which our trail wound in and out among clusters of thorn bushes and wild sisal. This place was literally alive with the graceful and shy dik-dik. These diminutive little animals are true antelopes, though no larger than a hare. As their flesh is very fine eating, I killed a pair with my shotgun, adding them to a greater bustard, a giant bird weighing about forty pounds, which I was taking to the mill boss. Driving up to the mine, we found everything quiet, the familiar noise of the stamps being absent. Upon going to the manager's house we learned that he had just died of black-water fever and that his assistant was down sick with pneumonia. Kill-a-man-ezy was keeping up its sinister reputation.

On the return journey we discovered that a new camp had been set up a short way from the road. In Africa strange faces are always welcome, so we drove over to the tents, where we were greeted by a noted African hunter, Jack Lucy, who hobbled out with a sprained ankle. He asked us to sit down and shouted for the boy to bring tea. When this arrived we grouped around our tea cups and cake, swapping lion and elephant experiences. Lucy had heard about my trouble with the lion that came to life after I had shot him through the eye, so at his request I told the story.

About two weeks after establishing Camp Simba we went to look for another camp, one if possible that would be close to a spring, for it seemed we were spending a great amount of time transporting water, this in spite of the fact that nobody was ever discovered taking a bath.

While on this mission we entered a country of rolling hills, threading our way through a parklike valley which was all green with new grass. Mimosa and camel's thorn trees were scattered in clusters over the landscape. Groups of topi, kongoni, and wildebeest stood in the shade of these trees, while here and there herds of tommies and zebra made moving patches in the sunlight.

Tanganyika. A white-bearded gnu, or wildebeest, on the Serengetti plains.

Tanganyika. A giant bustard. The white boy is Ted Cottar and the black man a gun bearer.

91

A herd of wildebeest, or white-bearded gnu, on the Serengetti plains of Tanganyika.

Toward some large hills, at the other end of this valley, we came to a deep donga which we followed for a while, hoping to find a spring. It was excellent lion country. As we walked along, every so often a reedbuck would spring up almost at our feet, and as these animals are nearly the same color as *Felis leo* under some light conditions, we received a few thrills.

We had almost neared the end of the donga when I came unexpectedly upon a fine specimen of Tanganyika yellow-maned lion. He and a lioness were having an afternoon siesta beneath a bushy thorn tree, whose shade made an inky-black spot in a landscape of dazzling white heat.

I was almost upon them before making the discovery, my eyes being unable to penetrate into the blackness where they were lying and watching my approach, but the tips of four ears above the short grass caused me to stop and throw off the safety of my Remington Springfield. I knew two of the yellow cats were there, a male and a female, but what I did not know was whether they would run toward me or away. As I stood waiting, the huge male slowly arose and faced me with his tail whipping from side to side, the usual sign of a charge. Then the lioness sprang up and bolted toward a donga at my right, some hundred and twenty yards distant. Seeing his mate thus in flight may have changed Mr. Lion's mind about the charge, for now he followed her at a slow trot, pausing just before entering the donga to take a last look at the strange two-legged creature confronting him. In that instant I drew a quick bead and fired. He dropped in his tracks as if struck by lightning, and the sound of the bullet's impact told me he was hard hit.

Knowing that a partly dead lion is bad business, I approached cautiously, stopping every few feet to throw stones upon the recumbent beast. Nothing happened, so I went up to him and, leaning my rifle against a near-by bush, began to prepare him for picture-taking. Meanwhile the rifle shot had brought up the other members of the party and all of us stood about admiring the huge cat. Mike remarking on the great number of lion flies in his mane, began a search to see where the bullet had entered the body. Shortly, he discovered that it had gone through one eye, not even damaging the eyelashes. While we were discussing this fluke shot, two of my boys were busily cutting down the grass in order to give a clear view for some photographs.

When this had been done I ordered one of the boys to take the lion by the tail and pull him over a bit, placing him in a crouching position, as this makes a better picture. When he gave a yank, the lion gave a roar, and all present made backward jumps. Austin suggested that air escaping from the lungs had caused the noise, but when the big cat began to breathe and his sides to heave, and then when one mighty forearm swept around with force enough to fell an ox, we consulted and came to the conclusion that the lion was not really dead after all.

As it was my lion, I hastened to get my rifle before the beast got up. From the time the boy pulled the tail until I gave the coup de grace at close range, only a few seconds elapsed, but during that time I remember having argued with Austin who insisted on finishing him with a twelve-gauge shotgun, which would have torn a huge hole in the skin, and of taking the soft-nosed bullets out of my rifle and putting in full metal patched instead.

Upon skinning the lion, it was found that the 220-grain bullet had entered the right eye, traveling across the skull without touching the brain, coming so close, however, that the animal had been paralyzed.

Lucy remarked that the beast would have been on its feet shortly and plenty mad, and that this experience simply helped to prove his contention that no lion was safe until made into a rug. Poor Lucy; how true his words! Not many weeks later he was to be badly mauled by an enraged lion, escaping with his life only because of the steel nerves and quick thinking of his companion.

Now the rest of the party came up and Lucy introduced us to Mr. Windsor White, of Cleveland, Ohio, and his son, Mike. For them he was managing the safari. After another cup of tea all around, we parted with an invitation to the newcomers to visit our camp the next day, promising to show them some excitement at our famous lion donga.

Early the next morning, with the Whites as passengers, we set out in two trucks to find our lions, arriving at the donga about three hours after sunrise. After the camera equipment had been placed inside, young White and myself, with his gun bearer and my boy, crawled into the boma. In a short time we heard one of the trucks coming back and, without looking, I knew that our actors would be in tow, so asked White to peek and see what was up. He did, then sitting down, turned to me, saying in a hoarse whisper that six lions were running toward us. One after another they sprang on the bait right under our noses, growling and snarling. They were a little bit hungry this morning, but I was used to them and paid no attention. This was White's first experience with wild lions, however, and here they were so close that you could have reached out and pulled their tails. I suggested this possibility, but he didn't think much of the idea.

While we sat there watching these huge cats as they fought over the meat and tore it away in great chunks, White's gun bearer sat as if petrified. He had seen lions before but had never been within fifteen feet of a whole group, and after awhile pushed a heavy rifle into his master's hands, at which my boy laughed, for he knew that I seldom touched a gun while in the blind. The fact is there was little room in which to use a rifle. By the time it could be swung into position to shoot, either the danger would be past or all need for the said rifle. During this time one of the lionesses made several trips to the lens opening, coming to within six feet where she stood on her tiptoes and leaned forward to look us right in the eyes. I don't know whether this gave White a thrill or not, but I didn't particularly approve of her actions myself, especially once when she came up with a little rush, growling while she switched her tail to and fro over her back.

A little later, after the lionesses had left the meat, two males came along and furnished us with a real thrill. The first to arrive was one we called the Bachelor, because he never ran with the troop, but would wait until the family had fed and then take his share. He made a majestic entrance, then after looking around carefully, started to feed. Just then another male strolled up and the two big brutes stood over the kill eying each other. When one would try to take a bite the other would slap him over the head or shoulder. This kept up for a while, then they got into a real scrap, during which one lion turned a complete somersault, while the very ground shook with their blows and roars. I was able to photograph this entire combat, and as we were only eighteen feet away were afforded a wonderful opportunity of watching the tremendous muscles as they rippled and played along the shoulders and forearms. The great strength of these animals is almost beyond belief.

During the several hours we were in the boma, Mr. White, Senior, first watched the proceedings from a distance, and then Mike Cottar took him close to several other lions with the truck. After we had called it a day and all assembled again, our guests both agreed that we had furnished them the most wonderful and thrilling experience they had ever had.

The lion has always seemed to me to typify Africa. Serene, majestic, inscrutable, like the soil from which he springs, and, too, like the vast continent he roams, he knows no law save that of his own making. Kill is the law of his being, even as it is of all Africa, where life swarms so abundantly that it would seem fecundity exists only that it may furnish prey. Cruel the lion is, but he is no brawler, no wanton killer, no foul glutton like the unspeakable hyena. He is brave and fearless, as anyone who knows him will freely testify.

I was greatly puzzled, therefore — and more amused — at the unusual experience of a friend of mine on the occasion of his first meeting with a lion. He and another Norwegian were having a short safari under the guidance of an experienced white hunter. This safari boss, however, had never before been in this district, but having heard of our great success with lions, and the Norwegians being very keen to obtain lion trophies, he had brought them here. While hunting water buck along a donga about eight miles from Camp Simba, we came around a bend and found this party in the act of putting up their tents.

Strolling up, greetings were exchanged; then questions were asked concerning the game in the vicinity, particularly about *Felis leo*. The one Norwegian who spoke English wanted to know if they were in a good position for lions. It was hard for me to keep a sober face, for just the day before we had fed six lions within a hundred yards of this spot. I had shot a reedbuck and after my skinner had removed the hide, we left the carcass to these lions, who had kept circling and growling at us during the skinning operations.

Ted was with me at this time and could not resist telling the newcomers about the big lioness we had killed near this camp a week before. It was three o'clock in the afternoon, when we found this old female standing over a young zebra she had just killed, with four hyenas and several score vultures forming a circle around her. This was the old lady who lived near one of our best water holes and, by her smelly presence, kept me from securing pictures at this point. Knowing I was on the outs with her on this account, Ted asked permission to shoot her. Before I could answer, the tenderfoot of our party blazed away with the .405; then Ted came into action with his cannon of .505 caliber. Each time he pulled the trigger the recoil would push him back about ten feet, but in his excitement he never noticed it. Between the two of them the old lioness came to an inglorious end beneath the small thorn

tree where the native cook of the Norwegian party
was now unpacking his kettles and pans.   The lay of
the land was such that for many generations lions had
followed down a depression and crossed the donga at
this point.   Water remained here longer than elsewhere
and there was always a certain amount of game near by,
which attracted migrating troops of lions.   Yes, it was
a very good position for contact with the jungle king!

That night my viking friend was unable to sleep.
Whether his trouble was due to the weird sounds of
the African night or to the unaccustomed viands he
had dined upon, I do not know.   Anyway, he failed to
woo slumber and at length gave up the attempt and
went outside the tent to stroll about in the starlight.
So far, all was well — quiet reigned along the gloomy
donga.   But, before leaving far-distant Norway, the
stroller had made what proved almost a fatal error;
for here he was walking about beneath the stars of
the African night in a suit of black-and-white pyjamas!
Suddenly he heard a sound as of galloping hoofs, and
presently made out in the distance a huge dark
form bounding toward him across the veldt.   He
stopped still, curious to learn more about the identity
of this galloping form.   In jig time he did learn, but
when the object became recognizable, he was too
frightened to move, standing frozen to the spot, while
a huge male lion came rushing at him with the speed
of an express train.   A few paces from the terrified man
the lion skidded to a stop in a cloud of dust, regarded
the object in black and white uncertainly for a brief
moment and then, with a low growl of surprise or disgust, or both, turned slowly around and trotted back
in the direction whence he had come.

The only possible explanation I can offer for this remarkable behavior on the lion's part is that, in the semidarkness of the starlit veldt, my neighbor's pyjamas had deceived the prowling beast into believing zebra meat was to be had for the taking and that, when he discovered his error, he became suspicious of a possible trap and so retreated into the donga as quickly as his pride would allow. I am not dogmatic on the point — it is anybody's guess. After all, "the only certainty about a lion is his uncertainty." Next day the Norwegian party moved alongside our tents, explaining that there was too much night traffic at their first camp.

Most of the photographic work was accomplished at what we called "our lion donga," and it was in this vicinity that the greater part of our experiences with the tawny cats took place. On one occasion we drove to the old manyatta and dropping four of our boys to lighten the load, circled the donga to give the lions a smell of the meat. Hardly had we done so when four pairs of eyes peeped over the bushes and then slowly one lioness walked into the open. She looked at us, less than fifty yards away, then turned and stood on tiptoe to catch a sight of the kill. Now another lioness with catlike tread followed her; then, after giving us a quick glance, walked to the bait, which was exactly fifty feet from where I stood in the rear of the truck. She smelled at the dead zebra, sniffed the air, gazed at us through slit eyes, then strode away about ten feet and lay down.

Meanwhile the third lioness had lost her last bit of fear and came to the kill at a fast walk, where with one mighty paw she turned the six hundred pound zebra over and started to tear at the belly.

Tanganyika. Lions on a kill. Although they look like big peaceful cats that would not mind being petted, no one in the party felt inclined to try.

Tanganyika. It is a curious fact that a lion will seldom quarrel with a lioness but often resents the presence of another male at the same feast. These two males must have been brothers.

Now, Mr. Lion had been watching all of this from the bushes, and finding that no harm had come to the others, he walked in all his majesty toward them, but for some reason all his own, passed them and the kill and went down the trail up which we had come until he was out of sight. Presently he appeared again coming slowly back the same way and continuing right up to the kill. As he came near, the big lioness sidled up to him, rubbed against him coyly, licked his face and then they both lay down side by side.

In the foreground we have this scene; a lion and his mate watching other members of the family eating. Now over the sky line appears another big male lion slowly but surely coming down the scented trail. He never slackens his pace until within twenty feet of the domestic scene described. The husband now gets to his feet, faces the rival and growls, whereupon Mr. Newcomer lies down and yawns, not once but several times, showing his huge jaws and teeth. About the second time he did this the only Negro we had in the truck looked at me and tried to smile, but failed.

The wife now got up and ran over to the intruder, whom she slapped twice in the face, to which he replied playfully by turning on his back like a big kitten with paws in the air.

All was quiet for a while until the first male thought he would have a bite or two, whereupon he looked at the other, growled and sprang upon the carcass, tearing fiercely at the meat. This was too much for the late arrival and he went right over. On his way the same lioness had another punch at him, to which he paid no attention, but which surely peeved him, for he made at the other male in a savage rush and for a few moments the ground shook, the air trembled, while heavy thuds sounded amid the uproar.

While this was taking place not a soul in our little party even so much as breathed, for without a doubt, it was the greatest thrill we had ever known. It was quite a different thing than watching lions in a zoo, to know that only a few feet of air separated you from them, and that in two bounds the whole lot could be right in the truck, settling the argument in your midst.

It must have been a draw, for both males began to feed at once, one on either side of the kill, eyeing each other and growling, while the lionesses kept at the side of their first love.

We could hear more lions in the donga, and as it was getting late, thought it best to move the bait into the old manyatta. As the truck started to pull the zebra away, the whole mob jumped on it and we could not budge an inch. I was afraid we would break the wire cable, but by slipping the clutch and jerking the zebra, we managed to get them off it until we could get going. The males now followed the kill, while the females remained behind, so after going half the distance to the boma, we stopped to let them all catch up and while waiting another lioness came out of the cover.

The four boys we had left in the old manyatta were lolling on the ground and could not see anything but the truck and us in it; they did not know that four lions were right behind us and another one coming at a dog trot, so when we drove into the manyatta and dragged the kill past them, they still remained in their favorite position. After the truck stopped, however, they stood up and then saw right under their noses, not more than thirty feet from them, five lions! They all dropped as if they had been shot, flat on their stomachs, and in that position they wiggled like a school of fishes into the boma, where we had told them to go in the first place, and where they will never fail to go when told again.

Now came the job of getting the lions away until we could finish the boma. By much jumping and shouting the boys managed to get them at about a hundred yards distance, then started operations. We had to cut down a lot of brush and grass so that when the pictures were made the lions would not be hidden. While this was going on, it began to grow dark and in our haste to finish the job we almost forgot the yellow cats, until one of the boys went over to cut down a bush and was met by a mighty roar. The big male had crept back and was within twenty feet of us and probably had been there for quite a while. It was time to quit, for darkness was coming swiftly on, and lions grow bolder as the shadows deepen.

Mounting the truck, which was standing alongside the dead zebra, we drove away about thirty feet and then stopped to see what would happen. What did happen was a most impressive thing, and we that beheld it will never forget the scene. Here was the old abandoned Masai manyatta with the grass huts outlined in the half light, as the sun sank blood red over the rolling veldt. Now with his fine head erect and the mane showing black, the big male lion strode slowly between two of the deserted huts and then continued his stride to the kill, where he stood over the zebra carcass in beautiful silhouette against the dying sun, a picture that no painter could ever transfer to canvas.

Daily they performed for us, doing things I never had dreamed this lordly beast could or would do, and always during that time we were in the position of men pouring nitroglycerine; if death were to come, it would be both sudden and decisive. I had ever in mind that saying honored throughout Africa, that "the only certainty about a lion is his uncertainty," and if one of our troop had suddenly taken a notion to charge home, who would know of its intention? Surely not the party charged! As a lion can cover more than fifteen feet at one bound and most of our filming was done within that distance, we were at all times more or less dependent upon their better nature. A lioness once rushed me and only stopped six feet from my crouching self. A split second before, she had been complaisantly feeding on a staked-down topi just fifteen feet distant, and what caused her to make this lightning charge and then to halt with her hot breath in my face, I do not know. It happened so quickly that I had no sense of fear, but after the danger was past I trembled like a leaf until it was possible to get my rifle trained out in her direction. A silly reaction, to be sure, for if she had continued six feet forward all the trembling and all the rifles in the world would not have made it possible for me to write this account.

My first intention had been to make a few scenes of these lions, for no one dared to hope that we could keep them around for long, but day after day we returned to find them playing among the rocks, climbing over the ant hills, chasing vultures in fun, cleaning

This photograph proves that, contrary to popular belief, lions can climb trees. While not making a practice of it, they do get up small trees, upon occasion, faster and easier than a man.

Tanganyika.   A young male and two lionesses on the plains of the Serengetti.

themselves like tabby cats with their huge paws, drinking and eating, loving each other; and so the days melted into weeks and the weeks into months before we had finished our work with the lions of Tanganyika.

Where I had expected to spend many hard days, I spent instead days full of interest and thrills, watching the king of beasts as he lived his natural life beneath blue skies, stalking from his cool lair out into the plains, not as a bloodthirsty killer, but because nature has so arranged things that he must use claws and fangs to live.   These were indeed wonderful days, during which we were given a marvelous insight into the true lives and habits of lions on their native veldt in the heart of an African wilderness.

CHAPTER SIX

VICTORIA NYANZA

BECAUSE we were operating in Tanganyika, it was necessary to obtain permission and hunting licenses from an officer of the territory, so shortly after establishing Camp Simba, Bud and I made a trip in one of the trucks to Musoma on Lake Victoria. It was the season of short rains and the terrain between the camp and lake is notorious for its swampy nature. There were, of course, no roads, although some wheel tracks going to a remote mine guided us part of the way.

After fighting mud most of the time and losing several miles on account of getting lost, our first day came to an inglorious end on the edge of a swamp. Toward dark we began looking for a camping spot, but finding nothing suitable continued on. Suddenly the whole front end of the truck sank down, giving us the sensation of tipping over a precipice, then came to a quick stop. Investigation proved that the front half of the truck was mired down in what seemed to be a bottomless mudhole, this mudhole extending as far ahead as we could see in the semidarkness. We tried to reverse, but the wheels simply spun around until the tires began to smoke. Darkness brought an end to our efforts. We were tired and hungry, so when a couple of lonesome hyenas began to moan off in the bushes, we decided to call it a day.

As it was too muddy to put up the tent, we placed
the tarpaulin over the truck in order to sleep inside.
Our boy made some hot tea, Bud opened a can of
herring, and I opened a can of beans. With these
and a loaf of bread supplied by pishi before we left,
we managed to have a very fine repast. The shadows
from the flickering oil lantern threw grotesque shapes
against the canvas. Outside we could hear the dismal
patter of the rain as it drizzled down upon the lonesome veldt. Its monotonous drip-drip as it fell off
the eaves of the cab and the end of the tarpaulin,
caused Bud to say:

"I know a country where sometimes a few rain
drops fall during the course of a year — where everything is burned to a crisp and not many white men visit.
It is the Land of Thirst, in the heart of the Taru, a
country of thorn scrub and scattered hills. Old Maniki
knows the place for it is the home of the Wakamba.
Dad, Mike, and I went out there in 1927, a short time
before they closed the district to elephant hunting.

"The day after we arrived the three of us went
scouting around to see what we could find and were
bouncing over the veldt in an old tin lizzie when suddenly from the other side of a large patch of thorn
bush, the biggest herd of bull elephants in all Africa
crashed out. We sat there in astonishment, counting
forty-two of them, I think, every one bulls, and all carrying good ivory. Not long after that we almost
bumped into all the cow elephants in that part of
Africa and the three of us decided to get out and look
them over — there might be a couple of good bulls
among them. We got separated and after awhile I
found a big old bull who looked like the possessor of

7

good ivory. Thought I could kill him outright with
a brain shot; knew I'd have to do it quick in order to
send the herd away before Dad and Mike got inside
of it, but the wind shifted and the bull charged me at
close quarters. I pushed my double-barreled .577 forward in a hurry as the enraged bull came tearing down
on me with his trunk on high and his ears outspread.
He could almost reach me with his trunk as I gave him
both barrels, which caused him to hesitate. This
allowed me a chance to do a little fast moving on my
own account, and as I was zigzagging about trying to
shove new shells into the breach, Mike popped up from
somewhere and dropped the old monarch with a bullet,
from his .505 Gibbs. It was sure a close call for me,
but I didn't mind it at all for he was carrying two
hundred twenty pounds of nice clean ivory.

"There was quite a party shooting in there for
several days. You remember Judd? He was there.
That was about three months before he was killed by
a Taru bull near Ndi station. Mike had a close call
too when two bulls charged him. This time Dad and
I helped him out. This is the country I want to take
you into for pictures of elephants and rhinos. We
won't have to worry about rain there, for I believe it
is the driest spot in Africa — it is even too dry to be
a desert!"

Outside the rain still pitter-pattered drearily against
the tarpaulin and dropped unceasingly on to the
ground below. Bud blew out the flickering lantern
and called to the boys for quiet. They had made
their beds underneath and were now shifting about
uneasily because we had heard several lions. *Felis leo*
always seems to prowl about a great deal when it

rains and tonight he was calling in every direction.
We had never heard louder roaring; the tremendous
vibrations seemed to roll right along the ground.
Then there would be silence for awhile until some
jackals commenced yapping, probably followed by
the weird sound of a hyrax. Then another lion would
start with a low grunt and keep increasing the volume
until he had reached the full height of his power and
his mighty roar rolled over the veldt like peals of
thunder. Silence again! Then perhaps a hyena would
give vent to his feelings in that long, indescribable cry
which ends in a weird laugh. Back of it all, a vast
chorus of bullfrogs which inhabited the swamp kept
up a continuous mournful croaking that sounded like
innumerable bass viols. Such is nature's stupendous
orchestra which nightly provides the song of the veldt,
for all those who are there to listen.

With this chorus in our ears we dropped off to sleep,
to be awakened by my boy, Kahindi, when he brought
us a cup of hot tea. After a hearty breakfast which
was commenced by Bud opening a can of beans and
myself opening a can of herring, we found it required
but little effort to get out of the mudhole and were
soon merrily on our way toward the lake. During
the day we motored through a very interesting parklike country of gently rolling hills. We seemed to have
left the soft ground behind, or maybe it had rained less
here — anyway were able to make good time. That
night we camped under a huge sausage tree near the
village of Chief Kitchamuli, who shortly came out
followed by three of his wives and presented us with
some butter and gourds of milk. The milk we gave to
our boys, but as we craved fat and the butter looked

fairly clean, decided to keep it for ourselves, first having Kahindi wash it with fresh water. It proved so good that we asked the chief to make some more before our return, so that we could carry it back to camp.

Like all chiefs in this district, Kitchamuli was able to carry on a conversation in Swahili, telling us that the tremendous valley which he overlooked from his village was at the present time alive with antelope and zebra; that on this account several troops of lions had moved into the district. He was anxious to have us stay and shoot some meat and lions for him. We had no time to hunt lions, but promised to remain long enough in the morning to kill him a few zebra or topi.

I guess he was afraid we would forget our promise, because when the first rays of the sun shone into my eyes, I arose up to find Kitchamuli squatted near the fire talking to Kahindi. He immediately greeted me with, "Jambo, bwana!" After our usual breakfast of herrings and beans, supplemented this morning with butter on our bread, Bud and I sallied forth into the plain below to fulfil our promise to the chief. Game was so abundant that we had little difficulty and within half an hour had shot two zebra, a wildebeest, and a topi. I noticed that the ever-present scavenger of the veldt was johnny-on-the-job, for hardly had the first zebra kicked his last, than a large spotted hyena gave a low laugh of satisfaction and darted forth from the nearest donga, as if he took it for granted we had gone to all this trouble for his handsome self. A well placed bullet dissipated all of his high hopes, and when we returned to the village a few days later his skin was adorning a hut wall.

We had heard plenty of lions that night; in fact one of them came entirely too close for comfort. Neither Bud nor myself can be classed as having nervous dispositions, but after listening to the chorus of lions hereabouts for several hours before going to sleep, who can blame us for springing up like a couple of jacks-in-a-box when, during the middle of the night, one of the large sausages fell from the top of the tree and lit ku-plunk near our cots? We both thought a lion had jumped right between us!

When we drove away, the chief with his wives and a few young boys were busily and happily engaged cutting up the meat, which they would afterwards dry in the sun. We got started on the wrong cow path, which brought us into strange country. Just as we were preparing to turn around and retrace our wheel tracks we came upon a big "n'goma" or native dance, at which many warriors were prancing and chanting. These men were dressed in skins, wore lion headdresses, and had wonderful big war shields. Some of them spoke Swahili, and so we talked to them about coming to my camp and spearing lions for picture purposes. It was all agreed upon and arrangements made to return for them at a specified time.

After getting started in the right direction again, we found the country gently sloped toward that immense inland sea, Victoria Nyanza, which covers roughly twenty-seven thousand square miles. Late that evening we drove into the place called Musoma. Our first call was at the police station where they were mighty glad to see us — not in the line of duty, but because it is very seldom indeed that a white man drops into their station. We were invited to have

dinner by the entire force, and he opened a bottle of
champagne to celebrate the occasion.

Next morning we paid a visit to the duka, where, in
addition to a few grocery supplies, we intended to pick
up twenty cases of gasoline which had been sent here
by lake steamer from Kisumu. We found that the
gasoline had duly arrived, but had been returned by the
brilliant Indian who operated the duka, his explanation
being that as he had ordered no gasoline, he thought
someone was trying to fool him. This was a fine situation; we didn't even have enough gasoline to get
back to camp. Things looked dark indeed until we
discovered from the black boys that the Indian had
a large warehouse full of gasoline. Then we surmised
what afterwards proved to be correct; that the wily
old boy thought by sending back our gasoline he
would be in a position to sell his own to us at an
exorbitant price. I had with me a letter from the
Vacuum Oil Company, which called upon him to supply
me with all the gasoline I wanted. As payment was
made through my New York office, I'm afraid his hopes
of an extra profit were not fulfilled.

People have asked me what Victoria Nyanza looks
like. Anyone who has seen the ocean can answer the
question, for it stretches beyond the horizon. One of
my boys who had been in Mombasa, but never before
to the lake, thought that by some mysterious route
we had arrived at the sea. He was not convinced
otherwise, until he had tasted the water and found
it to be sweet.

We did not envy our police friend's job, for although
it is a beautiful country around the shores of this
wonderful lake and there are many interesting things

to do and see, it is extremely unhealthful for white men. There were four whites in the place and every one of them full of fever. We were glad to finish our business and be on the way back to Camp Simba, one hundred thirty-five miles distant. This is not a great distance over good roads, but with a heavily loaded truck, plowing through mudholes, making your way over hills and through dry sandy river beds, it is quite a jaunt.

When we again stopped under Kitchamuli's sausage tree, the old fellow immediately darted out with his wives, each with a gourd of butter. He again asked us to stay and shoot some lions. I believe he was anxious to secure some lion fat, which these natives regard as a cure-all for most anything. From the lion fat they make an oil which they rub on their limbs for rheumatism, and take internally for all sorts of ailments. If administered in a certain way, it is supposed to make the taker as brave as the beast itself.

Bud was sure there were some fine black-maned lions in the district, so we decided to put out a couple of baits that evening and wait until next morning to see what luck we had. First killing a zebra, we dragged it for two or three miles in a huge circle to make a scented trail and then anchored the bait to a small tree near a likely donga. Another kill was placed two or three miles away, then we returned to camp fully confident that next morning we should see many lions. We listened to them all evening and away into the night, so imagine our disappointment upon paying visits to both baits, in failing to see a single lion! There were plenty of hyenas, however, as usual. This district was full of game and it is probable that the lions had become so accustomed to killing their own food that they were suspicious of a bait. If it had been possible to spend several days here, more than likely we would have found plenty of customers. Before leaving we shot three more zebras for Kitchamuli, thus leaving the village in a happy and prosperous condition. After fighting mud for the balance of that day and most of the next, we drove into camp, finding that the population had been increased by Mona and Ted, who had come down from the shamba in Mike's touring car.

After the work of the day, I would sit down to my typewriter and, by the light of a gasoline lantern, write my daily notes, but was finally forced to give up this night work by the thousands of bugs that came flying in from all over the continent of Africa to bang against my face, get into my ears, and to get squashed on the paper by the typewriter keys. When I would hit a key, instead of making a letter on the paper, it more often flattened out a beetle or sausage bug. The little foxes had now become very tame and as their principle diet consists of insects, they greatly enjoyed this deluge of bugs. One night I had a bright idea and placed the gasoline lantern on the ground. Immediately all the insects were attracted there and our wild doggies, as the bat-eared foxes are called locally, had the time of their lives scurrying around in high glee after everything from flying ants to huge beetles that weighed several ounces. As there was no end to the insects or to their appetites, I had to watch carefully and remove the lamp just before the little doggies popped. They had a friend who would join them once in awhile, a big bleary-eyed hop-toad, with an appetite as large as theirs, and I can still remember how he would get so full he could not budge. Then I'd carry him to some safe place, where nothing could step on him, until he was able to take care of himself again.

After switching my writing activities to the daylight hours, I was plugging away at the typewriter on an early morning, just after I had sent Ted with one of the trucks to the shamba for supplies, when my headman came in to say that four eland were just outside the camp. We had not shot an eland as yet and we needed some fat, but a look through the glasses revealed them to be four cows, which it is unlawful to kill. Later he rushed in again to inform me there were "twiga menge" standing about three hundred yards away. I went out more to show him I was interested than anything else, and for once was glad that I did, for there silhouetted against the morning sky stood a herd of seventy-two giraffe, one of the most remarkable sights I had ever seen. They were curious about our camp and hung around for some time, but before I could get the camera set, something frightened them, whereupon they galloped away in a cloud of dust.

Shortly afterwards three Masai came strolling up and, planting their spears in the ground, made signs that they wanted to talk to me. I sent for my Masai boy, who said they had come after the money promised to the chief for his coöperation when we photographed the cattle in the manyatta. Knowing that these people will accept nothing but metal coins, I had the agreed sum ready for them in shillings. When they seemed disposed to argue about the amount, I gave them the message sent by the D. C. — District Commissioner — at Musoma. They had no right in this part of the territory, and unless they were more careful of their actions, he intended to send soldiers to drive them out. While the boy was interpreting this to them, they stood there with exclamations of "Ah ah," "eh eh," "oh oh," then left without further ado.

We were still working with the lions, occasionally, and one day while enroute through the "valley of lions," I espied what looked like a leopard sitting on its haunches in the shade of a small thorn bush. As I was attracting Mike's attention, it sprang up and started to run, disclosing itself to be a large cheetah. So far we had obtained no film of this animal and taking advantage of this opportunity we raced after it in the truck. A cheetah is the fastest animal on four feet for a few hundred yards, but soon becomes winded, making it easy to run him down, which we did, getting some excellent close-up motion pictures. Then someone suggested we take him to camp for a pet. We had quite an exciting time tying him up and placing him in the truck, then realizing that he was too old to become very docile we turned him loose.

While making our way back to the trail we noticed a ring of vultures grouped around a slight depression and, upon coming closer, found the ever-present hyena and two jackals robbing an ostrich nest. They had broken most of the eggs and eaten their contents. Our arrival frightened them away, but there was very little left for the hen ostrich to mother. She hovered in the vicinity much distressed and was shortly joined by the cock ostrich, who made short charges toward us. After taking a few pictures of the unhappy pair, we left them surveying the ruins of what had been a happy ostrich home.

It is a well-known fact that tame ostriches mate for life and are very loyal once they have paired up. How true this is of the wild bird I cannot say, but I often observed a troop of hens attended by one cock ostrich. However, in the case of coming upon a nest, I have always found one cock and one hen in attendance. The average weight of a full grown ostrich is around two hundred seventy-five pounds, although, no doubt, some attain a greater weight. An ostrich is a very long-lived bird, the average age being about seventy years, while many live considerably beyond that.

Pishi had asked that we bring some meat to camp, so when a small herd of tommies went dashing by, I sat down on the ground with my Remington and taking careful aim at a young male, fired. My boy, Kahindi, who was standing up, shouted that I had killed two buck with one shot. He was right; the high velocity bullet had passed through one tommie and into another, killing them both. As the distance was one hundred twenty yards, and the animals were running, we classed it as a freak shot.

Ted was now several days overdue, and as we feared he might be stuck in a mudhole, or had gotten into some other serious trouble, had set a definite time at which, failing his return, we would go in search of him. We had the second truck ready for the road and were to start in thirty minutes when he came into view. I took a look through the binoculars and saw that he was not driving; that young Penfold from Gilgil had the wheel. The coming of the truck was comparable to the excitement of a stagecoach arrival in the old days out west. There was mail for everyone, and bits of news concerning the great world beyond the Serengetti.

There were good reasons for Ted's delay. Everything had gone along smoothly until the night before he planned to start the return journey. He went out that evening with a double-barreled shotgun to kill a buck for meat. At the edge of a wheat field, quite close to Mike's house — where Ted had complained not so many weeks before of being cheated out of a chance for adventure — he saw two large eyes gleaming in the semidarkness, and while swinging the gun into position there was a sudden flash as a huge leopard sprang toward him. In his hurry to turn he fell, but before doing so fired both barrels into the animal's face. Apparently no damage was done to the spotted cat except that one of his upper fangs was broken off and probably he got a little of the shot into his skin. This treatment didn't improve his disposition, and he rushed toward the boy with a savage growl. Ted held his right arm forward to protect his face, and the leopard bit him through the forearm. Now the three dogs who were with Ted distracted the beast's attention. He left the boy and rushed for the dogs, giving Ted a chance to regain his feet and reload his shotgun, which, however, he didn't have another chance to use, as the animal was not seen again.

Ted's father has been mauled twice by leopards, so he knew the dangers of infection and going into the house twisted some cotton around a small stick, then dipping this into a bottle of iodine pushed it down into the holes made by the cat's teeth. It was not a pleasant experience, leaving his arm so sore for a few days that it was impossible for him to drive the heavy truck over the terrible roads between the farm and the camp, a distance of nearly three hundred miles. He

finally managed to get as far as Gilgil, where young
Penfold, who had been in Africa for some time without
seeing a lion, agreed to drive to camp, if Ted would
assure him of a meeting with the king of beasts.

After Ted had completed his story, Mike said to
Penfold, "Guess we will have to take you out and
show you some lions," to which he replied, "No hurry
— saw plenty of them last night — in fact, I'm ready
to go home now!" Then it was Penfold's turn to tell
of what had happened the night before at the first
donga this side of the Gurmeti.

A light shower had softened the road and as they
were heavily loaded with food supplies and gasoline,
they got stuck in the bottom of this deep donga, the
truck not having enough power to pull up the opposite
bank. It was just at dusk, and while trying to get the
truck out, they heard a lion grunt within a few feet of
them. Penfold did not know what it was, but Ted
did, so casually turning to his companion he asked,
"Did you hear that lion grunt right over there?" and
as if in answer there were several more grunts; whereupon the men made a hurried exit, grabbing bedding,
a box of food and the rifles, as they abandoned the
donga. Going about one hundred yards from the
ravine they found a likely place to camp near a large
dead tree which would make a good fire. This had
hardly commenced to blaze brightly when darkness
fell suddenly, as it does in the tropics. Shortly afterwards, Mr. Lion stalked out into the open toward the
fire, followed by six lionesses. When Ted called Penfold's attention to the troop, he exclaimed, "I say, old
man, do they come in flocks like that?" Ted fired a
few shots to frighten them, but in spite of this they

hung around the camp all night, grunting and growling so that nobody was any too keen the next morning to get back into the donga in order to get the truck out. But it had to be done, and so here they were safe and sound after a little pleasure jaunt for supplies!

After things had been stored away and letters read, Mike and I set out to secure some meat for the boys — the intention being to get a zebra as I wanted the skin, but in Africa most anything can happen in one afternoon. As we were crossing the broad plain in front of our camp, I shot a fine topi bull with an exceptional head. This I had skinned out to return home for my collection. The carcass we placed for lion bait. Farther on I shot at a zebra, but missed, and while we were trying to get another shot at him, almost ran into a herd of eland. I promptly forgot all about the tiger horse and went after this giant animal of the antelope family. There was a noble looking bull in the lot weighing around fifteen hundred pounds. His head was nothing to brag about, but we needed fat badly and there is nothing finer than eland meat. Finally I took a running shot at between eighty and one hundred yards, placing a 220-grain bullet into his shoulder, which brought him down at once. We took all the choice cuts for ourselves and the boys, then dragged the remains to another likely spot for lions. While the boys were cutting up the meat, which took about two hours, hundreds of vultures and marabou storks collected on the surrounding trees waiting for us to leave the eland. When we dragged it away they swooped down to disappointment. This was one of the grandest days I ever spent in Africa. The evening was perfect, ending in a marvelous sunset

Hoefler holding up the head of a very fine water buck bull. The black boy is the author's gun bearer and skinner, Maniki, who plays a prominent part throughout the story.

The remains of the ostrich nest which had been robbed by hyenas and jackals.

Beneath the sausage tree near the village of Chief Kitchamuli. The gentleman standing at the extreme right is none other than the Chief himself.

of saffron and gold. Africa can be beautiful one moment and violently cruel the next.

Before dawn, as we bounced over the hazy landscape toward the place where I had killed the topi, we tried to solve some of the mysteries of the early morning; what sort of an animal a certain shape would turn out to be! In the dim light we would point out a moving shadow and call it a zebra, when in all probability it was a hyena, or you would name something a lion and find it to be an old-man baboon. So as this new day was born and we rode over the African veldt toward the dead topi, I saw a moving black shape and thought to myself, "Great Caesar, what a lion that is!" As we drew nearer several hyenas hustled away, which indicated there were no lions about. Upon getting a better look at the dim object, I was surprised to find that my lion was a rhino! The fact of its being near the kill was simply a coincidence. The prehistoric pachyderm was just ambling from one hill to another and happened to be passing our bait as we approached. Mr. Rhino gave a few snorts, then disappeared into some thick thorn scrub.

It was brightening into daylight now, so we hustled to where the eland remains had been left. Mike was driving the truck and in a position to see around the corner first, as we neared the clump of wild sisal. He took a quick glance, then whispered the magic word "lions!" In the next second I saw them, counting seven in all, four lionesses and three males. Two of the males had fair manes and as Austin had failed so far to shoot a lion we gave him first chance. He had brought an old .405, but as it was quite a distance, I handed him the Remington .30 and when it spoke the

8

lion went down in a heap, giving vent to several lusty
growls and roars. In the meantime I took a flying
shot at the remaining big one with the .405, but as
the gun was strange to me, only succeeded in nipping
him. This made him very angry, and he turned as if
to charge but changed his mind and went into the
thick bush, where he proceeded to raise a commotion,
shaking the small trees and making the ground rumble.

With the .30 in my hands again I maneuvered into
a position where I could see him. He was crouched in
the underbrush at about thirty yards and furiously
lashing his tail. I could only see his moving tail and
part of his head, the body being hidden by sisal and
scrub. Taking a careful bead at where I thought his
shoulder should be, I fired. More growls and I could
see him dragging himself farther into the thicket.
Not knowing where either of my bullets had hit, if at
all, took another quick shot. The growling ceased
and then the question was, "Is he dead or not?"
There is nothing more dangerous than a wounded lion
in thick bush, but the only way to find an answer to
our question was to go into the thicket. The fact that
there were five other lions in the same small patch of
cover, all of them in perfect health, made it quite exciting as Mike and I ventured in shoulder to shoulder
while the others watched on the outside. When we
found him lying in a small open place we noticed he
was still breathing, but in a short time he expired.

When Mike and I grabbed his tail, in order to pull
him into the open, pandemonium broke loose. The
other five lions had burst out of the thicket with such
suddenness that our companions were nearly knocked
off their feet, but amidst it all we could hear the voice

of Penfold, calmly and casually counting them as they passed! We found that the shot from the .405 had merely cut his paw, the first shot with the .30 had broken his shoulder, while the last had entered his head. Both he and the one killed by Austin were full-grown males with fair manes.

After the exercise of getting these into the truck, all of us were ready to enjoy a delayed breakfast. Later we proceeded to our lion donga, but, although we hunted high and low, could find no trace of our family. We came to the conclusion that they had heard of the tragedy to the other troop that morning and had left the country.

The time had now arrived to collect the Ikoma lion spearmen, who had promised to join us; so I sent Bud and Ted with one of the trucks into the lake country for them. The truck started early in the morning with rain threatening, giving prospects of a trying journey through mud and the tsetse-fly country. They took three boys with them and plenty of supplies, for, although it was only a two-hundred-fifty-mile round trip, in this country it is always wise to go prepared for a long trek. Bud had instructions to bring back twenty spearmen with all their equipment.

With Mike driving the other truck, his wife Mona and myself on the front seat, and three black boys for lookouts, we started out, intending to fulfil Mona's ambition to shoot a lion. She had been in Africa a long time and her husband is one of the greatest hunters the country has ever known, but it was the old story of the shoemaker's wife going without shoes. Mona had been living among lions, hearing about lions for years, and had never shot one. As we bumped along toward a likely spot, her possibilities of success were discussed. She had always dreamed of her first lion as being a huge beast which she killed with one shot, and now that the actual meeting was approaching she had two fears; one that the animal would be an undersized, scrawny beast, the other that she would be unable to hit him.

About two hours after sunrise we were going slowly along a donga when an impalla ram came running toward us. Now this was a very unusual thing for an animal to do so we watched him closely. He became aware of our presence and stopped to gaze at us, then turned around and stood rigid while he took a long look down the trail over which he came. We looked in the direction of his coming but were unable to see far because of wild sisal and cactus. When we turned a little corner, however, we saw what the impalla had been watching. There about two hundred yards away stood a beautiful lioness. Mona got all excited but Mike and I persuaded her it would be very unladylike to shoot another lady.

An hour or so later, and farther down the same donga, I noticed some vultures sitting in a tree and that all of these birds were looking in the same direction, so I climbed into the rear of the truck where I could get a better view. When vultures assemble there is usually a dead animal close by, and when they perch in trees this way, it means that something is keeping them from the carcass. I kept my eyes focused in the direction they were looking and stretching to full height tried to see over the edge of the steep bank. While in this position, the head and shoulders of a very big lion slowly arose in front of me. He was not more than

The Ikoma warriors who were keen to spear lions until the actual task confronted them.

Mike Cottar and the author with lions which they killed the same morning.

The "Clement Hill," on Victoria Nyanza.

The captured cheetah, with the pishi, Ali Ramazan, holding the rope.

thirty feet away, standing over a young zebra which he had just killed. Quietly I told Mona that a large lion was waiting to be shot, but she couldn't see him, the fact being that he was so close she was looking beyond the lion, never expecting to get that near without knowing about it. Mike had to point the rifle at his head before Mona sighted him. Now she banged away, but was so close she overshot. Up he sprang and ran diagonally toward a thorn thicket. Somehow she managed to throw in another shell and fire. I heard the 220-grain mushroom bullet thump as it struck the running lion in the shoulder. As he tumbled he gave a roar that shook the atmosphere. Now the old question arose: "Was he dead or not?" Some little time was spent in shouting and throwing stones into the bush trying to get an answer from him, but without result. Mike and I both pronounced him dead, but the black boys said no. As it was much better to be on the safe side, especially with a lady along, we were very cautious. While making a large circle around the spot, I got a good whiff of lion smell, and by following up the wind we found him dead. Her first shot was a clean miss, but the second had broken the right shoulder and then penetrated into the heart. He proved to be an exceptionally large lion and was certainly a grand prize for Mona.

While returning to camp we noticed a Grant's gazelle standing transfixed, and following his gaze, discovered a cheetah crouched beneath a thorn tree. During this one morning the antelopes and vultures had pointed out to us three beasts of prey; one had made its kill, while the other two urged by hunger, were on the hunt, for such is nature's decree here on the primal veldt.

That night I was up until about ten o'clock developing negatives. Shortly after putting myself to bed, a bloodcurdling chorus came from the native boys' quarters. I had been between the two scratchy blankets hardly long enough to get warm when the shrieks broke the night's stillness. Such a clamor from the combined throats of eight natives could only be occasioned by a mortal fright. That its cause was at least a lion standing right over some hapless black man and gazing soulfully into his eyes, I was all ready to believe.

My rifle was by my cot side, so grabbing it and a lantern, I rushed forth to save the man's life. On the way I stumbled over pishi who was crawling back into his own private lean-to. In answer to my inquiry as to what all the row was about, he told me that one of the boys had been bitten by a scorpion. This was the anticlimax. Here I was armed with a rifle and prepared to do battle with a prowling king of the jungle when it was the medicine chest I really needed.

I summoned old Maniki, gave him the rifle to return to my tent, and told him to fetch the n'dower, or medicine, bidding him hurry; because if I did not soon quiet the tumult, they would certainly scare all the wild beasts off the Serengetti plains. Making my way to the boys' quarters, where presently Maniki joined me with the first-aid kit, I found the scorpion's victim tossing on the ground and right manfully holding up his end of the din. When I could make myself heard I asked him if the scorpion was as big as a faru, which is Swahili for rhino, and my sarcasm had the effect of getting a laugh from the other boys and bringing down the volume of noise at least a few pitches.

In the feeble rays of the lantern I examined the boy who asked me tremulously if he was bleeding much. When I assured him not so much as one drop, his feeling of relief brought his lusty yelling to a low moaning. He was further reassured when I opened my kit and prepared to give his wound treatment, for the native African has a childlike faith in the white man's medicine.

Now my knowledge of medicine is limited, but what I lack in therapeutical skill I believe is made up for by a quite extensive knowledge of the black man's ways and psychology, which prompted a course of treatment which I carefully explained to my native clinic at each step.

First, with a small lance I opened the place where he had been bitten and rubbed into the incision several crystals of potassium permanganate. Next I swabbed the whole surface of the wound with a ten-per-cent solution of iodine.

My surgical ministrations performed, I produced from the chest two big black pills, technically known as CC, or army pills, explaining to my patient that it was these pellets that got our boys out of the trenches. I added that they were potent for the cure of practically all ills to which flesh is prone, with especial reference to the sting of scorpions. When he had gulped these down, I brought out two five-grain aspirin tablets, saying that in the white man's country, they were used for everything ranging from falling dandruff to fallen arches. He was duly impressed. By this time quiet had been restored, and, after inspecting the dead scorpion, I went back to bed.

Next morning, the scorpion's victim was apparently as good as new and quite happy. After examining the wound with professional mien, I felt rather proud of my efforts. It is true, I had not allowed the case to give me any uneasiness, for a scorpion's bite is almost never fatal and, while there are probably better methods of treatment than that I employed, I did the best I knew how and felt confident of the results. Usually the effect of this insect's sting is to nauseate the victim and to cause him a good deal of pain for the first two hours or so. Even with the primitive methods of the native medicine man, as a rule he is fully recovered after about twelve hours.

We had just completed lunch when off in the distance we heard the roar of our other truck. Soon Bud and Ted came into camp covered with mud and without the spearmen. They had found the village all right, but the chief would not allow his warriors to leave the country, asserting that the Masai had made war against them and all the warriors were needed to fight. Then again they did not want to go through the tsetse-fly belt that lay between them and our camp, saying they were afraid of the sleeping sickness. Both of these excuses were good ones, but my personal opinion was that when the bargain was made they were full of native beer, and now that its effects had passed away they had begun to look at the thing in the cold light of the possible results, and decided that they had no business fooling around the king of beasts with a spear. The fact that they would not come, however, put me up against a real problem. The spearmen were needed to furnish the climax to the sequences we were making around the lions, and their nonappearance made it necessary that I make arrangements with some other tribesmen.

CHAPTER SEVEN

THE ENDLESS VELDT

AFRICA is a vast stage upon which savage men and millions of wild animals daily perform their allotted parts, and lucky indeed is the civilized man whom circumstances permit to visit this alluringly beautiful but primitive country!

Wildebeest, zebra, kongoni, giraffe, ostrich, topi, and impalla were now trekking into our front yard in countless thousands, while the Grant's and Thompson's gazelles simply covered the landscape near and far. The innumerable small depressions filled by the short rains, were now commencing to dry up, and the game was coming back into the vast plains near the larger water holes, such as those along the Serra Nyiro.

Knowing that the lions would follow in the wake of the antelope and zebra herds, bright and early one morning we again took the familiar trail, which by a devious route, found its way to our lion donga. While bouncing along, a large herd of wildebeest stampeded and tried to outrace the truck. These animals and the zebra both have a habit which is unexplainable. Without any apparent reason, they will kick up their heels and race along parallel to any motor car, eventually contriving somehow to cross in front of it. It always seems that the last animal just clears the radiator cap by two inches — never more or less.

After they have successfully crossed your path and enveloped you in a cloud of dust, they will wheel about and come to a dead halt, standing lined up in a row to watch the strange object snort by. All African hunters have heard the zebra bark, but I am almost positive that I have heard some of them laugh on these occasions, while the wildebeest stood there with a silly grin on their faces.

A bull in this herd appeared to have a very large head. As we wanted meat for the lions and I wanted a trophy, I went to some trouble to shoot him, only to discover that his horns were not so fine after all. It is difficult to pick good trophies among such a large herd. My license allowed me an ostrich and as I wanted to take a skin home to be made into various articles for souvenirs, I took advantage of the fact that a big cock ostrich stopped at about two hundred yards to watch us pass. A Springfield bullet went singing over the veldt and Tanganyika lost another of its population. While Maniki, with the assistance of two other boys, was removing the skin, I made a little excursion on foot, shooting a young kongoni for meat and a little later made a lucky shot at a running Ward's reedbuck which proved to have a dandy head.

We arrived at the donga and circled the entire ravine twice with both trucks without finding our lions. This was a sad disappointment to all of us, for we had really expected to see our old friends again. While skirting the donga for the last time, we came upon a pair of hyenas, presumably mates. We shot one of them, and the unhurt animal started to run, but smelling blood it came back and commenced to eat its late companion while we looked on. After frightening it away, we found that the first one was still alive. There is certainly no other animal as low as these vile eaters of carrion; cannibal brutes which will rend and eat a victim before it is dead!

I had not shot a hyena for several days, feeling that, after all, they might not be so bad, but after witnessing this disgusting scene, I not only shot the offending beast, but another which, about two hours later, made the mistake of getting in the way. I had lost all count of the number of hyenas killed, but now that we had made up our minds to continue the war against them, decided to keep a score. One idea led to another until in a short time we had invented a new game which we called "hyena golf." The rules were that the hyena must be at least two hundred yards away — the shooter being entitled to four trys. If he killed the hyena first shot, it was a hole in one; if it took two cartridges, an eagle; three bullets made a birdie, and four was par.

Being unable to locate the lions, we started to camp, taking a roundabout course. While passing over some small hills, we encountered a herd of the graceful impalla. A look through the glasses disclosed an exceptional head belonging to a ram who was standing a short distance from the herd. As I placed my 7 mm. Mauser to my shoulder, he started to run, but I easily followed him with my open sight and ivory bead. I fired twice, the last shot assuring him of an honored place in my trophy room.

While Maniki was skinning out the head for mounting and cutting out the best meat for camp, we took a short jaunt over to a small water hole around which thousands of sand grouse had settled. These birds are about the size of a pigeon, very fine eating, and offer some excellent sport. We had found that the best way to shoot them was by hiding near a water hole late in the evening. As they flew in from the veldt in clouds for the last drink of the day, the hunter could obtain several dozen in a very short time. It was not possible to use that method here, so Mike circled the truck around, thus scaring up huge flocks. When they took to the air sometimes the flock would fly close enough for me to get in a shot. We gathered all we could use with four shells, using a 12 gauge full choke pump gun. It is to be regretted that so little has been written about the bird life of Africa, for the entire country teems with an infinite variety and quantity of feathered life, some species offering the finest kind of sport.

Picking up Maniki and my trophy, we continued our journey to camp, and while eating lunch, the conversation finally centered on vultures. I now made up my mind to carry out an experiment which I had often planned but had never had the time to complete.

It was a very hot afternoon, the thermometer registering close to one hundred thirty degrees in the shade, causing heat waves to dance over the veldt, making distant objects take on fantastic shapes. I scanned our front yard with the binoculars in search of a zebra herd, and spotting one in a likely location, strode out into the blistering heat. I walked about a mile from camp and, finding a suitable spot, crawled under the low-hanging branches of a dense thorn tree, getting into such a position that it would be impossible for anything to see me from the air. With the glasses I carefully searched the heavens in all directions.

This brave little Masai cowherd could not have been over twelve years old.

The Masai enjoy American jazz. Notice the cowhides which the women wear for clothing. The two young men are El Moran and are holding the "white spear," or battle spear.

They were as blue and clear as it was possible to be and minute search failed to reveal a single bird. Everything was hot and quiet, the hum of the insects and the distant barking of the zebras being the only sounds. Taking a careful rest, I killed a zebra stallion who was standing at about three hundred yards. As the balance of the herd ran away in panic, I noted the time by my watch. Ten minutes later by using the binoculars I could see afar off the circling of many birds. As I watched, they began to move faster and faster. I remained perfectly hidden, and soon they were close enough for me to recognize as vultures. A few moments more and they came dropping out of the sky like bombs out of an airplane. Upon reaching a certain height, they would fold their wings and fall at tremendous speed toward earth, making a loud hissing noise as their bodies hurtled downward. When they had almost reached the ground, they would extend their wings, circle a couple of times, and make a beautiful landing. Thirty-five minutes after the zebra was shot, several score vultures and a few marabou storks were standing in a solemn ring around the carcass; and before another five minutes had elapsed, the boldest bird had taken a bite at him to see if he were really dead.

The vultures of Africa are one of the phenomena of nature to me. I had often wondered about their appearance seemingly from nowhere, and had decided upon this experiment in order to ascertain the time which would elapse between the death of an animal and their arrival. There must always be vultures scouting beyond the range of human vision, their keen eyes making it possible for them to spot an animal as soon as it becomes lifeless.

In this vast country nothing goes to waste — animal feeds upon bird and bird upon animal, some even upon their kind, the insects and worms finishing whatever they leave. I have often returned after a few days to the scene of an animal's death to find absolutely nothing there. Although I have traversed many thousands of miles of African veldt and jungle, I can only remember finding a few bones, and these were being disposed of as quickly as possible by ants and other insects.

People have often asked me how the time was passed during the evening, suggesting that we must have been very lonesome. Personally, I never had time to get lonesome, for, after returning from the day's field work, all I had to do was write up my daily notes, develop films, load the magazines for next day, develop tests, pack films, number and file negatives, write caption sheets for motion pictures and still negatives, prepare packages for mailing, stick on several kinds of labels, eat dinner, doctor the sick natives, give orders for the next day, check up on the amount of stores and water in camp, chase a couple of hyenas out of the kitchen, and then, if nothing unusual came up to occupy my time, I would go to bed.

On this night I went to bed early for I needed the rest badly. I got into bed all right, but not to sleep, for we had a plague of hyenas around the camp. I had learned to take them more or less as a matter of course, but this night the place seemed to swarm with these pests and they proceeded to hold a laughing and growling contest right behind my tent. I became fed up on the noise and went out with a rifle, swearing vengeance on the whole hyena clan, but when I stuck the flash light around the corner, all was silent. I would hardly get back into bed before they would start all over again. Finally I gave up in disgust.

As I was unable to sleep, I called my boy, Kahindi, to prepare some coffee, then awakened Mike. After a light breakfast we dashed off in the fast car to see how many lions we could select for rugs. Two hours later we returned without having seen a single lion, but I had shot two pesky hyenas and hoped they were delegates returning from last night's convention. The first was a running shot and just managed to make him in par, while the second being too full to run enabled me to score a hole in one.

Today it was necessary to go after water so we went to the spring about twenty miles east of our camp toward the Blangetti. We took this route, hoping to find some eland on the way. We stopped at a likely looking donga long enough for the boys to beat through it, thinking that maybe we could scare out some lions, but all that the ravine yielded was several reedbuck and five hyenas.

Shortly afterwards we came upon the rotting carcass of a giraffe, and when we stopped alongside, all of my boys made a wild scramble to get the hairs out of its tail. It seems that these hairs are very valuable among the natives for ornaments. Later we found another dead giraffe. Both of these animals had been lifeless for several days and were practically eaten by hyenas, jackals, and vultures, so it was impossible to say whether they had died from sickness or had been killed by natives with bow and arrows.

Just before reaching the spring, a herd of impalla bounded across the path and ran in among some small trees where they joined five eland who were standing in the shade. All of them proved to be cows, but while looking them over I spotted among the impalla a marvelous ram with a very good head. Taking my 7 mm. Mauser I made a careful stalk, using a small ravine to hide my movements. Getting up to within two hundred fifty yards, I crawled out of the donga to behind a small bush and from there was successful in bringing down this prize with the first shot. He proved to be a fine specimen, so I had old Maniki carefully prepare him for my collection.

The shooting stirred up a large family of monkeys. These noisy little fellows are more difficult to catch than one would think, and chasing them certainly affords plenty of exercise. After a good deal of tree climbing and running about, we were successful in capturing three young ones, which we later took back to camp for pets.

During our absence some Masai women had made a visit to the camp, inviting us over to the manyatta for a special dance, their only request being that we bring some sugar along. We drove over hoping to secure motion pictures of the event, and, while waiting around came to the conclusion that the Masai were great believers in personal adornment. The women constantly carry around with them large quantities of copper and iron wire coiled about their arms, necks and legs. A fully outfitted Masai woman will have as much as thirty-five pounds distributed over her body. The men also decorate themselves to a small degree, stretching their ear lobes to enormous sizes, in order to retain such articles as strike their fancy. We met one such gentleman who was a collector of rare orna-

The author with a fine impalla ram.   Tanganyika.

A cock ostrich shot by the author.

Masai toto, or youth. These young boys tend the cattle and, in a country full of lions, have no protection other than the spear shown in the picture.

ments, with a preference for small milk cans. The
Masai have no music of their own, but, like the people
of all savage tribes, they go wild over American jazz.
We had a great deal of fun with our phonograph.
They could not understand where the sound was
coming from and would gaze all about, looking for it.
When we asked them what they thought made it talk,
their reply was that we had cut off somebody's head
and placed it in the box.

We had gone over at their invitation to witness a
dance but were now entertaining them with our phonograph. It became so hot that the records curled up
and after a while the stench and the flies got so bad
that I lost my patience and demanded to know where
the dancers were. All sorts of excuses were offered as
a reason for not starting the performance. The crux
of the matter, however, was that they hoped to stall
me and in so doing raise the price. As I was already
disgusted with this outfit, I told them in a few words
to either start the show as agreed or we would leave.
The spokeswoman then said they did not want to
dance until a certain girl who lived over the hill arrived
as she had prepared special medicine for the occasion.
I told her that regardless of the medicine we would
not wait, so packing up we started away. When they
saw the sugar leaving she called that they would put
on the dance at once, but in the meantime the flies,
the heat, and the odor had helped me to decide that
I did not care to see the dance anyway, so we left
them standing there, shouting and waving their arms.

The next day, November fourteenth, being my wife's
birthday, gave me an excuse for declaring a holiday
in camp. I ordered Ali to prepare a special dinner

for the occasion, which he did! The main dish came
out of a can. It was one of those flavor-sealed hams
and furnished a pleasant change from the monotony of
antelope meat; then there were canned peas, canned
tomatoes, canned jam, canned sardines, canned butter
— the tea also came out of a can but was mixed with
local water. Oh! yes, pishi was certainly proud of his
efforts! I often wondered what would become of us
if the cook lost his can opener!

While partaking of this holiday repast, my thoughts
were thousands of miles away in my mountain home,
but Mike's interests were on things closer to camp,
and while waiting for Kahindi to bring in some more
slices of ham, he remarked on the unusual and somewhat humorous fact of our unsuccessful daily quests
for lion trophies as contrasted to our photographic
attainments with the same animal; that not once
during all our early morning excursions had we been
lucky enough to find one lion with a good mane. He
recalled a particular morning when we had gone out
long before dawn with high hopes, only to return
empty handed, even missing a shot at a lonely hyena,
and that after eating breakfast, we had motored to
the lion donga to find our entire troop waiting for us
under a nice shady tree.

It was really funny to think of getting up early
each morning to search all over the landscape for lions,
and failing to find any, of then proceeding to our
rendezvous with Mr. Felis Leo and his companions
near the family donga, there to spend the rest of the
day visiting with these eight lions, all of them just
as wild and bloodthirsty as any we had hoped to
shoot; the difference being, of course, that these

animals had become accustomed to us and did not seek cover when we approached. Their confidence in us would have been destroyed immediately if any shooting was done in their vicinity, and should one of them have been killed, the balance of the troop would have, no doubt, left the country for good.

During all the period of our almost daily contacts, none of the party ever attempted to use anything against these lions more deadly than a camera; not only because this would have put an end to our picture taking, but because they looked upon us as friends and we were honor bound to treat them as such. We always feared that sometime during our absence a hunting party might happen along and upon having eight lions rush out to meet them, would think they were being attacked and shoot the entire lot. Now we were really worried, for we had been to the donga several times without finding them.

The morning after our holiday, during which everyone shaved and one man took a bath, we returned to make another search for them. Upon arrival at the donga it looked as if our wild friends had left the district for good, but we made a last search, dragging a topi behind the truck and circling the ravine as we had often done before. After passing all of the old favorite places, without a sight of our lions, we had given up hope and were preparing to turn homeward when I espied a tawny head and shoulders half hidden in the grass. I shouted to Mike to steer that way, and as the truck neared the spot another head appeared and then two more — we had found part of our old troop.

In a short time they were all around us again; one lioness even came to lie down in the shade of the

truck, where I could hear her panting like a dog.
Once in a while she would glance up at me and then
resume her siesta.   Later we dragged the meat over
to the old Masai manyatta in order to photograph a
few scenes and secured film of them going in and out
of the huts.   This wasn't our idea, but rather their
own.   They would go into the huts to seek the shade;
then when we would start the motor they would come
bustling out thinking we were running away with the
meat.   After working with them for a while we motored
three or four miles to an inviting water hole to have
lunch.   As we approached we saw several geese, so
stopping the truck I took my shotgun and commenced a wide circle in order to get behind some
bushes which would put me in range of the birds.
While stalking along intently thinking of roast wild
goose, I was nearly startled out of my wits when a
huge wart hog jumped out of a hole from almost under
my feet.   In spite of my hurry to shoot the geese,
I tarried to watch this most ludicrous of all African
animals, as he trotted away, with his head held high
and his tail straight up in the air.   Then I continued
my stalk, securing two fat Egyptian geese, whose flesh
would be another welcome relief from antelope steaks.

While we were eating lunch beneath a spreading
mimosa tree which stood near the pool of water, we
watched a small Masai boy who was attending a large
herd of cattle.   Later, with a sardine sandwich in one
hand and the ever-necessary rifle in the other, I strolled
over to visit this twelve-year-old ebon youth.   I had
often admired the courage of these totos, who, in a
country full of prowling Carnivora, with only a short
spear for a weapon, stood guard over the cattle of

the tribe. We exchanged greetings, then he told me he left the manyatta with his charges at dawn, fed them during the long, hot days, took them to drink before sunset and returned them to the thorn inclosed village just before dark. When I asked him what he would do if lions attacked his cattle, he replied he would shout and try to scare them away, and if they failed to run he would! He added that when he grew big enough to handle the "white spear" he would then rush at them and if they would not leave, he would kill them with the spear.

One of my outstanding memories of the Tanganyika veldt is the scene indelibly pictured on my mind of looking over the backs of lions to see in the distance one of these little boys leaning upon his spear, a lonely sentinel silhouetted against the African sky.

After lunch we returned to the donga, collecting another wildebeest enroute. Our arrival was the signal for eight lions to make their appearances. Six of them belonged to our old troop and these had brought along two new lionesses for our approval.

Lions seem to be very affectionate in their home life. We noticed that whenever new members would join our troop the others would go to meet them, rubbing noses with the newcomers. African hunters tell you that when a lion is killed, its mate will hang about the place for several days, roaring and kicking up an awful racket each night until fully satisfied that the lost companion will not return. They seem to be thinking beasts, for no animal could do the things they accomplish without thought. One day they took a spare tire off the truck and had a great time with it. This incident made a cute scene, but although it was a husky General Cord, their sharp fangs tore pieces from the side walls, making it necessary to have it vulcanized. This proved that a lion can bite, for we had traveled over hundreds of miles of rocky country on similar tires without getting a single cut, while these lions playfully bit chunks out of it.

I made a few scenes from the truck and later crawled into one of the bomas. It seemed there was no end to this lion photographing business, because no matter how much film I took of them, the next time they would do something different, presenting an opportunity I could not afford to miss. A short time after entering the boma I was photographing seven lions who were crouched all around the front of the inclosure. Two lionesses had lain down right against the thin wall in order to avail themselves of the shade, for it was an intensely hot afternoon. These two were within four feet of Maniki and myself — so close we could hear their breathing very distinctly. Quite often they would switch their tails when annoyed by flies and this banging against the thorn wall would always give us a thrill. While I was intently looking out of the peephole, Maniki touched me on the shoulder and conveyed the information that there was a lion behind us. Without turning my head I said, "What of it? There are seven in front of us so why bother about one behind?" "But, bwana," pleaded my gunbearer, "this is a bad lion, baya sana, and you had better take a look right away or I think we shall both be killed." Maniki had been with me in bomas many times, and knowing he wasn't easily frightened, I thought it best to find out about the matter. After turning around I was fascinated by the sight of a lion

stalking us.   He was acting just like a house cat
when it stalks a bird in the back yard.   When I first
looked, he was crouched flat against the earth with
his tail slowly switching from side to side.   Then, with
his belly close to the ground, he ran swiftly forward a
few paces, then sank down, his big yellow eyes fastened
fixedly on the opening through which we had entered
the boma.   This doorway was plugged with a very
thin thorn branch; in fact, I had never noticed before
how thin it was, and wondered why it couldn't have
been a very thick branch.   Mr. Lion was getting close
and it looked as if he meant to spring into the boma.

He was a stranger and probably didn't know we
were there making photographs.   It was quite a
ticklish situation — seven lions grouped in front with
this big fellow creeping upon us from the rear.   Something had to be done quickly so taking my little pea-
shooter, the .505 Gibbs, I shoved the thorn bush aside
and crawled out toward the newcomer.   Slowly I
stood up with my back against the thorn wall, then
commenced to jump up and down and wave my hat
while shouting at the top of my lungs.   I heard the
lions behind me move quickly and expected to see
them come around the edge of the boma any second.
If they had, I might have been seriously hurt, but my
jumping about had simply caused the two lionesses to
run out and join the others.   Upon this information
being relayed by Maniki, I felt quite comfortable and
gave my undivided attention to the stranger.   I felt
that with my young cannon I could push him back
about ten feet the first shot, so started talking to him,
explaining that I had a family at home, as probably
he did, and that after all I had no intentions of harm-

ing him; so why couldn't we be friends? While I was talking he stood there gazing at me in surprise. He couldn't quite make out what kind of an animal I was! I guess he must have figured it to be a trap of some sort, because after giving vent to a few low growls, he turned slowly around, trotted a short distance away, glanced over his shoulder, and then stopped to face me as if still uncertain what to do about it. Knowing I had the advantage of him, I now waved my hat some more, then bade him good-by as he disappeared into the grass.

Sometimes we would remain in these blinds for many hours and nothing would happen, while on other occasions there was something doing every minute. Once while in a boma near a water hole, I was entertained by the actions of a lioness who was stalking several vultures that had gathered around the remains of a zebra. This was her kill and she didn't intend to have these raiders from the sky take away the meat. As the birds were fighting among themselves she silently but swiftly shortened the distance between them and herself, using a small bush as a shield. When she had reached the shelter of this bush she lay down for a while, watching them and probably calculating the distance; then she doubled up, her ears went back, her tail slowly swung to and fro and after a lightning spring she went bouncing over the rocks in tremendous leaps, catching the panic-stricken vultures before they could lift themselves into the air. She struck one with her paw, sending it squaking and sprawling along the ground, then jumping into the air, reached out one mighty arm and pulled another vulture back to earth with her. This she quickly bit twice through the body, then dropped it to make a spring for another, but now the birds were too far up for her to reach. The one she had bitten made a feeble effort to fly away, going a few hundred yards before it tumbled to earth forever. The lioness now sat down on her haunches and surveyed the scene around her, evidently satisfied with results. It was one of those brightly hot days when you can easily watch the heat waves as they dance above the veldt. This unusual exertion during the heat of the day called for a short rest, after which she slowly walked back toward us to join another lioness who was dozing beneath the shade of a thorn tree.

This kill apparently belonged to both of these big cats who preferred to wait until the cool of evening before having their feed. As vultures work during all the daylight hours they continued to circle over this dead zebra, and about the time the lioness reached the tree they again settled near the carcass. Just as the birds were commencing to have a grand feast the other lioness left the shade and made a rush toward the kill. She did not carefully stalk the birds like her companion, but full of business, went straight to the zebra in long leaps. After driving the vultures away, she lay down alongside the carcass for a few moments to rest. The heat evidently becoming too great for her comfort, she returned to the shade, whereupon the vultures again circled and landed. As if by arrangement, the first lioness once more sallied forth to drive them away. I watched this performance repeated several times before the truck came to transport me back to camp.

We spent the morning of November twenty-third selecting sites near water holes for new blinds. We located a very good spot about five hundred yards from where Mona had shot her lion, the signs indicating that a tremendous amount of game came there to drink.   After completing this boma we returned to camp for lunch, intending afterwards to go beyond the hills in search of giraffe.   As we neared the camp, fifteen of these odd looking creatures came into view. We promptly forgot about lunch and rigging up the slow motion apparatus went to work.   As it was excellent country to photograph in, we were confident of securing some interesting film, but just as everything was going along smoothly, a serious accident occurred which put an end to all picture making for some time.

It is always dangerous to drive over the veldt at high speed, but this is necessary if interesting pictures are to be obtained, especially of the fleet-footed animals. We had the ill luck to strike one of the numerous pig holes that are scattered over the plain, jarring both camera and crew considerably.   Recovering our breath, we dashed on, Mike swinging the truck into position in front of the running giraffe in such a manner that we were all lined up for a beautiful shot. I reached up to turn the crank and found that the main drive shaft had been broken.   I was keenly disappointed as I gazed after the retreating animals, for I realized that no tinkering we could do with it in camp would suffice, and feared it might mean three or four months, delay while the camera was sent to Chicago for repairs and returned.

However, I knew an English mechanic in Gilgil whom I thought might have the skill and tools to repair it.   Returning to camp at once, we commenced preparations for a trip to Gilgil and Nairobi.

CHAPTER EIGHT

SPEAR AND SHIELD

THE Ikoma spearmen having failed me and it being impracticable to organize the Masai for a lion hunt, I decided, if possible, to bring the famed Nandi warriors into Tanganyika. With this settled, I took up the question of permits with the proper officials, the Provincial Commissioner at Kisumu and the District Commissioner at Kapsabet. There was much red tape to be unwound; it was necessary to secure permission to take them out of the Nandi Reserve, transport them through the Masai country, and, finally, to obtain sanction for the lion spearing. I hoped that favorable action had been taken on these requests and that permits would be waiting for me at Narok, the first telegraph station enroute to Gilgil.

Although the season of the short rains now prevailed, I did not anticipate much trouble in making the journey and expected to be back within a week or so. What you plan in Africa is quite a different thing from what you accomplish. Before returning to camp I drove nearly one thousand miles, crossed and recrossed the equator six times, and arrived home many days late. The lost time was a sacrifice to the demon of mischance.

Our first stop was at Kilimafeza gold mine where we picked up some mail to be posted and undertook a few other minor tasks for our nearest neighbors. After leaving the mine we went peacefully speeding along

159

over a lonely part of the trail. Suddenly, upon turning a sharp corner, we beheld a very exciting scene. Two impalla rams were engaged in a fierce conflict. They paid not the slightest attention to us, and for a few moments we were treated to a wonderful show. With their horns interlocked, they savagely butted and shoved each other around. While they seemed so intent on the battle, I tried to stalk them with one of the small motion-picture cameras, hoping to secure some movies of this extraordinary scene, but just as I got ready to press the button they gave a loud snort and bounded away.

We arrived at Narok just before dark, to find awaiting me the permits necessary to assure success of my plans with the Nandi. Next evening, after dinner at a little hotel in Gilgil, the mechanic took my camera apart. When I saw all the screws and springs and gears laid out, I thought that the expedition was sure enough at an end, but my friend informed me he could fix it okeh, although it might take him three or four days. This was the best news I had heard for some time. I drove into Nairobi next day, or as I had renamed it, the city of "Bardo Kidogo."

In the Swahili tongue, bardo kidogo is the expression perhaps most frequently heard. It is the shibboleth of the native, be he Swahili, Wakamba, Ikoma, Masai, Nandi, Turkhana, Suk, Lumbwa, or N'jemps. It is the African equivalent of the Mexican's ever-recurring *manana*, and to its lazy rhythm Africans live and have their being. Freely translated, it means "wait a while," and it is the ever-present answer, plea, or excuse of the natives when asked to do anything. Africa truly is the Land of Bardo Kidogo.

I have compared the trenchant phrase to the word
manana, yet the Spanish slogan pales into insignificance
when pitted against the African term in practical appli-
cation. At least the Spanish plea for delay names a
definite tomorrow, while the spirit of the African plea
is for "tomorrow and tomorrow and tomorrow," even
until "the last syllable of recorded time." It might
well have served as the sleep-laden refrain of the lotos-
eaters. I have also called the phrase the native shibboleth, yet the average white man in Africa in time
falls under its spell, until in his last state he out-
Africans the Africans in his surrender to its spirit.

It is in Nairobi that bardo kidogo reigns supreme.
Here some of the white men have succumbed to Africa's
slogan to such a degree that, by contrast, the native
often seems a model of industry and promptness. In
Nairobi one observes perhaps better exemplified than
in any other spot on the continent, with the exception
of West Africa, this disintegration of character wrought
upon some classes of white men. Of the four distinct
groups into which the white population in and around
the city may be assigned, I should say that two at
least have fallen signal victims to bardo kidogo. Of
course, their powers of resistance were probably weak
in the first instance, but it was my observation that
they had surrendered abjectly. Of the four groups,
there are the gentlemen farmers, "tuxedo tillers" of
the soil, who drive quite regularly into Nairobi in high-
powered cars, frequenting the bars and clubs, swizzling
whiskies and sodas *ad lib* and *ad infinitum*, dancing and
gossiping and frivoling; in short, doing everything and
anything but working. All their farming is done by
proxy, nor do they look upon their holdings as any-

thing more than an excuse to get away from home during the winter, for "home" to them is never any place but England.

An even more unworthy group is that composed of the chiselers — bounders who live precariously on what they can borrow, wheedle, or swindle from their too trusting or credulous victims. Whether or not the English term *rotter* was coined to describe them, it covers their case so perfectly that they surely have proprietary rights in the term. Over against the tuxedo toilers and the chiselers are the other two classes; one, composed of government officials: earnest, intelligent, and competent men, some of whom are representative of the highest type of British manhood; the other, made up of honest citizens who strive, too often ineffectually, to make headway against the spirit that is all too prevalent in Nairobi. How hard is their task I realized full well, for I was six days in Nairobi awaiting the completion of a job that could have been done easily in two.

During my enforced stay in Nairobi, I was asked to attend a Thanksgiving dinner to which all the Americans known to be in East Africa had been invited. I was compelled to go in my safari clothes, but when some of the others arrived in the same attire, I felt perfectly at home. Twenty-one citizens of the States were present at this banquet given at the Salisbury Hotel. The menu informed us that we were to have turkey and other things dear to the hearts of Americans, but when the meal was served, I again realized that no matter what you give a native cook in the way of ingredients, the result, in so far as taste is concerned, always will be the same.

During the dinner, I was shown an article from a Denver paper giving an account of my expedition. It announced to the world that I had reached Mombasa by driving from Capetown to the Kunene River and referred to this as a feat never before accomplished! I heartily agree to this, and add for the information of those who do not have a map handy, it is something which will never be consummated. This incident is impressive only because it shows how little most of the world really knows about the vast continent of Africa.

I was invited that night to listen to a broadcast from Pittsburgh of the Cornell-Pennsylvania football game. The reception was almost as clear as at home. It was indeed wonderful to meditate on the fact that this voice was coming through the air for many thousands of miles. At about two o'clock in the morning, as I was beginning to fear that dawn would break before I could get to bed, the voice from Pittsburgh remarked they would have to hurry up and finish the game, because the sun was commencing to set. I have forgotten who won the game, but remember that, in spite of the loss of sleep, I was glad of an opportunity to listen in. While a black boy pulled me in his rubber-tired rickshaw over the darkened streets toward the hotel, my thoughts of home were rudely shattered by the mournful howl of a hyena, who was lustily broadcasting the Call of Africa!

The next evening while having dinner at the Stanley Hotel, I became aware that someone in the room was talking American, and turned around to discover four of my fellow countrymen. I knew they were citizens of the United States because they wore horn-rimmed glasses and were smoking cigars. Going over to their table, I introduced myself and found that they were from Oakland, California, and had come to Africa for a vacation and incidentally to do some big-game shooting. We had an interesting visit, during which I obtained news from home and told them of our wonderful Tanganyika country and about our work with the lions. Before we parted, I invited them to visit our famous Camp Simba.

I had taken the truck into a garage to have the front axle straightened. The white man in charge was one of the shiftless kind and turned the job over to a black boy, who failed to tighten the bolts which hold the front springs to the axle, with the result that shortly after leaving Nairobi — while going down the steep Kikuyu Escarpment — the truck insisted upon wiggling all over the narrow road. When I stopped to find the reason, I discovered the bolts had dropped off and the whole front of the truck was out of place. The black boy evidently had screwed the nuts on loosely with his fingers and the rough roads soon jarred them off, leaving me in a fine predicament! My back and arms were nearly broken when I finally limped into Gilgil.

When my mechanic friend informed me the camera was ready for use, I forgot my recent troubles in the joy of knowing I could now go ahead with my picture making. With this equipment repaired and the permission obtained to use the Nandi, I decided to proceed at once to Kapsabet. Before leaving, however, I made arrangements to meet Mike in Gilgil five days later. With two boys as companions, I left the next afternoon, arriving in Eldama Ravine after dark — a trip of sixty-six miles from Gilgil.

Kenya Colony.   Young married woman.   These Nandi matrons are neat
and trim compared to the women of most tribes.

At a Nandi village. Spearmen preparing for the lion hunt.

We were now in the high country, and when we started at dawn next day, a cold mist was falling. We drove through this for many miles, and I shivered all the way in spite of my heavy sheepskin coat. As we were in a strange district and I was not exactly sure of the directions, I was much relieved when we encountered a signpost. I was so stiff with the cold that I could hardly straighten up, but after swinging my arms for a few moments to start my blood circulating, I strolled over to find that this post marked the equator! This information failed to warm me up, however, so I hurried on, and after traveling nearly one hundred miles over a slippery landscape, pulled into Kapsabet just before noontime.

The District Commissioner and his lovely French wife invited me to a most enjoyable lunch, after which I selected fifteen Nandi spearmen from the several hundred whom the D. C. had collected near the Council House. I regretted that I could not take more of these men along, but, unfortunately, we had no way of transporting them.

After loading the warriors and their equipment on board, we started back, arriving the same night at Eldama Ravine. We had driven one hundred sixty-eight miles that day over mountains and veldt, through rain and mist, besides bumping over the frozen equator several times.

I was struck by the fact that at no time during this journey had I encountered game herds; nothing but flocks of storks and golden-crested cranes and a few ducks and geese. The country was wild enough, but the cold of the high altitude evidently fails to meet the requirements of many species, although I under-

10

stand the forests covering these hills contain many
thousands of monkeys and a large leopard population
in addition to families of the rarer antelopes.

We arrived in Gilgil on schedule with both front
springs broken and several other truck parts missing.
Mike was not there to meet me as promised, nor did he
show up by the next afternoon. When repairs had been
made I decided to leave without him, because a storm
was gathering toward the Mau Escarpment and I did
not care to risk pulling up its steep sides when they
were slippery. An hour lost might mean the difference
between getting through and being stuck. When we
reached the Kedong Valley it resembled a lake; the
storm had preceded us after all. It did not seem
possible to get through, but I kept plowing onward,
expecting each hundred yards to be the last. My
warriors came in handy, pushing the truck up hills and
out of mudholes.

Just before reaching Narok, we drove through miles
and miles of flying ants which covered the truck and
everything in it inches deep. These insects are brought
out by the rain and issue forth from many thousands
of ant hills to try their wings. Things always run to
big quantities in this country, and this was certainly
an immense blanket of winged emmets. After passing
through this insect cloud, we were kept busy digging
them out of our ears and shaking them out of our
clothes, finishing the task after arrival at Narok, for
in spite of mud and rain we succeeded in reaching
our destination.

To the melancholy tune of the rain falling on the
hut roof and the fifteen Nandi chanting a weird war
song, I sat down to my dinner of herring, beans, bread,

and tea; then after reading some advertisements in a last year's magazine, went to bed. Some time later, I was awakened from a deep sleep by a motor car roaring into camp. It contained Mike and two of the Kerr brothers, who had set out to follow me several hours after my departure from Gilgil. Mike's explanation for not keeping his appointment was that he did not think it possible for me to return from Kapsabet so quickly. One brother back-tracked and the other three of us fought rain and mud all the next day, being barely able to get as far as Klein's Camp at the Gurmeti, sixty miles short of our wilderness home. Here we found comfortable huts for ourselves and for the Nandi warriors.

When the game country was reached and we began to go through huge herds of wildebeest, zebra, topi, Grant's and the lesser buck, there was much excitement on board the truck, for in the Nandi reserve there is very little game outside of the forest dwellers, and these are seldom observed. Near a place where we had seen lions before, a stop was made while Mike pointed out fresh spoor. This started a prolonged war chant, in which the spearmen told all the lions what to expect from the Nandi.

It was an interesting journey all the way, giving the three of us a great amount of pleasure at the expense of the Masai, for as we passed through their reserve, whenever we came to a manyatta our tribesmen would start their war yell and the Masai would rush out to watch us speed by. They stood in pop-eyed amazement, some of them, no doubt, thinking that their country was being invaded by Nandi warriors traveling in motor trucks!

After much digging through mud and pushing up
steep banks, we reached camp.   The two men I had
left there were mighty glad to see us again and told
about some weird experiences with hyenas and a leopard
which had tried to steal the baby foxes.   Shortly after
our arrival, I sent the chief and three of the spearmen
to a donga where they were shown eight lions within an
hour's time.   Upon their return they told me in Swahili,
"It is very good, bwana, there are many lions."

While enjoying one of the best meals which the pishi
had ever cooked, the talk turned into a discussion of
the big cats and Donald Kerr said he heard lions
prowling outside.   We thought he was a little bit
nervous — this being his first night at the now famous
Camp Simba.   There had been so many stories concerning our camp circulated that we felt a newcomer
would expect to see lions strolling among the tents, so
we quite naturally bantered Donald.   He was not convinced, however, and when the meal was finished,
walked out and switched on a spot light to have a look
around.   As the beam of light swept across the road
we had made toward the donga, it disclosed seven
lions standing within thirty yards of the dining shack!
Donald became excited, but the rest of us assumed a
nonchalant attitude and after watching them awhile,
Mike turned to me, saying in an offhand manner, "I
wonder where the rest of them are?"

It rained for several days without end; the Nandi
wanted to return home; some of my white crew lost
all interest in the plans; I meditated upon the situation,
then began to realize, as I had two years before, that
whoever aspires to conquer Africa must overcome her
omnipresent inertia, the procrastinating spirit of both

Oliatorio, the chief of the Nandi lion spearers. This young chief proved himself not only fearless but intelligent and light-hearted. He is wearing a neck piece, called "sombe," of ostrich feathers. His spear was also tipped with the chieftain's badge of feathers.

The chief, after some ancient rites, gives his men final instructions before the lion is attacked.

172

native and white, the wait-a-while plea of its terrain, its swamps and rivers, bush, jungle, and veldt. With an ever-growing but impotent rage it was borne in upon me that in Africa no one is disposed to do today what can be put off until next week — or longer — and that through the slow symphony of African life runs the insistent leitmotif of bardo kidogo, dominating the race and even, it seemed to me, Nature herself.

Even Tanganyika rains must come to an end, so after what seemed ages, the downpour ceased, but frequent clouds still obscured the sun for varying periods. The uncertainty of the sunlight and the fact that the ground was much too soft for fast moving, necessitated more patient waiting, for I knew that when a lion had been surrounded and the war chant started, neither the lion nor the Nandi would care whether the sun was shining or not, nor if the camera car succeeded in moving or remained stuck in the mud. But these things were very important to me, so I continued my best efforts to keep everybody in good spirits until conditions were favorable.

While waiting for the weather to clear up, we were joined by the Lieurance party, the Americans whom I had invited out while in Nairobi. Their camp was pitched alongside of ours and when my crew went out that day to keep tab on the lion population, young Bill Lieurance went along. After dusk they returned, bringing two lion cubs about three months old. While circling a donga they had found these cunning youngsters, captured them and were just getting into the truck when a very angry lioness came charging out of the bush. Ted managed to get the truck running in time to evade her; otherwise, there would have been

serious consequences. These cubs were quite large
and very husky. They did plenty of growling and
would rush at anyone who passed close. I had the
boys build a substantial cage for them, this addition to
our zoo making it a rather pretentious exhibit.

We sallied forth several times either to find the
ground too soft or to be rained upon. These delays
were worse than annoying, because I never knew what
would happen next and always feared that something
might transpire to disrupt my plans entirely. It was
cloudy at daybreak on December fifteenth but cleared
later in the morning, so with the entire crew aboard
the trucks, and the Nandi arrayed in full war dress, we
headed for the lion country. When we arrived at the
place where we had hoped to find a lion, we discovered
several about, and started at once to stage the big show.

We took the Nandi to a position between the lions
and the donga, with instructions to form their circle
from there while we attempted to separate an old male
from the others. They were to let all the others get
through the line. The lions paid no attention to the
trucks, but when they saw these warriors on foot,
things began to happen and continued to happen for
some time. It was all so quick that it was like trying
to watch a three-ring circus. My memory still pictures the barbaric and wild scene of lions running this
way and that, of warriors rushing hither and yon, of
the camera car being driven like mad over the veldt.
Every few yards we would hit a pig hole; each time my
thought being that the entire car would come to pieces.
Once part of my camera fittings came loose and scattered over the landscape, but I had mighty little time
to think about this, for Mike came to a sudden stop in

front of a thick bunch of grass where a lion was crouching and switching his tail. I got the camera into position and waited for the charge, for three Nandi were converging on him, and I knew it would not be long before he made a dash for one of them.

One slim Nandi youth walked slowly toward the crouching beast until within twenty-five paces, whereupon the lion gave a mighty roar and, springing as from a catapult, charged straight for him. He stood rigid as a rock in the face of the lion's rush until the space had narrowed to a few feet, then he knelt behind the shield and, raising the spear, hurled it into the lion just before it leaped upon him. The tremendous impact of the charge threw the warrior to the ground, but he fell beneath the shield at which the lion clawed and bit.

Within a few seconds the other two Nandi were driving their spears into the maddened animal. Others, rushing up, did the same thing, and shortly the lion resembled an overburdened pin cushion. He was dead and there was no mistake about it! The youth who received the charge came out of the encounter with only a slight scratch, a bent spear, and a hole through his shield where the lion had bit through as it bowled him over. He was at once named "Ngetuny Siiya," meaning "lion's claw." They should have named him "Lion Heart," for it takes a brave man to stand fast while one of these enraged beasts, all his energy bent on killing, rushes savagely forward. The other warriors looked upon this display of courage as a thing previously assured, for, after all, the young spearman had only proven himself true to the Nandi breed.

Next day while the Nandi rested, repaired broken spear shafts, took the many kinks out of the blades, and with the help of files from the tool kit, sharpened their swords for the next affray, I visited with them, learning something about their equipment. Most of the shields were made of buffalo hide, the others from the skin of the giant forest hog. After these skins have been prepared and stretched over the wooden frames, they are almost as tough as metal itself. The shields are called "long" and the designs painted upon them indicate to which clan or class the warrior belongs. Their name for spear is "ngotit" and these are made by their own blacksmiths from soft metal. After their first meeting with the lion, I had noticed that every spear was badly bent, some of them almost double, and inquired why they did not use tempered metal. Their reply was that the white man's steel breaks, whereas theirs only bends, it being an easy matter to pound it back into shape again.

There are many restrictions about the headdresses which the warriors are allowed to wear. The young chief Olaitorio wore a huge collar of ostrich feathers around his neck, while the point of his spear was tipped with a ball of fine feathers, this latter being the badge of his office. Three of the other men also wore the sombe, or ostrich pieces rather than lion or baboon headdresses. Most of the headpieces were shaped like a busby, the majority being of baboon. Three of the warriors, who had speared their lion, wore the mane as a headdress, this being known as "kutua" and representing the greatest honor a spearman can attain. Before the lion encounter I had been bantering the Nandi, telling them that the white women wore big hats, and now they came up to shake hands and ask if I still thought they were women.

Ngetuny Siiya (Lion's Claw), who speared the first lion. Notice the scratches
upon the shield and the hole where the lion bit through it.

After the king had fallen. Notice the bent spears.

The Nandi warriors bear away the vanquished but noble foe. It is part of their ceremony that the lion shall be lifted and borne away from the spot where it met its death.

Hoefler and his fifteen Nandi warriors after the spearing of a lion. The shield designs indicate the clan and class of the owner.

Next morning dawned bright and clear. We left camp before eight o'clock, the Nandi war chant rolling over the veldt as we sped toward the land of Simba. At a few minutes before ten, Mike and I espied four lions about one hundred yards distant. Plans were made, and Mike went to entice them away from cover.

While he was doing this, Olaitorio gathered his warriors around to give them final instructions. He reminded them that their fathers were all brave men, none of whom had feared the king of beasts; that no Nandi warrior had ever stepped back from the charge of a lion. It was the worst disgrace that could ever befall a spearman to falter or fail to place his spear. After this rousing harangue, the Nandi sprang to their feet, chanting their battle song which, like strains of martial music, inspired us all for the conflict.

During these proceedings I had arranged all the cameras ready for instant action. Upon the return of Mike, with the previous experience to guide us, we took it easy, with both trucks running together until a lion had been separated from his harem of lionesses.

While racing into position to film the lion charge, and desperately holding on to the tripod as we bumped over the veldt, I glanced over my shoulder to see how our visitors were coming along. Their two trucks were following a short distance behind and off to one side. One member of the party was perched on top of a truck cab preparing to make some pictures with an amateur movie camera. I looked ahead for a second and then glanced around again, just in time to see this man tumble from the cab and fall directly in front of the speeding truck, which passed completely over him. I thought surely he was killed, or at least seriously injured, but before I had time to say anything, Mike brought our truck to a stop with a loud squeaking of brakes and I knew we were close to the scene of action.

A lion had come to bay and made a false charge almost to the nearest Nandi, but then changed his mind and lay down. This gave us a chance to get prepared, but the lion then gave a sudden spring and dashed through a hole in the Nandi circle. Spears were hurled at him as he ran, but they missed, for which I was glad on account of the position in which my camera was placed. If a spear had struck him, the whole show would have been over and I could not have filmed it.

The lion now ran two hundred yards with the Nandi in pursuit, then crouched and roared defiance. He made another charge, which I got in the camera, but stopped short again. By this time, however, he was enraged and kept on his feet ready for action. The warriors slowly surrounded him once more, and I centered the camera on the spot which judgment told me he would charge. It was taking a long chance, for if he failed to charge that way, it would be over before I could change positions; but this time luck smiled on me, for with a roar and rush he came at the men whom I had picked as his likely target. It was an exciting moment as the raging animal bore down toward these three men who stood tensely waiting, none of them knowing which one he would choose as the victim of his anger. When he did swerve toward one warrior, that man knew his life depended on what he did in the next few seconds. His eye and arm must both be steady, for if he should fail to place his spear in that critical fraction of a second, when the lion gave him the opportunity to strike the right spot, he would

never have a chance to try again. He must calculate
the distance, permitting the beast to get close enough
to assure his aim, but not too close, for then the heavy
end of the spear toward him would not have sufficient
time to drop to the ground, allowing the lion, by his
own impetus, to push it through himself. Unless the
animal's attention was distracted by a deeply embedded
spear immediately after he had knocked the man down,
it would mean almost certain death for the warrior, for
with his strength unimpaired and no spear to cause
him pain, the lion would still be intent upon his desire
to kill this creature who had dared to challenge him.

But this Nandi threw his spear with a precision and
force that was truly remarkable, and when the lion
knocked him to earth, we could see from our position
that the spear had passed right through the animal.
It turned immediately to fight the weapon, thus allowing the youth to spring to his feet, pulling his sword
as he did so. In a few seconds the other two warriors
had hurled their spears and when the other Nandi came
up they commenced a wild dance around the fallen foe,
working themselves into such a pitch that when I arrived to make some pictures, I half expected one of
them to put a spear through me. The chief found it
necessary to take the swords away from two or three
who were swinging them around in a dangerous manner.

We had filmed this whole spectacle from the time the
lion started his charge, while he struck the first warrior
and sent him spinning, reached over and bit his shield,
and then fell before the tribesmen. Thus had my
Nandi twice within three days demonstrated their courage in hand-to-hand combat with the king of beasts,
conquering him both times with only slight injury

to themselves, and proving that they had not been overrated in regard to their prowess with the spear.

As soon as possible, I inquired concerning Mr. Lieurance, and was happy to find that he was only slightly shaken by his fall. He had tumbled between the wheels, the truck passing over but not touching him.

This lion spearing had furnished the greatest thrill that anyone present had ever experienced. One of the spectators, Lieutenant Commander Glen Kidston, had just crashed his plane in the great sudd swamps of the Sudan, while flying low over some wild-elephant herds, but he said he received a greater thrill out of the lion show. These fifteen warriors had proven themselves to be not only fearless but of high intelligence, while their chief, Olaitorio, had undertaken the task with a vim and comprehension which showed him to be a real leader among his people. The subchief, Koi Muren, "long warrior," had speared his lion on a previous occasion and was anxious to duplicate the feat, but neither of the two lions charged close enough for him to place his spear. He was a fine actor, however, and a great help to us in many other ways.

After the killing of each lion the spearmen would lift him from the spot on which he died and bear him away for a short distance. Then slowly to the tune of an ancient chant they gently placed back on the earth of his native veldt their age-old enemy, who killed their cattle and upon occasion members of the tribe, but who, nevertheless, always fought and died like a gentleman. It is part of their ceremony that no lion shall remain on the spot where it has met its death. Thus do the gallant Nandi pay honor in this parting tribute to a vanquished but noble foe.

Koi Muren (Long Warrior), the subchief. He proved a fine actor and a
great help in securing the spearing pictures.

The author's young Nandi friends crossing a stream deep in the forest near Kapsabet.

CHAPTER NINE

WINGED DEATH

THE great and small beasts of Africa, the picturesque and savage tribes that inhabit its vast forests and veldts, appeal to the imagination of mankind. To the average person, contemplating the risks of the dark continent from afar, its peoples and animals constitute a menace, the varied perils of which must be faced by the explorer. Actual experience teaches that, although both primitive man and savage beast are often dangerous, the real hazard of Africa lies in its winged couriers of death — the untold billions of mosquitoes and other insects that sing the song of fever during daylight and darkness. These little messengers of Satan are more to be feared than the animals that claw and bite or toss and tramp. Their surreptitious attack is far more deadly than an armed array led by a savage chieftain; more to be feared than spear thrust or poisoned arrow!

Modern man, with his high-powered rifle, is able to conquer the most ferocious of beasts; can withstand the attack of spear-throwing and arrow-shooting savages. He can see and hear man and animal and protect himself against them, but the presence of the tsetse fly is only announced by the feel of its bite, and then the damage is irreparable. The bloodthirsty mosquito makes its attack during the hours of sleep and flies away unharmed. Twelve to fourteen days

later, its victim is racked with pain, weak, and helpless,
a sacrifice to its deadly sting.   This hazard of the
jungles, the forests, and swamps, of the bush and hills,
is omnipresent to jeopardize all those who seek to wrest
secrets from Africa's mysterious depths.   Man escapes
claw and fang and the weapons of primitive tribes
only to succumb to the bite of a tiny insect.   And so
it was with me!

For several days following the second spearing, we
filmed scenes to fill in parts before and after the lion
charges, in order to make a smooth-running story.   On
a wonderful morning of blue skies, with gorgeous cloud
formations which gave a finish to every composition,
we completed our work with the Nandi.   This was
indeed a stroke of luck, for although conditions were
perfect until about two o'clock in the afternoon, suddenly a tremendous storm burst upon this dream day.
While the lightning flashed, Thor released his heavy
artillery and shattered the ominous thunderheads.
Rain then fell in torrents, deluging the camp and washing everything that was loose downhill.   The Serra
Nyiro became a river impossible to cross.

As I knew there would be a continuation of rain and
the ground was now too soft for further operations, we
decided to break camp, intending to return after the
short rains were past.

We left early next morning, hoping to reach Narok
that same night, but the spirit of bardo kidogo once
again interfered; once again made us realize that a
plan in this country is only a futile dream.   Halfway
to the mine, while pulling up the side of a very steep
donga, a rear spring was broken.   We had no extra
spring because our trucks had already depleted the

entire local supply. While Mike was rigging up things with some wire cable, a hungry horde of tsetse flies settled upon us, and long before the job was finished, our hands and faces were a mass of white blisters. When the task was completed, we limped to the mine where a spring was built from scraps.

We now learned of the tragic death of Major Warwick's wife, who had just succumbed to sleeping sickness, contracted during her stay at the mine.

Darkness prevented our departure, making it necessary to spend the night at this most unhealthful spot, and as my very efficient personal boy had failed to bring the mosquito net, I was bitten all night long. In the morning my arms were sore and swollen from the multitude of poisonous bites.

Daybreak found us on our way, but shortly we ran into more rain, then broke another main leaf on a rear spring. While Mike was fixing this with more cable, a passing Hindu was persuaded to transport eleven of the Nandi to the main road, some forty miles distant, and thus reduce our load. After repairs had been made, we hustled onward, expecting each minute that the whole rear end, or something, would fall out, but reached Gilgil safely just before dark. We were successful in finding the garage owner, who opened up his shop, and there we worked until midnight repairing the trucks.

At one o'clock in the morning we started for the farm some sixty-five miles away, over roads so bad it is impossible to describe them. As we climbed into the Aberdare Mountains, the cold increased; then we ran into dense fog, which made driving very dangerous. As it was impossible to turn around, we

continued forward, and with the first light of dawn
were presented with a magnificent sight. Clouds of
mist rolled over the hills and filled the valleys. We
would speed along for a while in semidarkness, enveloped
in sheets of vapor, and then by climbing upwards
would emerge into a fairyland where the first shafts
of sunlight were playing over the mountain tops and
painting the clouds that rolled beneath with brilliant
colors. Then we would dip down, passing through
the fog to drive beneath the clouds for a while, and
reëmerge as we climbed the opposite side of a hill, to
travel again through an enchanted world where mountains peeked through fleecy blankets and scudding
vapor formed fantastic and eerie shapes. Majestic
Mount Kenya stood sentinel to the left of us, outlined
against the pink light of dawn, as we roller-coastered
up and down through the Aberdare Mountains, from
clear heights to fog and back again, while the sun
slowly ascended, announcing to a waiting world that
this was Christmas morning!

Mona tried her best to make it a merry day for all
of us, and prepared a holiday dinner of roast wild
duck with all the trimmings. While enjoying this
meal, I looked out through the window at snowcapped
Mount Kenya and listened to the whining of the wind
as it swept down from Kenya's slopes. It was hard to
realize that this was Africa; that I was within gun-
shot of the equator, for the setting could be duplicated
in my own beloved Rockies.

After three days at the shamba we were again on
the road, the time between our departure and the first
of the year being a history of what happened to the
trucks rather than the members of the expedition.

We called at the farm of Sir Graham Moon to pick up
a lion cub which we hoped to use in a few scenes;
then left Thompson's Falls early one morning, expecting to reach Kapsabet the following night.   Did we?
We did not!   If I were to tell of all our minor misfor-
tunes this would be a chronicle of grief rather than
of adventure.   Just as we were approaching Eldama
Ravine, the truck Ted was driving burned out the
clutch, making it impossible to pull his full load over
level ground in low gear.   With all the boys pushing,
I managed to get him on top of the hill that overhangs
the Ravine.   With him safely perched up there, I
started to follow only to discover that another rear
spring had gone galleywest!

By making several trips with the burned-clutch truck,
we managed to get all our kit to the collection of ram-
bling buildings, which Bwana Chai referred to as
his hotel.   The natives always name an individual
from some outstanding habit or characteristic, so this
ancient mariner had been christened "Bwana Chai"
because of his fondness for tea and other drinks.   Ted
and I removed the broken spring and, emptying the
other truck, started for Eldoret, the closest place
where I could be sure of obtaining repair parts.
We succeeded in traveling about twenty miles before dark, then had to give up, for the truck refused to move another inch.   The fact is, it hadn't
moved much during that twenty miles, except from
the motive power supplied by our pushing it.   We
shoved off to one side of the road and, while Juma
was making tea and Ted searching for the can opener,
a car came along going in our direction.   The planter
kindly offered us transportation to Eldoret, where at

11

the local hotel I found the softest bed I had encountered in Africa and could easily have slept the clock around.

When the garage opened next morning, we found they had what was required, and hurried back in another truck with the needed parts. After installing the new clutch, we returned to Eldama Ravine, fixed up the spring on the other truck, and were all ready for traveling again. All the next day I expected something to happen any minute, but we reached Kapsabet without difficulty. We swept into the village in a cloud of dust, with our fifteen Nandi yelling at full blast. Little naked black boys came running from all directions, followed by the older folk, until soon we were surrounded by a crowd of shouting and laughing natives. The District Commissioner and his wife came out to greet us and, after a round or two of tea, we took up our permanent quarters in the Government Rest House.

Kapsabet, the administration point for the Nandi Reserve, is only a small place, the white population during our visit being seven persons. The D. C. lives here and, through his native police and tribal retainers, dispenses justice and punishment to those who need it, collects fines, taxes, and butterflies, and is, withal, a mighty fine fellow.

The two or three houses and collection of huts that make Kapsabet are situated atop a hill, and the entire place is one large grove of beautiful trees. There are no insect pests here to make life miserable, and the climate cannot be much improved upon, for the days are just hot enough to be delightful and the nights are cool. Green hills roll away in all directions and the valleys between are filled with dense forests. Wild

bananas, ferns, trees that look like the magnolia, long
creepers that hang from high above and swing to the
tunes of the whispering winds, all go to make up this
mysterious, intriguing forest where many wild things
hide away.

Leopards, giant forest hogs, and bush buck make
their homes in it, while in the tree tops many monkeys,
among them the rare and beautiful colobus, swing and
play. Through the sunlit lanes below, butterflies and
other insects flit about, fit prey for the many birds
that dart in and out of the shadows. It is such a
forest as many people dream about but few ever see.

Previous to 1905, the Nandi tribe inhabited the whole
of the highlands known as the Nandi plateau, a large
tract of land roughly bounded by the Uasin Gishu
Plateau extending to Mount Elgon on the north, by
the Nyando Valley on the south, by the Elgeyo Escarpment on the east, and by Kavirondo on the west. Since
that time, the entire tribe has been moved to the present
reserve which is a little to the north of the escarpment
that bears their name. This move was made necessary
by continued attacks of Nandi warriors on the Uganda
Railway and upon other natives traveling along the
right of way.

The Nandi are a fine, upstanding race greatly resembling the Masai in physical type. In talks with
different elders and warriors of the tribe, they have
told me that they are blood brothers to the Masai,
kinsfolk of the Turkana, Suk, and Samburu. In all
of these tribes one finds men and women with almost
Caucasian features. I have quite often found a man
that reminded me of someone at home. Some authorities class them as the remains of a Semitic race which

wandered southward from Arabia and became mingled
with African elements, but they are generally classified
as belonging to the Hamitic negroid group, a mixture
of Galla and Somali with Nilotic negroes. It is essentially a transitional type, and I have found examples
among the Nandi ranging from pure Hamitic to pure
Negro. The Nandi are very closely allied to the
Elgeyo, Kamasia, Sotik, and Lumbwa, who all inhabit
the Western Escarpment of the Central Highlands,
but that they are close kin to the Masai there is no
doubt, for we find that even today most of the Nandi
medicine men are from a Masai clan, and the Nandi
war song is sung in Masai.

Their speech is of exceptional interest, owing to its
peculiarities of structure and an interesting but per-
plexing fact is that most of the tribes leading a Bushman life in Eastern Equatorial Africa, such as the
Dorobo, Andorobo, and Wanderobo, speak a Nandi
dialect, this being true of such widely separated tribes
as the Dorobo of the Mau and Mount Kenya, and those
near Lake Natron in Tanganyika. I have seen men
among the Nandi who could easily pass for Heikum
Bushmen of the Kalahari Desert, with whom I lived
for some weeks, making it impossible for me to mistake
their characteristics. That there is a slight infusion
of Bushman blood in the Nandi stock has been admitted
by some anthropologists.

The Rest Camp consisted of one large hut which was
divided into two rooms by a low partition, a hut for
cooking purposes, and another hut for the boys. The
government maintains these places for visiting officials
and any others who may come along. They are comfortable; a great improvement over any camp in the bush.

Return of the warriors to Kapsabet from Camp Simba.

The big dance at Kapsabet in honor of the lion victors.

195

Kapsabet, Nandi Reserve.   Another view during the dance in honor of the victories over the lions. Note the splendid physique of the warriors.

196

I will always remember this *ménage* for several reasons; one because of the continuous parade of kukus of both sexes and all sizes that passed through the cook hut to end their journey on our table. The adjacent country furnished very little game, making it necessary for us to subsist on chicken most of the time. A properly cooked fowl is always acceptable, but pishi could never understand that it took a lot of boiling to soften a tough bird. He reasoned that if eggs boiled soft in a short time and got hard with long boiling, the same rule applied to the chicken. Toward mealtime I would stroll to the cook shack and ask for the menu. Pishi invariably replied, "kuku, bwana," simultaneously pointing to a scrawny looking fowl tied by a string to a near-by bush. When I asked him if the bird was for today or tomorrow, he would innocently say, "For today, bwana," and, sure enough, about one hour later, Ted, Austin, and myself would be struggling with this ancient fowl.

January second was the day set for the great n'goma, or dance, to be held in celebration of the lion victories. At about ten o'clock in the morning a runner came in to tell me that the dancers were coming from far and near and collecting at the n'goma grounds. Arriving there, we found several hundred already gathered. The El Moran were all in full war dress, with painted designs of varied colors covering their bodies. Soon they commenced dancing in a great circle to the furious beating of the drums. It was a fascinating sight to watch their gleaming bodies as they swayed and pranced to the wild rhythm. Adorned with monkey fur and ostrich plumes, with tinkling bells around their ankles, with their tall headdresses bobbing up and down, and the sun glinting on the spears as they twisted and turned, these savage sons of Mars presented a memorable scene of bright colors, frenzied action, and clamorous sound, as they rushed to and fro with a pounding of thousands of feet. During this violent orgy of rhythm, the rolling boom of the drums and the weird chanting of hundreds of voices rose and fell in unison. Many participants worked themselves into a high pitch of excitement, some dancing until they dropped from exhaustion.

At the height of this barbaric festival, the paramount chief of the Nandi, followed by three retainers, zigzagged his way toward the camera. His tall, powerful figure was partly hidden beneath many folds of brightly colored cloth. He also wore, as protection against the tropical heat, a pair of spats, a matched set of celluloid cuffs and a linen collar without a tie. One retainer proudly shaded his chief's head with a shiny new umbrella. He was coming over to inform me that, by common consent of the warriors, they had made the mane of the first lion speared into a ceremonial headdress and wished to present it to me as a token of friendship. I greatly appreciated this display of regard on their part, knowing as I did that it represented a real sacrifice to the man who had speared the lion, for no greater honor could ever be his than to wear this selfsame headdress as a badge of courage and manhood.

It was a savage and colorful show, but I was glad when I could leave, for I had been feeling badly all morning and shortly after the dance commenced was shaken with chills. We were close to the equator where it was fairly warm, but even after putting on my heavy sheepskin coat, I continued to tremble with cold.

Working under a tropical sun, lugging a heavy camera from one place to another, trying to catch the high spots in the fastest of wild action, that of savages going through a ceremonial dance, is hard work when in good health, but to jump around this way during a bad attack of jungle fever is just about all a human can stand. After three hours of heartbreaking effort, I hurried back to camp and went to bed, where my boys piled eight blankets over me. These and several hot drinks warmed me up, but for three nights and days I suffered with the fever. My temperature was around one hundred four most of the time; my back and stomach pained so much that I thought surely the end was near. Large doses of quinine only seemed to make me worse, so on the third afternoon I had my boys place me, army cot and all, on one of the trucks, over which was rigged a tarpaulin to keep off the burning sun.

Ted drove me to the Eldoret Nursing Home, twenty-eight miles as the car bumps. Of all the rides in my life I shall never forget this one. Every time we hit a hole, which was every second or so, it seemed as if someone were sticking knives into me. The miles seemed ages long, but all things must have an end, so finally we arrived where I could get proper medical attention and rest. A very efficient English doctor and two white nurses constituted the staff of this hospital. A soft clean bed and the realization of skilled attention at hand made me feel better immediately. They gave me injections of liquid quinine twice daily until the fever broke; then once a day for a while. I had nothing to eat for six days, and on the sixth day of this fast I received a bunch of letters from home. One of them from my wife contained a kodak picture of a picnic in the mountains. In the same letter she went into detail — in fact, too much detail — concerning the fried chicken, shrimp salad, chocolate cake, and ice cream. When the nurse made her rounds about two hours later, I succeeded in talking her into serving me a small cup of beef broth and one small cracker.

After returning to Kapsabet, I was still very weak and rested as often as possible in order to regain my strength. One hot afternoon I lay dozing on my cot in the hut, listening to the song birds and insects outside and trying to picture in my mind what would confront us on the journey which we would soon attempt across Africa. My boy, Juma, came in to say that two white men and two white women were out in our yard looking at the lion cub. We see very few white faces in this country, so I at once strolled out to extend greetings. As soon as I took a look at the visitors, I knew they were missionaries.

Walking up, I introduced myself and immediately one of the women started to tell me how cruel she thought it was to keep a poor little lion cub in a cage. I explained to her that it didn't belong to us, that we were simply taking care of it for a friend. It had everything it needed in the way of food and was perhaps better off with us than out in the jungle, and as far as we knew it was perfectly happy, for we had heard no complaints. I noticed the taller of the two men had a peculiar gleam in his eyes, and now he suddenly wheeled on me, pointed his finger straight into my face and shouted in an accusing tone, "Has your soul been saved?" You could have knocked me over with a feather. I was so dumbfounded for a few seconds I couldn't think, then searched the man's face in an attempt to discover whether he were joking or not. It was plain enough that he was serious, so not wishing to offend any of them, I used my best diplomacy in attempting to change the subject. One of the women gave me an opportunity by suggesting that I visit them the following day for services. It was only forty miles away. I promised I would, if possible, and the tall fellow evidently thought he would have another try at me when I came to the mission.

This same young lion was the cause of a clash between Austin and a lady missionary at Bwana Chai's place. Some boys had gathered around the cage and were teasing the cub. Austin was standing inside a hut door shaving and becoming annoyed at these totos rushed out to chase them away. He had never mastered the native language and was falling back on a few popular cuss words to emphasize his remarks, when up from nowhere popped a young white woman, who was mothering this flock of blackbirds. Without preliminaries she started a tirade against Austin, telling him that it was the most disgraceful language she had ever heard an Englishman use; that in America, especially that part from which she came, no man would ever speak that way to children. Austin politely inquired where she was from, to which she answered, "Los Angeles," whereupon, assuming a gallant attitude, he said, "Well, well — I'm certainly glad to see you — I'm from Hollywood!"

During my convalescent period at Kapsabet we put in a few interesting days with the Nandi totos, or boys. One time we took the lion cub out and turned him loose, offering a prize to the first boy who caught him. He was full of pep, and there was certainly a mad scramble and plenty of excitement before he was overtaken and captured. With these totos as companions, I often strolled into the deep forest, where I seated myself on a recumbent tree trunk, and gathering my little friends about, would swap stories. I tried to explain to them how far away my village was, tried to describe the mighty expanse of ocean, the big ships, and the tall buildings, but am afraid they doubted my veracity.

In return for these fantastic tales they related to me some of the Nandi folklore, repeating the stories told by their mothers and by the elders of the village. There was the narrative of the origin of the leopard and the hyena:

"A lion once had two cubs, who, when out one day, came upon some warriors in war paint. 'Let us paint ourselves like those men,' said one cub. So they procured some paint and one cub painted black spots on the other cub. When this was done the other cub started to paint his companion, but just then they heard a cry of, 'A goat has been lost,' and thereupon the spotted cub threw the paint pot over his friend, and ran to see if he could find the goat. The spotted cub became the leopard and the other one, whose coat had only been streaked with paint, became the hyena."

They told me that cattle were once like human beings, with feet like men, that they lived with men and could talk like men. Dogs also at one time were

just like men, but went to war with men, who threw
sand into the dogs' eyes and so blinded them that they
have never to this day been able to find their way home.

Then there was a boy who slew the giant. This
demon ate people and cattle until he had cleaned up
everything on earth except one woman and her small
son, whom he had overlooked. One day he found
them and made ready to finish them off, but the small
boy by a clever ruse put a lot of red-hot stones down
the demon's throat and thus finished off the demon.
As the giant was dying he told the boy to cut off his
little finger and his thumb; and this being done, all the
people and cattle issued forth to populate the earth
again and they made the boy their chief.

One of the aged elders told me about the famous
Nandi Bear, and assured me he knew of its existence
when he was a small child, having heard his father
talk about it, while his mother warned him to keep
away from the forest when alone, as otherwise the
bear would get him. The young chief, a Nandi of
more than ordinary intelligence, told me that one of
his warriors had been chased by this terrible animal
a few nights previous to our talk. I asked him to
fetch this man so I could inquire of him about this
experience, but he said the warrior in question had
gone on a long journey.

From several descriptions of this beast supplied by
the Nandi, it must certainly be a horrible animal.
They describe it as larger than a leopard, but not as
big as a lion. Its front legs are longer than the hind
ones, after the shape of a hyena. It has sharp claws
and is very swift in running, sometimes leaping over
bushes fifteen feet high. It has a face like a human

being, only that there is a long snout like that on a wolf. It is light tan in color and has an odd call like that of doves.

It will attack anyone, and after it has killed its victim it breaks open the skull and eats the brains. When the Nandi find a person dead with his head in this condition they know the Nandi Bear has been about. Sometimes very brave men will stand their ground with spear or club and then the bear will run into the forest and not harm them.

Such is the tale as told by the Nandi themselves. That some strange animal prowls about in their country is possible, but when it comes right down to producing the Nandi Bear itself, something always prevents. I tried to organize a hunt to run this weird beast to earth, but was unsuccessful. They will spear lions and leopards, but when it comes to creeping through the forest in search of the Nandi Bear, that is something else again—a thing to be whispered about.

The Nandi do not live in large villages like many African tribes, but sometimes one or two families will group together for sociability. The Nandi women ornament themselves in a similar manner to the Masai, but, in contrast to the Masai, they are neat and clean and, while they do most of the work, still they seem to have plenty of time for leisure, enjoying life in a much greater degree than most primitive women. Nothing worries them, either past, present, or future, and in such a state of mind they go merrily about their daily tasks. The young Nandi women must go through many strange rites before marriage, one of them being circumcision, without which no woman may marry.

Young married woman, Nandi Reserve. These people are of a much higher type than most East African tribes.

Nandi boys who have just been through the circumcision ceremony, wearing the strange headdress called "kimaranguchet."

At the end of a seven-year period, all the boys who have passed a certain age since the last rites are required to go through a long and intricate circumcision ceremony. After the performance of the operation they must remain in seclusion for several weeks, during which they may see no woman, not even their mothers. On a certain morning they go down to a stream and if the cattle come to drink while they are there, it is a good sign; but if certain birds appear in the trees, it is a bad sign and they are required to perform new rites to overcome the evil omen. After a lapse of time they are garbed in women's clothes, and over the head and shoulders of each is placed the odd headdress, called kimaranguchet, without which they are not allowed to appear in public. During the wearing of this they must always carry a bow and arrows with which to shoot small birds, these being suspended from strings strung across the top of the headdress. The killing of these birds and the hanging of them in the rigging of the headpiece is an important part of the rites of circumcision. All boys must go through this tiresome ceremony; otherwise they can never become warriors, nor will their spirits live after death.

One day we undertook the task of paying the Nandi warriors and of giving presents to everyone who had assisted us. This required a lot of patience, for if we were not careful one little word would start an argument which required fifteen minutes to straighten out. These people are still primitive, but it seems that there are certain basic traits in human nature reposing in each individual, no matter of what race or color. Every person, regardless of where found,

always considers his particular services worth more
than those of anyone else.

The aged father of Ngetuny Siiya came to thank
me for my presents of money and other things to his
son. He was very proud of his boy and with fatherly
pride enumerated the many benefits which would
accrue on account of the opportunity I had given
the Lion's Claw. With the money he would buy
three wives and a few head of cattle, sheep, and goats.
He would have enough left to pay his hut tax for many
years and the position attained in the tribe by having
speared the lion would place his whole clan in a favorable light, so that, all in all, it was a great event in
the history of this particular Nandi family.

While he was discussing the price of wives, I did a
little rapid calculating and figured that these women
would cost his son about sixty-five dollars each, which
I believe anybody will agree is very reasonable,
especially when it is considered that the first cost
is the last cost, as, thereafter, the wife not only
earns her own way but contributes to the riches of
her husband.

As soon as I had regained my strength sufficiently
to go on safari, we bade good-by to all our friends at
Kapsabet and left for Eldoret. On the way down,
pishi informed me that he was a Nandi! Of course,
I knew he was not, but in spite of that, he insisted his
father had just died, leaving him two hundred head
of cattle, plenty of sheep and goats, and some almost
new wives and he wanted to remain there long enough
to get his new affairs into shape. This "father-dying"
business in Africa is parallel to our "grandmother"
story during the baseball season. Every year thou-

sands and thousands of unfortunate fathers "die" throughout the dark continent, for one reason or another, and to suit almost any case.

My boy, Juma, was absorbing the high points of the conversation and this is probably where he got the idea which he sprung on me a few days later. Juma had some education, so he went into the thing with refinements. His father not only died but he had a telegram handed to me telling of the sad event and requesting that I break the news to Juma! So imagine my surprise when a few days later I met his father face to face in Nairobi, accompanied by the son whom I had just a few days previously sent home so he could attend the funeral! When I inquired of Juma how many fathers he had or whether the medicine man had brought this one back to life, he just grinned sheepishly and made no reply. There was nothing to say!

After these two sudden deaths, I lined up my remaining boys and took a census on the paternal situation, finding to my great satisfaction that there were only two more fathers left to "die."

Pishi promised to meet me in Nairobi within six weeks' time. I doubted that he would do this, because, if what he said was true, he was now a wealthy man and it would never again be necessary for him to labor day after day opening cans with a dull can opener.

After bumping our way into Eldoret it required a few days to make repairs, such as putting new leaves in springs and in having a dentist recement my bridge work which had been jarred loose at the same time the springs broke. Between Eldoret and Eldama Ravine, which is some sixty miles eastward, a person

travels through one of the coldest parts of Central
Africa and, after the sun goes down, the thermometer
drops to near the freezing point. Once again I shivered
in my sheepskin coat as I drove past the signpost
which marked the equator, and once again marveled
that I ever thought this band around the earth was a
belt of heat!

Upon arrival at the tavern run by Bwana Chai,
we found the old gentleman was sober! He greeted
us like long-lost brothers and soon we were sitting
down to hot chakula. On the next day the expedition
would split into two parts for a while, so I was up late
explaining to the other members what they were expected to do during my absence.

A few miles east of Eldama Ravine some wheel
tracks turned off into the bush, these indicating the
way to Lake Baringo in the bottom of the Great Rift.
Here I left Ted and Austin with the greater part of
the load and most of the boys, while I, with only my
personal boy, Juma, and another lazy cuss whom I
was taking into Nairobi to fire, kept on the road to
Nakuru, where we arrived in the forenoon. From
here I attempted to reach Thompson's Falls by way
of a short cut which would save me about forty-five
miles. I got started on the proper path all right, but
in this country there are no signs, so I suddenly found
myself at the end of the road.

. Near this point was a police post and the officer in
charge told me I should have turned off on to another
road about twenty miles back. He drew me a map
showing how I could cut over a range of mountains,
thus saving ten of the lost miles. Still being an optimist
or foolish, I don't know which, I attempted to follow

his directions, after a while ending up in a beautiful
valley. I was glad I got lost this time, for this trip
took me through the finest agricultural district I had
yet seen in Kenya. Many beautiful farms and coffee
shambas passed in review as I followed down the center
of this vale. Later I came to a large bungalow in front
of which stood a lone white man, and, stopping the
truck, went to inquire if I was getting any closer to
Thompson's Falls. He refused to discuss the question
until we had lunch, during which I learned he was the
well-known Colonel Lean, who here operated one of
the most successful farms in East Africa. Another map
was drawn — this time an accurate one — which led
me through deep forests and over narrow roads. I
met several long spans of oxen, pulling heavy wagons,
and on these occasions there was a delay while the
teams passed around the truck; otherwise things
went along smoothly until the boy riding behind
shouted that the lion was loose. The jarring had
shattered his cage, and finding the cub lying with his
head out of a hole, I pushed him back and shoved
some boxes where they would hold him in for the
balance of the journey. I reached the falls just at
dusk, after having traveled through fifty miles of
sure-enough wilderness. I delivered the cub safely
at Sir Graham Moon's, but there being no white folks
around, found it necessary to have tea by myself,
then pushed on the remaining forty-five miles to
Gilgil.

The next day found me in Nairobi where I met
Mr. and Mrs. Modder of Kibuku Estate, old friends
from Limuru, with whom I had traveled from Mombasa to Marseille, France, in 1926. They insisted on

12

my paying a visit to their shamba on my return journey
to Gilgil, and gave me detailed directions, but in spite
of these I got lost again and wandered around the
landscape several hours. Eventually I found the
place, however, which proved to be a beautiful spot,
situated on top of a hill, and laid out like an English
park. Looking southeast from their veranda, I could
see Nairobi below, with Mount Kilimanjaro's peaks
reared skyward in the distant haze. Toward the
north, snowcapped Mount Kenya and the Aberdares
seemed near at hand. Beyond these was torrid
Legumukun, deep in the Great Rift.

CHAPTER TEN

INTO THE GREAT RIFT

WHEN I again journeyed to Eldama Ravine and stopped at the tavern, I found Bwana Chai anything but sober. He had closed the bar, for, on account of his persistent sampling, it could not be made to pay. In order to cinch the matter, he had undertaken the task of drinking up, all by himself, the remaining stock on hand, and when I arrived had not quite recovered from his labors.

As I drove down the main street next morning, I was hailed by a boy who looked familiar. It proved to be Bwana Chai's cook, who had quit his job and wanted to go with me. Being minus a pishi, I hired him to take Ali's place. I found the path toward Lake Baringo rather good in spots, so made fair time, arriving at the Maraget River about noon. There a runner was waiting with a note from the D. C. at Kabenet, giving my party and self official permission to enter the Lake Baringo area. I had tea here with an officer in charge of a crew fighting the locust swarms, and from him borrowed a boy to guide me to Legumukum.

This whole country, after driving down into the bottom of the rift, reminded me of Southwest Africa. I found the same small hills, the same fiery hot depressions where burning blasts blistered the skin, the same sandy stretches that held the heat and threw it back into our faces, the same thorny trees and bushes, with over all the white-hot sun suspended in a dome of turquoise blue. In this part of the Great Rift Valley, which lies about forty miles north of the equator and directly south of Lake Rudolf on the thirty-sixth degree of longitude east from Greenwich, is a little-known region called the Baringo area. At the hottest spot in this valley of heat, we located Legumukum.

Ted and Austin had found a locust officer named Joe Pedley occupying the most favorable location, so we combined the two camps. Pedley knew the district very well and had expected to show me around upon my arrival, but was now down with a touch of fever, so I spent the hot afternoon talking with him.

He had planned on making headquarters at a place called Sandi, some ten miles distant in the shadow of the Laikipia Escarpment, but had found the river dried up. Thirteen months previously the Sandi River was a clear cool stream flowing out of a crevice in the escarpment and winding its way through the parched valley floor southward. Along its course were many villages of the N'jemps Kidogo, a warlike people depending on their herds for sustenance. During the night a tremendous earthquake had shaken the country and next morning when the women went down to the stream for water, they found the river had disappeared. The earthquake had changed the course of the stream before it debouched from the cleft in the escarpment, leaving the villages isolated in a semi-desert. This sudden failure of the water supply was a calamity to the N'jemps; many people and hundreds of head of stock perishing before they could adjust themselves to the new order of things.

The hut at Kapsabet in which the author was stricken with fever. He is shown on the left.

Nandi totos perched on the limb of a very odd tree.

Camp Legumukum in the Great Rift Valley. N'jemps Kidogo were constant visitors at this camp. The white men in the picture are members of the party.

While we were talking, Maniki came in with the information that many elephants were near. Going out to the edge of the camp, I counted over one hundred of these ponderous beasts. Through the glasses, I watched the herd, which was less than a mile away, as they milled about and blew dust into the air.

Camp Legumukum was situated near a running stream, approximately midway between the two lakes of Baringo and Hannington, the latter being some twelve miles south and Baringo seven miles north. On January twenty-ninth we went on an inspection tour to Lake Hannington. I was anxious to see with my own eyes the wondrous sight which had been described to me by a previous visitor to this remote section. For many weeks I had been looking forward to the gorgeous spectacle presented by the tremendous multitude of flamingos, which for untold centuries have painted acres of this African lake with vivid patches of pink and scarlet. We had been told it was impossible to reach the place by truck but, although the country we traversed was enough to discourage almost anyone, we continued on over sharp rocks, winding our way up and down hills, crossing deep gullies, until we finally succeeded in approaching within sight of this tranquil water, which, like a huge mirror, reflected on its surface fleecy clouds which were leisurely floating overhead through an azure sky.

Long before our first glimpse of the lake, we heard a roar like that of a distant waterfall or the whistling of wind through a dense forest. My N'jemps guide said it was the noise of the flamingos and we found this to be so. The commotion from these millions of birds produced one continuous sound which increased in intensity as we picked our way forward over the hot sharp stones. This ceaseless noise, the hissing and kronking of millions of birds, has probably disturbed the solitude of this remote vale for many thousands of years.

After climbing down some steep rocks, we passed through a small grove of stunted trees and emerged into the open. There before us was one of the most romantic and compelling scenes any man has ever witnessed. The nearest shore line of the lake was a solid mass of birds as far as the eye could reach, while toward its center floated many pink islands. As we approached closer we realized that there were millions of flamingos within sight — not hundreds nor thousands, but millions. I paced off one mile along the shore line and estimated the width of the block of birds at this point as one eighth mile, thus making an area of flamingos one mile long and one eighth mile wide, eighty acres of pink birds, packed solid side by side. These were not all of them, for the glasses disclosed greater multitudes in the distance. It does not seem possible that there could be so many birds of one kind in the world.

Lake Hannington lies in the bottom of a deep bowl formed by the sheer walls of the escarpment on one side and by small brush-covered hills on the other. That it has been the undisturbed home of the flamingos for centuries is proven by the bird feathers and other remains, which are piled layer upon layer many feet deep along the beach for miles and miles. The water is very heavy with soda and lime, the decaying bodies of the dead birds having something to do with this. The N'jemps say that a devil lives in the lake and if the cattle, sheep, or goats drink the water they die. I could not quite understand this, for I found many rhinoceros tracks leading to pools along the shore, but it is possible that these animals were attracted by the smell of the water and upon tasting it went away without drinking. We found the heat near the lake to be simply terrific, while the glare from the soda-incrusted ground almost blinded us.

On the day following our trip to Hannington we paid our first visit to Lake Baringo. It was open veldt country and we were able to drive almost to the water without great difficulty. From the shore of the lake, a person gets the impression of being in the bottom of a great crater, hemmed in on all sides by mountainous masses. But there are no mountains visible. The encircling cliffs are escarpments; the Laikipia on the east and the Kamasia on the west. These precipitous walls tower on either hand almost two thousand feet from the floor of the rift, then twist and turn, giving the appearance of a solid barrier inclosing the valley on all sides. The bottom of this tremendous depression is so deep below the surrounding plains that no cooling breezes ever find their way into the inferno.

Africa is fascinating in many ways. Its terrain, its wild denizens of forest and veldt, its romantic coasts are all alluring — even its heavens are mysterious. At night the stars seem to hang almost within reach, while the moon is glorious beyond description. When the last stars fade in the morning, they leave the sky an azure blue, and a search far and wide will disclose not a single cloud. In the afternoon a few wisps of white vapor appear from nowhere and these increase in size until shortly the heavens are full of beautiful cumulus clouds. They have not drifted from over the horizon but have created themselves right above your head. Toward the end of day, when you stand silently, almost reverently, to watch a magnificent sunset, you suddenly realize that the gorgeous clouds have melted away as silently as they came.

My poetic reveries were interrupted by a school of snorting hippopotami who were thus telling us of their displeasure at our coming here to disturb their peace and quiet. Lake Baringo supports a large population of these ponderous water horses, and for every hippopotamus there are a thousand crocodiles. They seem to get along in perfect harmony while alive. Upon the death of a hippopotamus, it is a different story; then the crocodiles swarm around the carcass of their departed neighbor, fighting for his flesh.

While watching the playful hippopotami splashing and diving, I became aware that a crocodile was sleeping in the shallow water about sixty yards away. All I could see was the top of its head, but taking a careful bead with my 7 mm. Mauser, managed to hit it. The reptile's tail furiously lashed the muddy water, stirring up an awful row and frightening all the birds along the shore line. I took another shot, putting the second bullet alongside the first, but as the crocodile continued to move lakewards, fired again. This time the bullet glanced off its armored back and went whizzing toward the escarpment. This did not matter, for the crocodile was quite dead and had only moved a few feet from the spot where the first shot struck it. Two bullets had landed just above the eyes, the best place to hit one of these carnivorous reptiles. When the boys dragged this flesh eater ashore, I was surprised to find it measured twelve feet. Sunk in the mud with only the top of its head showing, I had thought it to be only a small crocodile.

It was now commencing to get dark, but Ted and I had noticed a bull hippopotamus hanging around close to shore, so, hiding ourselves in a blind, waited for him to come out of the water. After it was pitch dark he decided that all was safe and slowly splashed his way landwards. These heavy animals cannot leave the lake at any spot, but by repeated comings and goings build themselves a sort of canal, leading from the water on to the solid earth. These channels, or hippo paths, extended in all directions from this part of the lake.

Ted and I listened as this huge amphibian passed within ten feet of us in the dark, remaining perfectly quiet as he ponderously made his way up the canal. Not considering him dangerous, we left the blind to follow, and the ground being soft and the wind right, he failed to become aware of our presence until we spoke to him in Swahili. With a surprised snort he wheeled around and dashed straight for us as fast as his short legs would carry him. Without hesitation, we did a little quick moving on our own account, allowing him plenty of room for his journey to the lake.

The hippopotamus is a very interesting as well as an odd animal, spending his days in the cool water away from the heat and possible enemies on land, coming ashore at night to feed on the green grass bordering the lake or stream. I found out more concerning the habits of this enormous pachyderm from the N'jemps, when I tried to arrange with them to form a human barrier between a herd and their aquatic home. Finding to my dismay that I could not photograph them in the lake, and it, of course, being impossible to film them at night, I planned on holding a herd ashore until daylight. When I explained my idea to the N'jemps they went into spasms of laughter; then told me that all the warriors in the valley would not be enough to prevent one hippo from getting to the lake. It seems they had tried this in the past — their object being to obtain fat meat. They went through a pantomime showing how the hippo had charged through the line of men and trampled some of them into the ground. We got a great laugh out of their description of the encounter, especially where they demonstrated how it was necessary to dig some of the warriors out of the mud.

After our friend had noisily splashed his way far into the lake, we returned to our truck and started campwards. We had only gone a short distance when we almost bumped into a cow hippopotamus that was grazing on our private roadway. It was now very dark and she was feeding several hundred yards from the lake shore. Getting sight of what looked like twin moons hanging halfway between heaven and earth, we had speeded forward to investigate, finding this corpulent lady waiting to see what sort of a creature was roaring toward her. Upon discovering that humans had something to do with this apparition, Mrs. Hippo made for home posthaste, with us in hot pursuit. I believe this to be the only instance on record of a hippo being chased by a motor truck. There was no intention on our part to harm her, but she, of course, did not know this, and we had an exciting but short race which the galloping lady won by diving into Lake Baringo and leaving us stuck in the mud.

Our camp had been established several days, when early one morning a boy came running in wildly shouting that we were being attacked by a horde of savages and should all be killed! This was quite interesting news so early in the day; so unusual, in fact, that all of us left our cots in a hurry to hustle out and meet the visitors. A band of warriors in full regalia, with the early sun glinting on their spears, were rushing pell-mell toward the camp, uttering bloodcurdling war whoops as they swept forward. It looked serious, but our judgment prevented us from shooting, because we realized that this might be only a prank. If any of the warriors were killed or wounded, it would then turn into a real raid, without much hope of our surviving, so with bated breath we waited to see what would happen. Shortly they rushed up, prancing like high-spirited horses, with shields thrust forward and spears held on high, and when almost upon us we could see they were laughing. I cannot recall whether we laughed or not, but I do remember I was much relieved. After the dust had settled the chief explained they were out seeking excitement, and sighting our camp had dropped in to say "good morning!" I was not able to ascertain whether or not the young warriors in this district still made raids upon neighboring tribes, but this band seemed very keen to engage someone in battle, and it is more than possible in remote districts such as this that some tribal conflicts still occur.

The N'jemps were not yet accustomed to the white man or his ways, and still being raw savages, were most childlike. Whenever I worked about my dark-room tent I would be surrounded by them, for they seemed much interested in watching me mix the photographic solutions. My boy recounted some tall stories about what the magic mixtures would do; one being that I could take their spirit from their body and transfer it to a piece of paper. They were quite awed by this, but not a bit frightened. The people of some tribes would be panic-stricken at such possibilities, but these primitive folk seem to have no fear. When I would hold a developed 8 x 10 negative so they could look through it, their first reaction was to stand perfectly still, struck by the wonder of the white man's sorcery. Then they would start to laugh and shout, the particular interest in the negative being that their features had turned light. The bwana was a great witch doctor, for he had turned them into white people!

My most uncomfortable task was the nightly handling and developing of films in the dark-room tent. On account of the intense heat at this camp, I could only remain inside long enough to complete one operation and then had to rush out for air. Stripped to the waist and armed with a big Turkish towel to keep the perspiration from falling on the films, I would reënter, but after a short period in the stifling interior, during which I would hastily load a magazine or film holder, it would be necessary to burst out for another breath in time to avoid suffocation. This is but one of the tribulations of a photographer in the tropics.

At this camp a most heroic encounter between man and beast came to my knowledge. One afternoon a

Kenya Colony.   N'jemps Kidogo war chief, who commanded a roving band
that visited the camp.

Some of the N'jemps Kidogo warrior visitors.   Note the elaborate shield markings.

warrior strolled in from the bush to ask for medicine, and we found that he had been badly mauled. He explained that a troop of lions had been bothering his cattle, so he and a friend had gone out to chase them away. A male lion had charged him and his spear had missed the mark; whereupon the cat bore him to the ground, biting through his arm and shoulder. The friend then ran up and jumping on the lion's back took hold of its ears, which he twisted until the animal turned and bowled him over. They both lay there for some time, probably unconscious, for he said when he awoke the lion had gone away but the friend was still sleeping. Although the shoulder and arm muscles were badly torn, this man entirely recovered, but his companion died — a sacrifice on the altar of friendship.

When another journey to Lake Baringo proved fruitless in the securing of crocodile pictures, I came to the conclusion that our methods would have to be changed, for when we arrived the water was seething with these cold-blooded reptiles, and although I counted thirty heads close to our bait, there was nothing on the hook. This lake is simply alive with animal, reptile, and bird life of many kinds. On this occasion we counted fifty hippopotami in addition to the hundreds of crocodiles and spent some time watching a huge snake as it swam shoreward with its head lifted about three feet out of the water.

Inland and along the shore were many thousands of birds — geese, ducks, flamingos, white ibis, pelicans, storks, cranes, herons, snipe, fish eagles, hawks, vultures, plovers, and some others. On our way back to camp we encountered wart hogs, zebra, impalla,

Grant's gazelles, Thompson's gazelles, dik-diks, oryx, kongoni, eland, sand grouse, and plenty of guinea fowl. The first part of the night in this valley is so hot that sleep is impossible, and while tossing beneath my mosquito net listening to these little pests buzzing around, other sounds came from the direction of the river; baboons, hyenas, jackals, night birds, and a distant lion. Becoming restless, I reached out and, picking up my boots turned them upside down to empty out the scorpions, then putting them on to protect my feet against the fleas, ants, snakes, and lizards, took a short walk around the camp, almost bumping into a black rhinoceros and his wife, who, after giving a couple of loud snorts, disappeared in the direction of an elephant herd, which was trumpeting close to a near-by pool. While walking back to bed, an enormous flock of flamingos flew noisily overhead between myself and the moon. When I again lay down I was fully satisfied that at last we had made camp in a real wilderness.

High in the rocks around Sandi and also in the vicinity of our camp lived thousands of baboons. Ordinarily I would not care to shoot one of these animals, but I have a doctor friend who is collecting skulls and I thought that a baboon's cranium would be an interesting addition to his museum. I never realized what evasive creatures baboons could be until I started after them with a rifle. Upon my approach to their rocky home, there was a great clatter of small stones as the entire troop scampered up the face of the escarpment; all except one old man baboon who sat on a huge boulder shouting at the retreating members of his family until they were out of sight. Then he commenced reviling me and shaking his fists. The first time he did this I shot at him, and he ducked behind the boulder, only to reappear immediately, using the most violent language I have ever heard, so I fired another shot, whereupon Mr. Baboon made for the higher elevations. I did not try again because it seemed almost as if I were shooting at a human being. These animals are sometimes very destructive, but here in this remote country they cannot possibly do any harm and add much to the interest of the wild places.

Upon returning to Lake Hannington for more photographic material, I decided to obtain a comprehensive view of the lake and country, which could be used as an opening view for the film story of the flamingos. With four boys following, each carrying camera equipment, I led the way up the steep side of the escarpment. Mountain climbing in a cool climate is not so bad, but here under the equator it certainly cannot be classed as sport. The worst part was that I had to ascend this sheer wall twice on the same day; once in the early morning and then again just before sunset to make a closing scene. After a difficult climb over rocks and through thorn scrub, with the scorching heat adding its share to the hardships, we finally struggled to a small ledge, which projected from the face of the cliff, almost at its top. There was just room enough here to place the large camera and from this vantage point I made a panorama of the scene below. Perched here with the binoculars I could see for many miles, finding that over all the visible expanse of lake flamingos floated in solid pink blocks, some of them acres in extent.

Leaving the camera in place and a boy to watch it, I crawled and slid back to the bottom, where I went on a short exploration trip. Through the glasses I had noticed steam arising along the western shore of this volcanic lake, and upon trekking there, found several boiling springs, many steam vents, and small geysers, miniatures of those located in our own Yellowstone Park. These springs were bubbling, boiling, and steaming like an old-fashioned kettle on a red-hot stove. We found the water to be very hot — so hot that meat could easily be cooked in one of these natural caldrons.

The scenery in this entire vale gives one the impression of being on another world. The boiling springs, the intense heat, the sheer walls of the escarpment, the slimy blue-green water through which protruded the trunks of trees long dead, with their limbs held heavenward in a gesture of despair, as if imploring aid before they should sink forever below the surface of this poisonous lake, all these things combined to make me feel as if I were treading on a strange planet where I should suddenly encounter monstrous and grotesque animals similar to the dinosaur, or mayhap come face to face with counterparts of the enormous fifty-foot-long and twenty-foot-high carnivorous Tyrannosaurus.

Farther on, near the edge of the lake, we found the nursery where the flamingos have constructed their nests year after year by the piling up of mud into what looked like exaggerated golf tees or miniature volcanic craters, on the top of which, in a small hollow, the one or two eggs are placed. The soda and salt crust which surrounded these nests reflected back the bright

rays of the sun until its heat almost blistered us and
at each step we broke through this thin layer, stirring
up a powerful odor which was almost thick enough
to be visible. This aroma arose from the mass of
decaying matter scattered about this section, and I
was amazed that even a bird could survive such an
overpowering stench.

Returning to the northern end of the lake and finding the mud a bit too thick for swimming and not
quite thick enough to walk upon, I waded out almost
up to my armpits through the oozy slime in order to
place a small camera with an electrical attachment, so
that it would be possible to secure close-up views of
the birds. At my approach they edged out into the
lake, and when I continued farther, there was a great
uproar, a confused kronking and hissing, as the birds
took to flight. They first ran awkwardly over the
mud for a short distance, bouncing up and down like
an airplane taking off from a bumpy field; when they
gained enough momentum to raise their weight into
the air, their long necks were stretched forward and
their equally long legs behind, both being in a straight
line with their body. When thus in flight, with their
beautifully shaped scarlet-splashed, black-tipped wings
gracefully flashing in the sunlight, it seemed there
could be no more exquisite bird in all the world than
the African flamingo, and while watching them wing-
ing their way overhead I was reminded of the poetic
lines: "Where the red flamingo flies, hunting fish
before his eyes."

After placing the camera, I returned to take up my
station behind a big boulder which the earthquake
had shaken down from the mountain side. The heat

13

was enough to bake a person alive and soon dried this
poisonous mud on my skin.   Then the fun commenced.
It started to itch and burn until, in desperation, I made
a flying trip to the truck where I used up all the drinking water in my frantic efforts to secure relief.   Partly
successful, I returned to my station by the rock
to find out after a while that, although flamingos
are interesting and comical, they are also extremely
camera shy.

They would crowd around from all points excepting
in front.   There was probably a reflection from the
glass which frightened them, but I could think of no
way to take pictures without a lens, so had to be
patient.   Gradually they approached closer and I
eventually secured some scenes of these long-legged
birds parading down the beach, strutting before the
camera, with their bodies swaying from one side to
another.   Some would stop and, with a coquettish
angle to the head, glance here and there, at the same
time pulling their feet out of the mud, reminding me
of a high-stepping fly on a sheet of sticky fly paper.
As they marched back and forth I involuntarily started
to hum "The Parade of the Wooden Soldiers."

The word "flamingo" is derived from the word
"flame" and was given to this bird on account of its
brilliant plumage.   There were two species represented
at Lake Hannington.   We found the smaller but more
highly-colored *Phœnicopterus minor* to be more numerous than the larger species, *Phœnicopterus roseus*,
although this latter lived here in hundreds of thousands.
The larger bird will weigh approximately thirty pounds.

The long slender legs and webbed feet are scarlet
and purple; the odd-shaped beaks are of the same

color and, excepting for the crimson under the wings and the black-tipped pinion quills, the bird shades from a pale pink to a rosy hue. The flamingos feed on tiny Crustacea which thrive in the mud, and it is this invisible food which attracts them here in their many millions. They go about the business of securing their nourishment in a methodical fashion. I watched them as they waded about, combing the lake with their beaks which they thrust upside down into the mud to scoop up food and dirt together. They would then swish their bills through the water, straining out the unwanted parts through a sievelike arrangement in the side of their beaks and retaining the minute particles of animal matter upon which they subsist.

Before returning to the ledge high upon the face of the cliff, I stationed my boys around one end of the lake with instructions that on a signal from me they were to shout and rush upon the birds in order to make them fly. So when the sun had dropped to the point where I could obtain the best scene, the prearranged sign was given and a few moments later a million wings were flashing in the air as the seething mass of flamingos bumped against one another in their mad haste to rise from the lake. Even from my lofty perch I could hear the thunder of their beating wings and the mighty clamor produced by thousands of throats as this multitude complained in reproachful tones of their ill treatment. They arose in long graceful curves to fly between me and the setting sun, resembling a huge rose-pink cloud as they drifted across the lake to disappear in the shadows of the escarpment.

While scrambling down the cliff, one of the boys spotted a cloud of dust across the valley. The glasses disclosed this to be stirred up by a large herd of elephants who were ambling in the direction of Legumukum. A day or so later we unexpectedly encountered this herd, following them all afternoon in the hope of securing a few scenes. But although we drove many miles, we succeeded in catching up with them only as they entered some thick bush where it was impossible for us to follow. During our wild ride we got into many tight places, once finding ourselves almost completely surrounded by the herd. When a cow elephant screamed, the bushes began to crash and the ground to tremble. I don't mind confessing that I felt a little bit uneasy, for there were over one hundred animals in the herd, bulls, cows, and calves, and if a major section of this group had charged our way, the truck might have suffered more than a broken spring.

Upon our return to camp we found Joe Pedley packing his equipment and learned that all the locust officers had been recalled to Nairobi. There was much excitement at Legumukum, for to the primitive N'jemps this was an event of extreme importance. They came in from all the near-by villages to watch the white man prepare for safari, each one bringing along his own private swarm of flies, so that soon the place was buzzing with activity. Our savage neighbors spent the balance of the evening with us, then danced and chanted far into the night. We had long looked upon them as real friends, for they had helped us in many ways, and next morning when Pedley left there was sincere regret on both sides at the parting.

The author with a crocodile he shot in Lake Baringo.

A N'jemps Kidogo bowman.   These men are expert marksmen.

Millions of flamingos around the shore line and on the surface of Lake Hannington. Laikipia Escarpment is seen in the background.

I made another trip to Lake Baringo in a last attempt to secure some motion pictures of crocodiles. On the way I shot a young impalla for meat and later a Grant's gazelle and some spur fowl. I found our fifty hippopotami still in the same spot, snorting and splashing and having a great time. It was one of my ambitions to photograph them at close quarters, but this was impossible here, for we could not find suitable material from which to build a raft, and only on some such contrivance could we hope to approach them.

The crocodiles were swimming all about but none had been obliging enough to get itself caught, so we reset the hook with a wart hog as bait and then started on a trek around one side of the lake to a distant rocky point where the N'jemps informed me the reptiles came out to sun themselves. After hours of arduous work in an attempt to get through thick thorn bush and over big boulders, I called a halt. Upon learning from my guide that it would be easier to reach the point by taking a wide circle, I decided to make another effort later, so returned at once to our crocodile blind. Finding that the crocodiles were still avoiding the hook, I took my Remington and commenced shooting at them just for spite. After firing all the cartridges I had with me, I started toward a marsh with a shotgun, hoping to obtain a few ducks and geese.

While trekking along, my boy called attention to what looked like a distant cloud of black smoke hanging over the far shore of Lake Baringo, where it curved over the earth's rim toward Abyssinia. In reply to my questions the N'jemps explained that it was a great mass of bugs. From his descriptions of former visitations, I surmised this to be a swarm of locusts, and this proved to be the fact. Late that evening before the humming mass had reached our camp, we were able to compute its length and breadth by familiar landmarks along the Laikipia escarpment and estimated the cloud to be about twenty-five miles wide and sixty miles long. A small part of this tremendous multitude of insects came to rest around our encampment, feeding all through the night, so that when morning came we found the district absolutely devastated. This offered an opportunity for an unusual film, and I abandoned the balance of my plans in the Baringo area in order to follow the locusts, eventually securing some marvelous material of this insect plague near our old camp in Tanganyika.

CHAPTER ELEVEN

BEYOND THE HILLS

ON a stifling hot day we started our trek to follow the locust swarm. The cool breeze caused by the moving truck was a welcome relief from the oppressive temperature of the camp, but just as we were beginning to feel comfortable, a broken front spring halted our pilgrimage out of this inferno. We were forced to stop at a point where sizzling blasts swirled through a deep depression, and what we said concerning springs in general, and this spring in particular, added much to the heat of the surrounding atmosphere.

Toward evening we ran into a section of the locust swarm, and as these insects rained down from the black cloud sweeping overhead to settle on the trees and vegetation along the roadside, I realized for the first time what a real menace they were. Soon they had covered the trees in a solid mass, breaking and bending limbs under their weight. We stopped to make some photographs, and as I watched them chewing the green leaves, I could visualize from past experience the scene of devastation which would be left behind. We drove for several miles through this swarm while it was descending to earth for a night of rest and incessant feeding, the insects pelting us like hailstones as we moved along at thirty miles an hour. When we had passed beyond this living cloud, we stopped to shake them out of our clothes, and old

Maniki commented that it was a bad year for the black man when the heavens rained bugs.

Upon arrival at Gilgil, we unloaded everything into the warehouse, and I sent Ted to the shamba with one truck while Austin and I in the other hustled on to Nairobi. Just before reaching the bottom of the Kikuyu Escarpment we frightened a troop of dog-faced baboons and remarked on their resemblance to lions when they scrambled away through the grass. Shortly afterwards we met a car containing some tourists coming down the hill. That night at the hotel I overheard these tenderfeet telling a circle of amazed listeners about their exciting adventure at the bottom of the escarpment, where they had encountered a troop of lions!

Finding it necessary to visit Mombasa in order to complete final details concerning my gasoline supplies across Africa and to pick up a shipment of motion-picture film that was waiting there for me, I made arrangements with Mike to go down in his touring car. He was glad of the opportunity because he wanted to visit his dad's mine on the coast, so in the early morning of February thirteenth we started seaward over the dusty trail that bumps for hundreds of miles across fields and rock-strewn gullies, hills, and veldt. This is the main highway, being without doubt the worst road of its length in the entire world. At the end of the first threescore miles, all that could be seen of Mike, the native boy, and myself, was the whites of our eyes; everything was buried under inches of fine red dust.

There are many stream beds crossing this boulevard, but we found only two bridges in place, one at Stony

Athi and the other at Voi. We reached the Tsavo River just before dark, to find it running in flood and the flimsy bridge about a foot under water. To our left stood the new railroad bridge which was constructed to replace the one made famous by the man-eating lions of Tsavo. The old span could no longer stand the heavy railroad traffic, but instead of using this historical structure, built at the cost of so many human lives, for a highway bridge, the railroad administration had this world-famous monument torn down, fearing road improvements would invite motor-truck transport and lessen the railroad's revenue.

We slept that night at McKinnon Road and had breakfast next morning with a white man in charge of a black crew working on the railway. He was mighty glad to meet someone who could speak English, and upon finding I was from Colorado, told me he had spent a few years before the war riding the range in Wyoming, and that he wanted to go back.

When we penetrated into the coastal zone the heat became sticky and oppressive, but this is the Africa of song and story — the land of tropical scenes, of color and romance. As we rolled down the green hills toward the distant blue of the Indian Ocean, we passed huge mango trees, waving palms, banana plantations, ferns, and flowering shrubs of many kinds. What a contrast to the dusty and burnt countryside of the interior were these lovely pictures of valley and hill, where rainbow hues were set like jewels amid the many shades of green that covered the landscape!

While on the native ferry, crossing to the island, I became impatient to visit again my friends, the Dohertys, and shortly afterwards we were gathered on their wide veranda, the coolest spot in Mombasa, kept so by refreshing breezes from the ocean.

After a cool bath, I had donned civilized clothes once more, and while reclining in a comfortable chair, with a cold drink at hand, talking to my own kind of people again, I watched a passenger liner move slowly out through the channel toward the open sea. As it nosed its way through the narrows I was overcome with homesickness and wished that my work were completed so that I could return to my family who were so far away. Seven months had now passed since I left Denver, and, although many adventures had befallen us, there was much still to do, and the steamer which I hoped would bear me homewards sailed from a port on the opposite side of this vast continent!

When Doherty's house boy awakened me the next morning with the East African greeting, "Chai, bwana," and placed the tray of hot tea at my elbow, it required a few seconds to gather my thoughts, for I was not accustomed to such luxuries as china cups, clean linen, and a soft bed. It was the season of fruits and at breakfast the pishi served mangos, pawpaw with lemon, and the most delicious bananas I had ever eaten.

On the way to town, I stopped to say "hello" to my friend the tortoise. This giant land turtle is one of Mombasa's most interesting citizens. He is looked upon as a pioneer, for according to the accepted story, he was brought here many hundreds of years ago by a sailing ship, hailing from the coast of South America. Regardless of where he came from, or when, it is certain that he is not a native of Africa, and that he only understands commands given in Italian.

Continuing on my way toward the Vacuum Oil Company office, I passed the shop where a few months previously I had undergone the most uncomfortable hair-cutting experience of my life. It made me itch even to glance into this torture chamber which brought back vivid memories of the slow-moving barber, of the hairs floating down my neck and back in trickling streams of perspiration as I sweltered in this Turkish bath disguised as a barber shop.

On the next corner stood the open-air cinema, or picture theater, where every once in a while, conditions permitting, they display to the public gaze, for the price of two shillings and sixpence, an ancient film. I recalled that on my first visit to this movie palace I had assisted to kill a cobra in the lobby, and I remember that they stopped between each reel for a smoke and refreshments.

Even Mombasa has its traffic problems and occasional smash-ups. At the main intersection a heavily loaded wagon, pulled by a dozen husky black men and pushed by as many more, had jammed traffic. A gray-bearded, white-robed Hindu came buzzing along on a motor cycle with his robes and beard fluttering and trailing in the breeze. In trying to avoid the wagon he crashed into a rickshaw. No one was hurt, but I was heartsick because I could not photograph this scene in sound. The actions and facial expressions of blacks and Hindus, who joined in the argument, the shouting in six different tongues, each individual trying to top the others, offered a comedy that no one could ever stage. The show was stopped by three native policemen who waded into the center of things using their clubs right and left.

The balance of the day was spent with Mr. J. L. Oates of Colombo cocktail fame. He was East African manager for the Vacuum Oil Company, and I was happy to learn of the arrangements which had been completed, whereby I would pick up gasoline and Mobiloil at Arua, Buta, Bangui, Fort Archambault, and Maidugari. These points were hundreds of miles apart, but, by carefully planning the loads, it would be possible to carry enough to get us through from one depot to another.

When we again reached the Tsavo River we found the bridge missing. This meant either a several-hundred-mile detour or that we must build a new span. We found some boys loafing about and put them to work, constructing, after several hours labor, what we thought to be a passable bridge. But the car got stuck in the middle when the front wheels pushed the crosspieces ahead of them and dropped into the hole. It was late at night when we gained the Nairobi side, and after a simple repast of herring and beans, washed down by a little hot tea, we spread our blankets on the warm ground. Looking up at the marvelous sky, wherein millions of bright stars twinkled and danced, I remarked to Mike about the beauties of the African night. His answering comment was that he had started out, years ago, to count these stars, but that the darn things kept increasing in number and moving about so fast that he finally gave it up as an impossible undertaking.

Before dropping off to sleep, I recalled to mind the thrilling story of the man-eaters of Tsavo; of their nightly kills of human beings; of how they would drag their screaming victims out of bed, the

Another view of flamingos along one shore of Lake Hannington.

Flamingos, Lake Hannington. These birds live here in greater multitudes than in any like area on the face of the globe. Note the countless numbers along the distant shore where they are so thick as to resemble dense grass.

morning's search by companions revealing only a few gruesome remains. With these thoughts in mind, I fell asleep beneath the ghostly abutments of the old bridge.

Some time before dawn I awakened with a start — an animal was moving close to my head. Immediately visions of man-eating lions flashed before me and when I slowly turned to face a large wild dog leering at me from only a few yards away, I received a shock that left me numb for a few seconds. Finally comprehending that this was merely a wild dog, I began fumbling around for my rifle. My movements frightened the animal and he loped away into the mist.

Upon arrival at Gilgil, I sent a note to the farm by Ali, our old cook, who had rejoined us, instructing Ted to hustle down with the safari boys and kit. Then, loading the other truck with supplies from the warehouse, I dispatched it in charge of Austin and Jones toward Camp Simba. Jones had just been added to the staff, his job being to keep the trucks in repair, which task he lightly undertook, little knowing what confronted him on that long journey across Africa. Ali rode as far as Thompson's Falls, then walked the eighteen miles to the farm before ten o'clock that night. Ted loaded at once, arriving in Gilgil at four o'clock in the morning, giving me one of the greatest surprises of the entire expedition.

After a day's drive, we overtook the other truck at Narok. Next morning one of my best porters came in complaining that he was very sick and wanted to go home, so I paid him off and arranged for his transportation back to Nairobi; then, after a visit with the A. D. C., we collected the mail for Kilimafeza and buzzed off "into the blue."

A broken front spring delayed us, tsetse flies bit us, and some canned fish poisoned Jones. I recommended CC pills, and Jones swallowed two, thus starting a string of events which were to give him an unusual and thrilling initiation into African safari life.

Camp was made that night near a large outcropping of rocks, and hardly had we stopped when our friend, Simba, welcomed us with a mighty roar. While eating our meal, Ted, Austin, and myself discussed some lion adventures, incidentally mentioning how bold they were at this particular spot and how one man had spent the night in a tree because they insisted on walking around his bed. At first Jones tried to laugh about the matter, saying we were talking like this to frighten him, but when the lions continued to grunt and roar all around the camp, and the pills began to take effect, his attitude changed. It was the first night of a full moon; it was the first night that Jones had ever slept on a lion-and-hyena-infested veldt. The prowlers circled close to camp all night long, thus preventing Jones from going too far afield, but next morning he told us of the shadows cast by the moon, of night birds that uttered strange sounds, and of his undying hate for canned fish and army pills.

A pair of these lions awakened us with a final burst of roaring within five hundred yards of our beds, so we got up for an early breakfast, after which we drove onward through a parklike country, enjoying to the full the clear morning air. We had crossed the Border River and with each mile the game increased in variety and number. About midday we reached Kilimafeza, where we stopped for a cup of tea with Major Warwick, whom we found sick in bed with fever. After we had pulled up the Benogie hill, a large herd of zebras crossed our path, making it necessary to stop until the dust had settled. When it cleared away, we found a baby zebra standing there all alone. Upon espying us he came running to the truck, so Ted picked him up. Austin was appointed nurse, and for several days fed this little chap on a bottle. He was named Dapper and became a great pet around camp.

It takes only a short time for the jungle to regain its own, and several days of work were required to put Camp Simba into order again. We found the dining shack standing at a slant due to the fact that white ants were busily engaged in trying to consume the timbers which supported it. At each meal they would flavor our soup and other liquids with fine sawdust. This was very annoying and vengeance was sworn against them.

We made a scouting trip toward the Blangetti, paying a visit to an old water hole about eighteen miles from camp. On the way we were successful in filming several groups of giraffe. While stalking a large herd of wildebeest to photograph them, a sudden change of wind gave them our scent and they stampeded away in a panic, running through a group of gazelles that happened to be in their line of flight. When the dust had settled we found a young tommie struggling on the ground. The wildebeest had taken these antelope by surprise and this little fellow had failed to get out of their path.

The whole country was teeming with buck, the Thompson's gazelles being in the majority. No matter where we went, there were countless thousands of these graceful little animals; they were never out of sight. Arriving at the water hole, we found the tsetse fly very bad thereabouts, while the water was green and evil smelling.

We noticed several vultures perched in some near-by thorn trees, and while going to investigate jumped a wart hog boar from behind an ant hill. He ran a short distance, then stood broadside on. It seems I could never miss one of these porkers no matter whether it were standing, running, close, or far away, and although in this case it was a long shot, my first bullet finished him for good. Upon discovering that one tusk was entirely broken off, I was badly disappointed, for I was certainly having bad luck in securing a wart hog trophy. Shortly afterwards I shot a Grant's gazelle for meat, never giving a thought to the head until Maniki called my attention to it. The steel tape said it was a close second to the world's record, so I had it carefully skinned in order to bring it home with me.

The long dry season was almost at an end. The short rains had freshened the country for a period, refilling the smaller ponds, but these were now dried up, making it necessary for the game to congregate in enormous numbers close to the larger supplies of water. The long rains would soon begin, replenishing the pools in dry dongas and causing these herds to scatter again over an immense territory. Now was the time to secure pictures of animals coming to the water holes, and, with this aim in view, we sallied forth to locate suitable bomas along the course of the Serra Nyiro. We split into two crews, in order to rush the work, constructing blinds at six likely places. During one afternoon, while the boys were completing the work on one of these camera-hiding places, I strolled across the veldt with my gun bearer and a toto, shooting a nice fat zebra for the boys, and collecting two young wart hogs, one goose, one duck, one yellow-legged partridge, two emperor partridges, and twenty-two sand grouse for our own larder.

The camp was astir next morning just before the sun peeked over the edge of the Serengetti plains, for it is necessary to get into blinds while it is still dark. Three of us spent the entire day in bomas without much success, the net result of our combined efforts being a ten-foot scene of one lone tommie whose thirst overbalanced his fear, and a view of two golden-crested cranes that came down to drink.

Several days were spent in these blinds with varying success. On one occasion Jones reported that, as the animals seemed to avoid the place, he circled around the boma to see if he could discover the cause, and had found a big male lion peacefully reposing beneath a near-by tree. This explained things to his entire satisfaction but failed to improve his nerves.

Ted had gone to the mine for drinking water, with instructions to return for us before dark. When the shadows began to deepen, Jones and I moved our things out into the open plain to await his belated arrival. Darkness came down black as ink and strange noises began to fill the air, while dim shapes prowled around among the bushes and in the grass. About this time we thought of making a fire and Jones produced four matches, all of which went out. The shapes moved closer. A lion grunted; Jones made another frantic search, finding two more matches.

14

We carefully piled up some dry grass, protecting it from the wind, then struck the first match, which followed its predecessors to wherever a match goes when it goes out. The next one started the grass blazing, but then it was a problem to find sufficient fuel, for we were out in the plain and all the wood was in the donga or on its banks. Necessity forced us to take a chance in our efforts to keep the fire burning, as otherwise some hungry carnivore could walk right up to us in the darkness, without either our knowledge or permission. While engaged in the ticklish task of picking up wood along the donga, a near-by lion growled and we raced back to the fire, losing part of our precious fuel on the way. When the blaze was leaping brightly we made a second round trip to the donga, then sat down feeling somewhat secure. As the lights of the truck flashed around a bend in the road, Jones absent-mindedly pushed his hand into his largest pocket and found a full box of matches!

To vary the monotony of waiting in blinds, Ted, Austin, and myself went out to photograph impalla, but although lucky enough to find a large herd, we were soon convinced that these animals were going to be most difficult to film. Deciding our chances would be better with two trucks, we started campwards, recording enroute some good herd shots of zebra, wildebeest, and topi. While buzzing merrily along, a wart hog sow, followed by several youngsters, crossed our path. We badly needed scenes of baby animals, so started out to capture as many of this litter as possible. The race was through a tree-strewn country and while going thirty miles or more an hour, we hit a large pig hole, breaking a front spring and causing the wheels to lock. The truck swerved toward a large tree and Ted, being powerless to stop our onrush, hit it with a terrific crash. He was not hurt, as the wheel held him in place, but Austin struck an upright post, receiving a nasty cut. I was pushed against the cab roof with such force that for several days afterwards, whenever I chewed, my face hurt. There were three boys in the back, each one of whom received some minor injury. All hands piled out to survey the damage, Austin finding his sun glasses twenty feet in front of the tree, although they had been on his nose when the crash took place. About the same distance away, we found a box of rifle shells which had continued their journey after the truck stopped. The truck itself was in bad shape; the heavy bumper was wrapped around the tree, the radiator was smashed and the frame broken. In fact, it not only needed repairs, but some new parts.

The least injured boy, a raw savage, was sent on the run to camp, which was four miles distant, with orders to tell Jones about the accident. He made it in jig time, and Jones told afterwards how this Ikoma rushed up all out of breath to say that the other masters had run into a piece of wood! When Jonesy arrived and reviewed the result of our race after the baby pigs, it was easy to gather from his expression that the romance of his job had lost part of its appeal.

One night while waiting to take some negatives out of the hypo bath, I watched the moon rise from beyond the hills. It was almost a full moon and flooded the landscape with a mysterious mellow light. In a near-by lair two lions had been kicking up an awful rumpus. I had never heard *Felis leo* roar louder or keep at

it for such a long time. They came so close I could
hear the intake of their breath. Farther away, from
the direction of the blinds, another lion was roaring
back at them, while the scattered hyena population
was letting the world know how mournful it felt. The
baby zebra became very nervous, finally running into
the dining shack, where he hid under the table. Poor
little fellow — he was not old enough to know what a
cruel world he had been born into!

With a Masai as my only companion, I started out
on foot next morning to explore the district where I
had heard the lions roar the night before. While
walking along, I collected a fine silver-backed jackal
which I killed with my shotgun when it jumped up
forty yards away. We circled around back of the hill,
then down into a little grassy valley. After crossing
a hollow and climbing a short way up the side of the
opposite slope, we sat down beneath a shady mimosa
tree to rest. The Masai's quick eyes detected movements below which heralded the raising of the curtain
on a drama of the veldt. Very few are privileged to
behold a troop of wild lions actually stalking and
killing their prey.

From my box seat I gazed down on this beautiful
vale of the Serengetti, and through my eight-power
glasses watched three lionesses and their consort,
assisted by an unwilling kongoni, enact their alloted
parts in a tragedy of the wilderness. The four cats
were crouched in the grass between myself and the
intended victim, which, of course, was unaware of its
danger. The wind was blowing from the kongoni
toward us, but slightly to the left. The three lionesses
slunk forward through the grass and took up positions

The locust swarm in flight.   Notice them on the ground.

A close view of a section of the locust-covered trees.

255

A section of the tremendous locust swarm which devastated the country.

down wind, while the male slowly made a wide circle to get back of the antelope. When the kongoni got a smell of the lion, he threw up his head and after gazing in that direction for a few seconds wheeled about, dashing straight toward the three lionesses who were now spread out fan-shaped, but some yards apart, in the yellow grass. As he galloped toward them, thinking only of the danger behind, they ran catlike along the ground to intercept his flight, and when he discovered their presence it was too late for retreat. The closest lioness bounded forward and running alongside the unfortunate kongoni for a few paces, sprang upon him, and with one mighty paw twisted his head downward, at the same time biting into the neck. The others trotted up and in a few more seconds it was over. The lion took his time about joining the females, seemingly confident of their ability, and that a meal would be waiting for him. The show was ended, and so, with the Masai bearing my rifle, I slowly descended from my seat on the hill.

During my absence Jones and Ted had prepared the truck for towing to the mine, so next morning we undertook the difficult task of dragging this dead weight over roads and through dongas that were sufficiently hard to negotiate under a truck's own power. Our progress was so slow and our stops to repair the towing cable so many that it required an entire day to cover the twenty miles. During that time all of us were nearly eaten alive by mosquitoes and tsetse flies. We were literally covered with blisters left by the bite of the fly, which caused us considerable worry, for this country is notorious for sleeping sickness. We could not be sure whether or not we had escaped its dread clutches until many days later.   Once at the mine, it took two days to make necessary repairs before Ted could get under way for Nairobi.

On the night of March fourth, a big event took place on the plains of the Serengetti.   The first banquet ever given in this part of the world was held under the stars, attended by the largest group of white people ever gathered together in the game country of Tanganyika.   Seventeen sat down to dine at the long table, the party consisting of the Lieurances, who had returned for a short visit, accompanied by their wives; Major Warwick, who had driven from the mine to join us, and the members of my safari.   The menu included native products, although most everything came out of cans.   For a cabaret we had hyenas and jackals, howling as if they objected to being left out in the darkness, and beyond the hills lions grunted to remind us that this was still their domain.

Three nights later, the Lieurances invited us to their camp for a return banquet.   A feature of the affair was the menu card which Barney drew by hand. While the courses were being served, I arranged the 8 x 10 camera, and with a crudely rigged apparatus, endeavored to make a flashlight photograph of the group.   Having no caps to ignite the powder, we used some movie film for the purpose.   After all was set, I opened the shutter, Jones lit the film and we both rushed to get into the picture.   We all stood or sat tensely waiting as the fire gradually approached the powder and just before it reached the pan, everyone set his teeth and batted his eyes — then the light went out!   This was repeated several times, until we

were all upset about the thing and uncertain of what
was going to happen.   At a moment when no one was
expecting it, there was a mighty flash and the camera
recorded one of the most unusual and extremely
flattering photographs ever made, reproduction of
which would probably bring on several lawsuits.   As
we were leaving, a native driver came in with supplies
and reported he had met Ted on top of the Mau, and
that he was getting along toward Nairobi, slowly and
with difficulty.

Several days were spent in the blinds with scant
results, so it was suggested we stay away from the
bomas for two or three days, allowing the animals an
opportunity to drink at the water holes without any
chance of our presence disturbing them.   In order to
keep busy, we went exploring into the country back
of the low ridge that faced our camp.   I was anxious
to locate giraffe herds and make some motion pictures
of them, so kept the big camera always ready, and
along the way secured some excellent scenes of zebra,
topi, and wildebeest.   In crossing over a saddle
between two large hills, we surprised a herd of water
buck and among them a very fine bull.   After a careful stalk, I succeeded in hitting him at four hundred
yards, but he ran into a stony and hilly country where
it was almost impossible to follow.   In trying to locate
him, I climbed to the top of a steep rocky hill.   From
this height I could see for many miles in all directions,
getting an excellent airplane view of the entire country.
The veldt rolled toward a range of distant mountains,
and dotted here and there upon the plain were large
patches of thorn tree and scrub.   Down the center
ran a big donga with green trees outlining it along

both sides.   In the open spaces could be seen thousands
of head of game, mostly wildebeest, topi, and zebra.
I knew that for every animal visible there were fifty
more hidden by trees and bush.   This is no exaggera-
tion, for while only three species were discernible, in
that same stretch of country roamed many thousands
of lesser buck, such as impalla, Grant's gazelles, tommies, dik-diks, and, of course, hundreds of lions,
hyenas, and jackals, to say nothing of the immense
number of giraffe.

We went in another direction the following day in
search of wildebeest herds, for some film was needed
of these animals.   We found plenty of them but they
were mixed with zebra which seemed to be more
timid than usual.   It is probable that they had been
bothered a great deal by lions, for the country was now
overrun with the big cats.   The smell of the tawny
prowlers is enough to send the zebra off in a stampede,
while the sight of one throws them into a panic, so it
is no wonder these black-and-white horses of the
plains were timid.

We did not secure what we wanted in the way of
wildebeest film, but the day was not lost, for we photographed some excellent close-ups of a huge old bull
giraffe, who obligingly posed in the most suitable
settings of light and composition.   We followed him
around for an hour or more, until finally the old fellow
became annoyed at our persistent attentions and,
kicking up his heels, made off in that long rocking-
horse gait which seems so awkward but which carries
them over the ground at surprising speed.

Upon returning to the blinds again we had fair
success, obtaining a few scenes of gazelles and other

animals coming down to water. One of the most interesting features of our vigil in these thorn inclosures was to watch the clouds of sand grouse that flew here in the evening to drink. They would usually arrive too late for photographing, so, after I had become acquainted with their habits, I would take my shotgun in hand as they came swarming in from the veldt, collecting enough in two or three shots to supply us for the ensuing day. They are delicious eating and we never tired of them.

During these long days in the blinds, I had ample opportunity to muse over things past and present and to dream a little bit about the future. Once I took stock of my experiences, the surroundings causing my thoughts to revert to my first night spent in a boma, and I came to the conclusion that one of these blinds not only offered the most interesting way to study the nocturnal prowlers but that a night so spent furnished enough thrills to last anyone a lifetime.

After building a boma and placing a bait, you crawl inside to await the darkness. As soon as the long shadows melt into blackness, you will hear the yapping of the jackals and a distant howl of hyenas, and later the first ones will appear at the kill. You first become aware of their presence by using the flashlight; you have heard a noise and becoming curious as to its cause, turn on the light to see, discovering a pair of shy little jackals hungrily eying the meat. Later, losing fear of your presence, they sneak up and hastily take a few bites; then tearing off a good sized chunk of meat, they run back into the shadows to devour it.

Now you hear close at hand the unearthly cry of a hyena and, although you have heard it hundreds of

times before, it will still cause cold chills to run up
and down your spine. When this gruesome beast
slinks up to the carcass you again use your spotlight
and he stops to gaze toward the boma with big red
eyes. These carrion eaters now approach from all
directions; you hear their laughs and cries far and
wide and soon fifteen or more are grunting, jabbering,
and growling within a few feet of where you sit, tensely
listening as they tear at the flesh and crunch the bones
with their powerful jaws. When they have started
to feed you again flash the lamp on them; they stop
for a second to glare in your direction, and then, entirely
disregarding the light, continue their meal. While
watching them you notice how each one tries to eat
faster than the others. You also catch sight of a
jackal dashing in now and then to pick up pieces of
meat and run out again. Suddenly they all stop, every
head becoming erect, then you hear away off in the
distance the roar of a lion, which trails off into a
whisper, then dies away. A few seconds later the
hyenas are busily feeding and it seems they are eating
faster than before, if such a thing is possible. After
a short silence, you again hear the lion roar, this time
much closer; he has scented the kill and is on his
way! The mere thought that the king of beasts is
stalking toward you makes you tingle with excitement. You reach over to be sure that your heavy
rifle is where you put it, and picking it up open the
breach carefully to see if it is loaded. As you place
more shells where they will be handy, you notice that
your gun bearer is intently listening, and now he leans
over to whisper in Swahili, "The lion is coming
fast——"

Now you look out the opening again; the hyenas have redoubled their efforts and you conclude they are the most gluttonous animals in all creation, but they know the lion is near, so are trying to gulp down all the meat possible before the time of their departure. As you watch, they suddenly stiffen, then with one final bite slink away into the darkness. Now all is still for awhile until you hear the heavy tread of the lion as he stealthily circles your boma. You wish that you could see him, but it is too dark, so you listen as he stalks around you — once, twice, three times. Then your boy whispers, "There are three lions, bwana," but you think to yourself that his imagination is playing tricks with him, because you have heard only one. You keep your face to the peephole, your eyes focused on the dimly outlined carcass, and suddenly a heavy body hurtles through the air and lands with a mighty thud on the other side of the dead zebra! The king of the jungle has arrived! He is facing you; his big yellow eyes are fixed on the opening; his tail is lashing slowly from side to side. Fascinated you watch him — then two lionesses stalk out and lie down beside the zebra, and after a casual glance in your direction they leave the matter of your presence entirely to the male and commence to eat. If you are a real sportsman you watch them until they have completed their meal, and then you will allow them to return to the jungle unharmed.

No one can have a more thrilling, more memorable experience than to wait in a boma for the Lord of the Donga. Some people brag of having shot lions under these conditions, but they certainly cannot claim the title of a true sportsman, and it is to be regretted that such methods of hunting this majestic animal are allowed.

We spent many hard days during this period of working in bomas; days that started with the dawn and ended with midnight; days of patient waiting in blinds for scenes that never happened. About this time Mike returned to camp and, with his experience to guide us, I hoped to secure some special scenes I wanted, but we had a series of minor annoyances that prevented success. One day Mike was just on the point of securing a fine scene of zebra and wildebeest drinking together when some natives came along and scared them away. The next day a leopard hung around his water hole and frightened everything. At my blind the wind shifted as the animals were coming to drink, causing them to stampede out of camera range. Next day it rained like the flood and drowned me out.

I was not prepared for this, so, when the deluge came, Maniki and I sought shelter under a fair-sized thorn tree, but in spite of it were soon soaked to the skin. The cameras were well protected in their waterproof cases, and as I didn't mind a cool shower bath, I was not particularly peeved, excepting that it did seem to take Jones a long time to come after us with the truck. While waiting for him, I amused myself by counting the vultures as they dropped out of the sky to seek shelter. Later I watched countless millions of flying ants as they issued forth from numerous ant colonies close to the tree, and wondered where they were going. When I pointed to them Maniki grinned and said they were very good to eat, especially when fried in butter! The season of long rains had com-

Dapper, the baby zebra.

A close-up view of locust on tree leaves.

Once when the party left this truck near the lion donga they returned several hours later to find six lions grouped around it. It had become a familiar and friendly thing to them, bringing them meat, and so they gathered around waiting for a meal. Note how readily the lion on the left conceals itself in the grass.

menced in earnest and all our prospects of securing
pictures at water holes were ended.

On a dark, cloudy morning, I looked out of my tent
and thought this would be another wasted day, but
about eleven o'clock it began to brighten up. Mike,
Jones, and I had an early lunch, then with all the
camera equipment on board one truck, went in search
of material for pictures. We had no particular plans,
just hoped that something worth while would show up.
Three miles from camp we turned off the road to circle
a low ridge and there before us saw the edge of a vast
army of locusts. In the valley beyond, we could see
the main swarm hovering over the veldt like a black
storm cloud. As we approached toward the center
of this winged horde, with the insects swarming over
us and pelting us from all directions, we appreciated
that by the merest chance we had either met again
the swarm which had passed over Lake Baringo, or
another of like magnitude.

The ground was pulsating with the crawling mass
of purple insects, while the heavens in all directions
were black with them. They obscured the sun and,
as we sped through this plague of whirring bugs, it
was impossible to see more than a few yards ahead.
The noise produced by these billions of wings was
deafening, resembling the roar from a fleet of airplanes.
We almost ran into a wildebeest herd fighting its way
through this pestilent flood, and upon stopping to
photograph them, the animals stampeded into the
swarm and actually faded from sight, engulfed by
the cloud of insects that arose in front of them.
These beasts and the gazelles were panic-stricken,
for whenever they would try to take a bite of grass

they got a mouthful of insects instead. The locusts
struck them like falling hail until the herds sought
refuge in flight, but no matter in which direction they
ran, escape was impossible, for this cloud filled the
air for many square miles with a whirring mass of
locusts.

We all worked frantically to secure as much film as
possible while the light remained. An opportunity
such as this seldom presents itself, so we took full
advantage of it, only stopping the cameras when the
sun commenced to set. While we were recording this
devastating army of invasion, the words of Moses kept
running through my mind:

"For they covered the face of the whole earth, so
that the land was darkened; and they did eat every
herb of the land, and all the fruit of the trees, and
there remained not any green thing in the trees, or in
the herbs of the field, through all the land."

CHAPTER TWELVE

LAST DAYS ON THE SERENGETTI

THERE came a short period of clear weather, so for a few days we gave all of our time and attention to photographing the skyscrapers of the veldt — Mr. and Mrs. Giraffe.

In a grassy valley about twenty miles from camp, we found fourteen of these mottled creatures standing beneath a cluster of thorn trees to escape the sun. The herd consisted of a few old bulls, several cows, and four youngsters. Placing the camera up high, so as to photograph over the cab, Mike started after the family with care and caution, for this was now our only truck; our sole means of getting back to civilization. The veldt was full of hidden pig burrows and ditches varying in size from the small ones that only broke a spring to enormous trenches that the whole truck could fall into. Filming giraffe proved to be dangerous work, for, in order to get close enough for good pictures, it was necessary to race after them at thirty miles an hour or more. Once you have gained a good position and made a short scene, the process must be repeated all over again. Were the ground smooth, recording these animals would be an easy matter, but no such conditions existed in the giraffe country, every foot of which contained some hazard, either pig holes, ditches, hidden rocks, or tree stumps. It was possible to strike a hollow and turn the truck over, or to hit a tree as you went dodging in and out among them, just missing some by inches, or you might plunge into a deep donga, with serious consequences. But to secure pictures of giraffe that would be of any interest to spectators, we had to take these chances.

Immediately after starting we struck a hole which threw the camera into the air and myself and the boys to the floor of the truck. Nothing was seriously hurt, so putting things together we went after them again. This time we raced over a large plain and, as the truck went speeding along at thirty-five miles an hour, often hit small holes which shook things up, and once we nearly capsized. Mike had barely dodged a large boulder, turning so suddenly that we ran along on two wheels for a few yards, when I saw directly ahead of us a big wide ditch. I yelled at Mike just in time for him to stop at the edge of the chasm. If we had tumbled into this, the expedition would have come to a sudden and untimely end. Circling the donga, we tried again, this time getting into position for a fairly good view as the giraffe raced by, but after grinding out seventy feet of film, I discovered that the iris on the lens had jarred down to a pinhole, which meant we had nothing to show for the morning's work, excepting a few bruises and some underexposed film.

On account of our recent accident which had put the other truck out of commission, we were almost nervous wrecks after this day's effort, and I would much rather have been back in a boma photographing lions.

Next morning we made another early start in search of giraffe, this time going into a district where we had seen many of the animals in the past. After a

A lion and lioness playing with one of the Mobiloil cans stolen from the truck.

A lion and two lionesses with a spare tire which they carried from the truck.

short tour, we found a good-sized herd, and setting the camera up for slow-motion work, went after them. On this occasion I secured eighty feet of pictures, showing these odd but graceful animals running across the screen in single file, giving a remarkable study of their peculiar rocking-horse gait. An interesting fact is that the long neck seems to take up the motions of the body in such a way that it would be possible for a giraffe to carry a glass of water balanced between his miniature horns without spilling a drop. The head seems to float along on an even keel, while the rest of the body wiggles all over. The babies, no matter how small, keep up with their parents, and once in a while, becoming annoyed at eating all the dust, the youngsters will put on an extra burst of speed and rush around into the lead. Nature seems to have so arranged matters that most of the African mammals are able to run with the herds almost immediately after birth.

The giraffe is the tallest of living creatures, a full grown bull towering as high as eighteen feet. They are purely browsers, especially addicted to the leaves of the camel's thorn, a species of acacia. Their upper lip is prehensile; it is long, tough, and covered with short hair, thus enabling them to browse on their favorite trees without getting stung by the thorns. They vary greatly in color and I have observed in one herd individuals which were a light chestnut shade and others of a dark brown. The markings also differ considerably, once in a while a freakish design being found.

This animal must be mute, for during all of our associations with him and his family, we never heard them make a sound, and inquiry among hunters and the native boys also indicated the giraffe to be incapable of any utterance. He is able to live for great lengths of time without water; in fact, can abstain from drinking longer than a camel. He undoubtedly obtains a great deal of moisture in the form of dew which collects on the leaves on which he browses, but regardless of whether or not he secures enough liquid in this way, it is a well-known fact that in semiarid country where lions are a menace at the infrequent water holes, he will stay away for great periods of time, for when he does go to drink, it is necessary for him to spread his forelegs in order to bring his mouth to the water. When standing in this awkward position, he is more or less at the mercy of a lurking lion, which could easily pounce upon him, breaking his neck before it would be possible to regain his feet and seek safety in flight.

When out on the open plain, his keen eyes can spot the approach of enemies from a great distance. It is difficult to detect him when standing motionless among the thorn trees, his spotted body blending into the surroundings so perfectly that, unless he moves, you are likely to pass him by. I found it was much easier to locate giraffe by looking for their heads above the tops of the trees, for although their bodies remained stationary, their heads often moved and betrayed their presence.

To me they are the most interesting of the harmless animals, and I cannot picture a scene of Africa without including a few of these strange left-overs from the dim past dotting the landscape or silhouetted against the sky.

Another bright morning found Mike and me again chasing giraffe over pig holes and through the trees; he driving at top speed to get the camera into position, and I striving with might and main to hold on to the careening truck, at the same time keeping the camera together so that when we did get ready to photograph there would be something left to take pictures with.

These animated towers are capable of running nearly forty miles an hour, but they cannot keep this up for a great length of time; in fact, it is injurious for them to be chased in this manner for more than a short distance. For that reason, after securing two or three scenes of a herd, we would leave them and go to look for another. I have often marveled that we came through all of our giraffe filming without a serious accident, but we did, and when the last scene had been photographed, Mike and I shook hands and thanked our lucky stars that we were still alive and that this dangerous bit of work was finished.

While searching for picture possibilities, we strayed into a strange country, finding a valley where thousands of antelope were holding a convention. It must be almost inconceivable to one who has not visited Africa, that so much wild life still exists in the modern world. To the hunter at home, such numbers seem impossible; to us, these vast herds had become commonplace, part of the landscape. It is likely that during such days as this we encountered more game than the average man sees in his entire lifetime.

While skirting a donga which winds through this previously unexplored region, I espied a spotted head and shoulders suddenly appear out of the tall grass. I was suffering with a splitting headache caused by a

touch of the sun, which I received the day before
when my helmet was lost for a short time during a
race with giraffe. Not feeling very well, I only gave
this apparition a casual glance, thinking it to be a
hyena, but a second look disclosed a large and very
fine leopard. I told Mike to stop the truck, and
without moving from the seat, attempted to get a
bead on the snarling cat, but when Mike saw what
it was, he hopped out of the truck in order to secure
a shot. The members of the Cottar clan had sworn
vengeance against all leopards, because of the serious
maulings Mike's father had twice experienced from
these bloodthirsty brutes and the more recent attack
upon Ted. His jumping from the truck upset my
aim, and before I could draw another bead on the
animal, it disappeared in the grass, and although we
hunted around for a long time and got three more
glimpses of it, neither of us had a chance to fire a shot.
I think Maniki was more put out than anyone else,
because he told me in Swahili that it was an exceptionally big leopard and would have made the bwana
a nice rug.

Being unable to find the leopard, we continued
onward, keeping a sharp lookout for spotted animals,
and had only gone a short distance when we encountered one of the little tragedies of the veldt. Africa
is pristine country where the law of survival deals
death to the weak; where the strong have no sympathy
for the unfortunate. We found an old wildebeest
bull who was sick almost unto death. His companions
had left him behind, and here he was, deserted, standing on unsteady legs, watching through dimmed eyes
a circle of hungry hyenas waiting for him to lie down

before they would pounce upon him. On the near-by trees solemn looking vultures surveyed the scene, probably estimating their chances of securing part of the feast. Mike turned to me and exclaimed, "The poor devil!" and while he was putting this suffering animal out of his misery, I turned my attention to the hyenas. They were a little too close to come within the golf rules, but, in chasing them away, two of the bunch were accidentally killed.

Now we started back to camp, but had not gone far when Maniki pointed out a water buck bull standing under some trees. I was very keen to secure another of these graceful animals for a trophy, so made a careful stalk and landed him with the third bullet. After Maniki had skinned out the head, we continued on our way, eventually coming into a small valley where forty-five giraffe were having a family reunion. The light was bad, but we decided to try to obtain a few scenes of this large herd and spent over two hours with them. During this time we noticed that the giraffe would not cross a certain donga; nor would they approach very close to it. This excited our curiosity, for experience told us there must be a lion or leopard hidden in the brush. Mike and I walked through the donga, finding the grass so high that it was necessary to carry our rifles at arm's reach above our heads to prevent seeds from getting into the actions. The donga proved only a few yards wide and upon stepping out on the other side, we found ourselves face to face with three lions.

The males and the lioness eyed us for a few seconds, during which we realized what a ticklish situation we had walked into. Both of us carried our lightest rifles, the 7 mm. Mauser, shooting a 139-grain bullet. If they had charged us en masse, we could not possibly have stopped them at that short distance with these small guns.

One of the males was an exceptionally big lion, and I made up my mind to take him home with me if possible. Mike agreed it was a good idea, provided we allowed them to get farther away before starting any trouble, so we stood still until they had finished their inspection of us and trotted off. At sixty yards the one I wanted stopped, while the others continued on another sixty yards or so. This appeared to be the time for action, so, taking a careful bead, I placed an expanding bullet into his back, which made it impossible for him to move; however, he was not dead by any means and raised enough commotion for six lions, causing his late companions to wheel about. For a few seconds it looked as if they might charge, but after a little growling and tail swishing, the lioness bounded away and her consort followed. While Mike went to fetch the truck, I walked up to within twelve feet of the wounded lion, finishing him with a hard-nosed bullet.

Now came the task of loading this heavy beast aboard. There were only two of us and one black boy, and, in spite of our best efforts, we were unable to lift this huge cat into the truck. A storm was brewing and Mike estimated we were at least forty miles from camp by the nearest way. A hard rain would make the ground impassable, besides filling the many dongas with water, thus effectually trapping us. In spite of these hazards of delay, I did not feel like giving up my lion and finally hit upon the plan of

digging holes for the rear wheels to set in, thus lower-
ing the end of the truck down to the ground.   This
idea worked fine and, after a little tugging and
pushing, we managed to get the lion safely aboard.

Now it commenced to sprinkle and we found ourselves up against another problem — that of getting
the truck out of the holes.   After working frantically
with the jack and pieces of wood, we successfully
overcame this difficulty, but it was now commencing
to rain and we felt sure it soon would be pouring
down in bucketfuls.   On this occasion our pessimistic
forecast was wrong, because after running through a
drizzle for a short while, we reached dry veldt and
continued on our way to camp without further trouble.

After completing our work with the giraffe, we
expended several days in attending to minor tasks,
expecting every hour that Ted would return.   We
went down to the lion donga to see if our troop were
still there.   We found them at home, evidently hungry,
for they trotted out to meet the truck and gave other
evidences of being glad to see us again.   We had long
ago learned to judge their hunger by the sort of reception we received; if famished they would eagerly run
toward the truck when it approached, but if a kill
had been made by themselves, it was a different story.
In that case they would look at us with a far-away
expression, seeming to say, "Where have I met you
before?" and sometimes would even yawn right in
our faces!

Driving to the water hole, we left the truck, making
a foot trek to some rocks out on the veldt.   Upon
returning an hour or so later, we found the lions
grouped around the truck, and, while photographing

this scene, discovered that the spare tire was missing; also that the row of Mobiloil cans, which we carried on the running board, had gaps in it.

After a few thrills and some maneuvering, we climbed into the truck and from this vantage point found that these curious and playful animals had taken the tire a few yards away into the grass and were having a great time. It was a sturdy General Cord, so we had little fear of any damage to the tire, but the question arose of how to recover it. Nobody volunteered to take it away from the lions, and all of our shouting and horn tooting from a distance had no effect. They were having a glorious time with this new plaything and did not intend to give it up, so we contented ourselves with making a few photographs, also securing a very cute motion-picture scene, which was later used in the completed film, "Africa Speaks."

As they didn't seem inclined to leave the tire, we went in search of the Mobiloil cans, finding them scattered within a radius of a few hundred feet of the truck. Taking up a station near two of these tins, I waited to see what would happen. After a while two lions abandoned the tire and came over to sharpen their teeth on the cans, puncturing these containers full of holes, allowing the oil to run out. I did some fast work with the graflex and movie cameras, obtaining a few unique pictures and scenes while this was going on.

This experience convinced us that lions have a many-sided personality. We knew one phase of their nature — that of the cruel killer, the flesh eater, the blood drinker; the powerful cat that strikes down the giant antelope with one mighty paw. We had witnessed these things and had photographed a lioness as she stalked a wart hog which incautiously stuck its head out of its burrow. Stealthily coming up from behind, with a quick bound she lifted this two-hundred-pound animal out of its hole by the nape of the neck, killing it almost instantly and bearing it away as a house cat would a mouse. So we thought everything that was possible for them to do had previously been performed for our benefit, but today had discovered another side of their nature, proving them to be inquisitive and playful animals. As I watched them I wished it were feasible to tame one and take it home for a pet.

As this was to be our final day with the lions, I remained with them until sunset. My last remembrance of the prowlers of the Serengetti is of a majestic male lion silhouetted atop an ant hill with five lionesses grouped below him. Another female walked across this scene with her head held high, carrying in her mouth a piece of meat which she was taking to her cubs near by. Her shadow was reflected in the drinking pool across which played long shafts of golden light, making it glint like diamonds, as the blood-red sun dropped from the cloud-filled sky to sink below the flaming horizon.

The heavy rains came on suddenly and, as Ted had not returned, it was decided to load the one truck as heavily as possible and push beyond the Gurmeti, for all potential trouble in getting out of the district would be between our camp and that river. I stayed behind with two black boys to pack up the remaining equipment, which would go on the second load.

Shortly after the truck left at noon on March twelfth, a regular cloudburst deluged the country, making me wonder if Mike would be able to get through, and if he did reach the Gurmeti, could he return for me. In the hurry of departure, some brilliant individual had placed my food box, prepared by the pishi, back on the truck, so when I took stock of my supplies, I found a very scant larder. If flooded rivers should make it impossible for Mike or Ted to return to Camp Simba, my situation might indeed prove serious.

As usual when it was dripping wet, the lions began to prowl about and roar, even before darkness. They always kicked up a big fuss after a rainstorm, but now both they and the hyenas seemed to know I was all alone, so they did their best to keep me company with roars, growls, laughs, and howls, until I commenced to wonder if they intended to move into camp. Lions, being cats, dislike dampness, but my personal opinion is that, in addition to their natural repugnance for water, the storm itself — the lightning and thunder — makes them uneasy; then the water, of course, floods them out of their lairs in the bottoms of the dongas. Once out of their accustomed locations, they go roaming about, complaining to all who care to listen, until they find a dry spot. This night the lions circled my camp within five hundred yards, while the hyenas came within that many feet.

Old African hunters had told me that upon occasion hyenas would imitate the roar of a lion, but I could never be sure I had actually heard one do it until this evening, when one big spotted fellow stood within plain sight and gave me an excellent imitation of a lion's roar. I suppose his intention was to scare me, but it only made me mad, and I ducked into the tent to get my Remington. He seemed to sense my intentions, for when I came out with the rifle he was loping away as fast as he could go.

Later, as I sat picking at my typewriter, I was serenaded by a circle of animals around the lonely camp. About midnight some of the hyenas came uncomfortably close, so with my rifle and a gasoline lantern, I went out to chase them away, but it was not safe to move far from camp, so I accomplished nothing. My two boys were almost frightened stiff and asked permission to move their shelter alongside of mine. After this had been done, the lantern was hung up between the two doorways beneath the canvas awning, and I went to bed with this unearthly chorus of animals and the monotonous drizzling of the rain as a bedtime lullaby.

I was awakened about three o'clock in the morning by the purr of a motor. Rising up on my cot, I watched the rain falling in the glare of the headlights as Mike pulled into camp, dripping wet and covered with mud. He had been driving through the storm for hours, with plenty of trouble from the truck to make it doubly interesting. Shortly after his arrival at the Gurmeti, he thought it wise to return for me at once, so started right back, for which I was duly thankful.

Before daybreak we were busy packing the truck in preparation for our attempt to join the others. Several hours were lost on account of a gasoline leak which had to be stopped, but just before noon we were ready for the road. We said farewell to Camp Simba by setting fire to the dining banda; thus avenging ourselves upon the colony of white ants which had been dropping sawdust into our food for weeks.

The Serra Nyiro had risen to flood proportions, but we managed to ford it without injury to the motor. At Baboon Crossing it required over two hours to pull the truck across with a rope and then reload it. This gave us something to worry about, because if the deep Benogie Gorge was filled with water, we should be marooned. As we rolled along, Mike told me about the leopard he had shot the day before near Gurmeti and of the three lions that had crossed the road at Benogie. We found no lions at the Benogie Gorge, but, instead, a swift torrent that leaped and roared toward Victoria Nyanza, carrying huge logs and all sorts of débris on its foaming crest. As it was over forty feet deep, we erected our tent and prepared for a long wait. Old Maniki then came forward and offered to swim the river and take a note to Major Warwick at Kilimafeza, seven miles away. Finding a bend where the water was not so turbulent, we placed a rope around his waist and allowed him to try. He proved to be a powerful swimmer, but was almost knocked unconscious when he was thrown against the opposite bank. However, he made it all right, and we then threw him the note tied around a stone. Carrying our S O S, he disappeared from sight.

Mike and I took a long walk, hoping to encounter lions or leopards, but saw neither. We found many dik-dik, reedbuck, water buck, zebra, and kongoni, in addition to plenty of birds. Our food supplies were practically exhausted, now consisting of one can of beans and three onions. We poured the beans into a frying pan and sliced the onions in with them. Upon this mixture, with the addition of whatever meat we could eat without salt, we subsisted during our enforced

stay.   It rained hard throughout the night, and on
the following morning the gorge was full to the top
and over two hundred feet across.

After a spoonful of beans apiece and a drink of
Benogie River water, we sat down to await the return
of Maniki, who shortly appeared with a note from
the major, saying that he was watching the river
farther up, near the mine, and as soon as it seemed
possible for us to cross, he would come down with
ropes, trucks, and plenty of boys.

After a noonday feast of broiled young kongoni,
without salt, we set up a stick at the water's edge and
timed it with a clock to see how fast the river was
falling.   One hour's interval showed it had receded
nineteen inches; so, in an optimistic mood, I figured
we might be able to cross about midnight.   I was
wrong, for the sky darkened, rain clouds gathered,
lightning flashed, and thunder rolled; the resultant
flood carried away our crude watermark, while the
river attained new heights.

Next morning Major Warwick arrived in his seagoing flivver, inviting us to spend the week-end with
him.   The water had again receded, being now about
fifteen feet deep, but it looked as if it might rain some
more and delay our crossing indefinitely, so we planned
a rope bridge to span the chasm to get ourselves and
the motion-picture material over.   One of the major's
boys climbed out on an overhanging limb and swung
a light rope to us.   With this we pulled a heavy hawser
across, which was made fast to staunch trees standing
on opposite banks.   A canvas sling was rigged up to
hang from a pulley and in this improvised breeches
buoy we passed load after load across the raging tor-

rent. I held my breath while the big movie outfit
was swinging over the river and also as the films, that
represented months of hard work and danger, were
slung across. Everything made the passage safely,
however, Mike and I going over on the last load.
Things were then dumped into the seagoing flivver
and the Major headed for the mine, his ancient Ford
throwing water like a motor boat going at high speed.

Next day, with fifteen boys, Warwick and ourselves
piled into his land-going motor boat and returned to
the river. We found the water only four feet deep, so
hastened to get the truck across before anything
happened to make it impossible. It was easy enough
to get down the hill and through the stream bed, but,
when the bank on our side was reached, we discovered
that silt had made the road bottomless. It required
several hours of digging, and much hauling on a block
and tackle, before the truck was able to move under
its own power.

Arrival at the mine brought news by one of their
drivers who had just fought his way through from
Narok. He had turned his truck over in the Sand
River and reported that Ted was there with my other
truck, unable to cross. It is not very far from Kilimafeza to the Gurmeti, so we loaded as quickly as possible,
and, while the boys were fastening down the tarpaulin,
had a farewell cup of hot tea with Major Warwick,
then roared off into the gloaming, hoping to reach the
Gurmeti that night. Our luck had changed, and we
arrived there in less than three hours, finding that our
appearance reunited the entire party again, for both
Ted and Bud had driven into camp about an hour
ahead of us. With both trucks again on the job, next

morning we made wheel tracks back to the Sand
River, the best country in which to secure pictures of
impalla, and, making our new camp some three miles beyond the stream, remained until our work with these
interesting and graceful antelopes had been completed.

While the camp was being arranged, the discovery
was made that some important equipment had been
left at the Gurmeti, so Bud and I went back to fetch
it.   While returning late that night, four big lions
jumped across the road about fifty yards in front of
us, two of them having magnificent manes.

Nothing else happened except that we broke another
front spring.   Morning disclosed that most of the
leaves were gone, also other items that could not be
replaced, so once again we back trailed to look for
the missing parts.   Upon arrival at the spot where
we had encountered the lions, Bud, Mike, and I followed their spoor for quite a while, over the veldt and
through thorn thickets, but the ground was too hard
for successful tracking and we finally gave it up as a
hopeless job.   Maniki and the boy whom I had paid
off at Narok, when he complained of being sick, were
with us.   When Ted came through that post, enroute
to the Gurmeti, this latter boy had rejoined our safari,
hoping to get my permission upon arrival.   He had
not returned to Nairobi, but had spent his time and
money gambling with the native soldiers at Narok.

Bud had just started the motor when this boy
suddenly yelled he had lost his tobacco pouch.   Mike
told him to forget it, but, in spite of our commands, he
jumped from the moving truck and ran back to search
for it.   After waiting some time, we continued our
hunt for the truck parts, then returned to camp, think-

ing that maybe the boy had taken a short cut, for the camp was only seven miles from the lion thickets. When we arrived, he was not there and all of our searchers failed to find trace of him. Two or three days passed, then one of the parties came in to report they had found the remains of our unfortunate porter. He had evidently been successful in locating the lions on his second trip through the bush.

Our first day after impalla was spent by Bud and me chasing them through a bushveldt that was almost impassable. We found these graceful antelope fairly abundant, but always in the thick bush where it was hard to secure good pictures. The morning sped by without a single foot of film to reward us, but the afternoon presented three good scenes; one of them exceptional, easily worth the whole day's efforts.

Bad luck seemed to dog my footsteps, at least as regards accidents to the trucks and cameras. While returning to camp, still on the lookout for fresh impalla to picture, Bud failed to notice a low-hanging limb, driving under it with the camera set up, the resultant smash-up bending the tripod all out of shape.

During these hectic days, I often wondered whether or not a movie audience would appreciate these scenes of the graceful impalla in slow motion, as they leaped and sailed over small bushes and trees like birds in flight. My reward for these dangerous days of dodging through trees and over the veldt, at the risk of breaking my neck, to record these "Leaping Lenas" has been ample. The pictures of impalla flying through the air on their thirty-five-foot leaps has been commented upon as one of the outstanding features in the film production, "Africa Speaks."

The Benogie River, ordinarily dry, with the water over forty feet deep.

En route to Nairobi from Sand River. The trucks at the Guaso Nyiro River.

Lions resting in the shade on the plains of Tanganyika.

The author with the large lion which was so difficult to load aboard the truck.

Bud and I would work for hours without seeing a single impalla, then sometimes sudden showers would cost us a valuable scene. On one occasion we raced like mad to get into position, but when I put my hand to the crank, the sun ducked behind a cloud; when it came out again, we made another try, only to be exasperated by a repetition of the same thing. Finally I called a halt, as there was no use risking our necks and taking chances of wrecking the truck when the light was playing tricks like this.

During the times when the sky was overcast, I did a little shooting for trophies. On my first expedition I had passed up all of the common animals and regretted it afterward. Although millions of zebras roam over the veldts of Africa, still no two are striped alike, and I had been watching for a well-marked animal to add to my collection. When a herd of punda milia, the "donkeys of the plains," raced out of some near-by trees, led by a magnificent stallion, I sat down and, taking a careful bead with my 7 mm. rifle, was lucky enough to hit him. Now his mounted head looks across the room at a bull kongoni which I collected in the same locality.

For a few days we chased after the impalla herds, through bush, down ravines, and over the veldt. After securing one excellent slow-motion picture showing these antelope leaping in all directions, we followed them for a short distance, hoping to obtain another shot of the same animals, when suddenly we burst through the bush upon a scene of destruction. A large herd of elephants had just passed through the district, tearing down and uprooting hundreds of trees, leaving a wide swath through the country, comparable to the wake of a cyclone.

16

On another occasion in this same locality, we beheld a picture that will long remain in my memory. In a beautiful green glade near a water hole stood an enormous drove of impalla, a large group of eland, several giraffes, while hundreds of zebras, kongoni, and tommies were grazing near by. Before we could film this happy family, a gust of wind announced our presence. The animals took to flight in all directions. One bull giraffe, who was so old he had nearly turned black, became confused, running toward us instead of away, enabling me to obtain some excellent views, for he passed so close to the camera that I just managed to get him all on the film. We then followed the herd of mixed eland and impalla, both of these agile animals performing their feats of leaping as they bounded away. They crossed a rocky donga, which forced us to make a long detour, during which they escaped.

A great deal of this virgin country resembled a cultivated park, making it hard to realize that we were in the wilds of Africa. Gently rolling hills of velvet-smooth grass, with clumps of small trees dotted here and there, swept toward distant mountains of purple and blue. Overhead, wisps of white clouds hung motionless in a clear sky, and scores of vultures circled like monoplanes through this turquoise sea, never moving a wing as they drifted and glided, while watching life on the veldt below.

Frequent showers, then a heavy storm warned us it was time to trek into Nairobi. Hurriedly, in the middle of the day, we abandoned camp, scurrying before the wind-blown sheets of rain. The god of storms had at last triumphed, and we were forced to leave our beloved plains of the Serengetti.

CHAPTER THIRTEEN

SOURCE OF THE NILE

WHEN Easter Sunday came to the capital of Bardo Kidogo, Jones and I cleaned up a bit and went to church. Few were there, most everyone taking advantage of the four-day holiday to go on short safaris. It was more important, after they left East Africa, to be able to say they had shot one of this and two of that than to brag of having gone to church on Easter Sunday. Besides, maybe they thought, as did one old-timer, "The wilderness is God's greatest cathedral!"

Upon my return to the hotel, I took a seat on the veranda, to watch the full-dress pioneers and the silk-hatted frontiersmen, as they sped into town in their Rolls Royces, Packards, Cadillacs, and other simple conveyances of the struggling settler. They did not visit the city to sell steers or sheep, grain or poultry, nor to attend land sales or to learn about market conditions of crops, but to attend a dance, and incidentally to drink their share of whisky and soda.

I strolled back into the lounge to have refreshments with an acquaintance, who, during the conversation, gave me the definition of a white hunter. According to him, "A white hunter is a man who wears a big hat and shorts, speaks Swahili, and takes tenderfeet out into the blue, eats their grub, drinks their liquor, and keeps them away from the game until their money

293

runs out." There may be some like this, and probably
are, but my crew were not of this type. Mike Cottar
knew animals and where to find them, and I was sorry,
indeed, to learn that he would not be able to accompany me on my journey across Africa.

Three weeks were spent in Nairobi, securing government permits, reorganizing the expedition, making
changes in the personnel, overhauling the trucks,
replenishing stores, and renewing equipment. When
I look back and consider the Easter holidays and the
many officials that had to be consulted, I wonder
how I ever got started. While Jones was rebuilding
our Durant marvels, endeavoring to make them into
trucks, I attended to everything else, even having
time to visit Jack Lucy in the local hospital, where
he was convalescing from his lion mauling. Propped
up in bed, with a soft pillow behind his injured arm
and shoulder, he explained how it occurred.

"I was walking down the bottom of a donga, not
expecting to find lions there, but as is usual in Africa,
the unusual happened. It has always been my habit
to carry a heavy rifle, but on this day my leg was
bothering me, so I carried a light bore, which made the
difference between being mauled and getting away
scot free. I saw a flash of yellow over my shoulder,
and almost automatically threw my rifle around and
fired. The aim was true, the bullet entering the
lion's mouth, but was too small to give a killing blow.
The lion threw me to the ground, mauling me badly.
I recall no feeling of pain during the time this was
happening, but after my companion had shot the cat
off and I tried to get up, my painful bites became
only too apparent."

The party at the rest house on top of the escarpment which overlooks Albert Nyanza.

The author at Ripon Falls, the source of the Victoria Nile, beside the tablet commemorating Speke's discovery.

View of Ripon Falls near Jinja, Uganda. It is here that Lake Victoria spills itself into the Victoria Nile, which leads to Lake Albert, the source of the true Nile. This fall was discovered by the English explorer Speke in 1862.

The day following my visit to Jack Lucy, I added Joe Pedley, the former locust officer, and a new black boy named Onyango to my safari. With Jones, Austin, the new boy, and Maniki riding in one truck; Pedley, Ali, the cook, the boy Masai, and myself in the other, we left Nairobi on the thirteenth day of April, 1929, for our long trek to the West Coast.

We traveled over familiar roads toward the precipitous Kikuyu Escarpment, down the face of which we glided until bottom was reached in the Kedong Valley. The long, dusty trail taking us via Naivasha, Gilgil, and Nakuru to Eldoret, was well known to us all.

After passing Gilgil, the road shortly drops off the plateau into a deep valley which gently slopes toward Lake Victoria. From the rim of this escarpment a marvelous panorama of wild beauty unfolds itself to view. Below lies the rippling waters of romantic Lake Elmenteita, now covered with pink patches of flamingos. The beauty of this lake and of Lake Naivasha, with the volcanoes of Longunot and Suswa towering behind it, have always appealed to me as scenes symbolic of Africa.

The second night out we camped at Turbo, twenty miles beyond Eldoret. Joe had the camp awake at dawn, and while the pishi was busily preparing breakfast, I took a stroll through a near-by vale and shot an oribi, *O. cottoni*, a species of diminutive antelope which we would now encounter in increasing numbers.

When Mount Elgon, 14,140 feet, called The Weather Prophet, lay before us, its summit was covered with clouds that boded rain in large quantities, so we hustled along as quickly as the abominable Kenya roads would allow, knowing that every mile brought us closer to the hard highways of Uganda. Not the deepest-dyed pessimist could do justice to the shortcomings of the Kenya trails. Not even that panegyrist of the road in India, which he declared was "not passable, not even jackassable."

We ran toward the mountain until within its shadow, then bore westward to Malakisi. About thirty miles before reaching this place we came to the village of the paramount chief, Murunga, who was here holding the regular Monday morning baraza, at which the Elders gather to try petty offenses against tribal law, and to fine the convicted as many sheep or cattle as they deem advisable.

From Malakisi to Tororo was a delightful drive. The whole aspect of the country changed. Green shrubbery took the place of dusty hillsides, while a smooth road wound through the beautiful tropical landscape like a broad white ribbon. Kenya was behind us and Uganda under our wheels.

The road then ran straight, for many miles, toward an enormous rock which rises perpendicularly from the plain. It is the famous Tororo Rock, at the foot of which lies the village of the same name. We stopped here to visit with the police and obtain our passes through Uganda. Now we bore southward to Busia. Signs of cultivation on a large scale began to appear; banana groves, cotton patches, coffee farms, sweet-potato fields, and small gardens of tobacco followed one another in close formation. In Uganda the native is allowed to expand and attain toward a real civilization. He is encouraged to cultivate cotton and other crops for export, and being able and willing to earn some of the king's shillings, has money to spend on the white man's goods. The result is that the natives of Uganda are economic assets, doing their parts toward making it a prosperous and happy community.

Now we pressed westward again until we had passed Iganga, where we made camp near some native bandas. We arrived at Jinja the next morning, and were quartered at the rest house. It stands on a bluff below which roars the Ripon Falls, source of the Victoria Nile. Here it was that John Hanning Speke stood on July 28, 1862, after tracing out this beginning of the Nile, during an exploration of Victoria Nyanza.

We went down to the falls and watched the huge volume of water as it poured from Lake Victoria into the Nile, and reflected that so it had been spilling this flood for many thousands of years, even while the Pharaohs were on the throne of Egypt. Now a bright flash attracted my eyes; fish were attempting to jump up the falls. They would leap high, but always short of the top. Being in a speculative mood, I wondered how many fish, since fish were fish and began to leap, had tried to conquer this avalanche of water to no avail. Not a single fish has ever attained the top, but still they keep trying, and the hawks and crocodiles hope they never stop. Between the first and second fall, a rock supports some treelike shrubs. Here a colony of weaver birds have made a village of nests. These were hanging over the swirling waters safe from all harm, for unless their homes should drop into the whirlpool below, nothing could happen to them on their unique island.

While I was photographing the jumping fish, the Captain of the "Clement Hill" happened along. He informed me that unless we hustled to Butiaba, we should fail to make connections with the boat on Lake Albert. Not wishing to be delayed, within an hour's time we had eaten lunch, packed the trucks, and were on our way, only to find, after all this haste, that the ferry which crossed this arm of Lake Victoria did not run until two o'clock in the afternoon.

While waiting, I watched a gang of Buganda shifting a heavy wooden crate to the tune of a weird chant, and some others loading two-hundred-pound sacks of grain into a scow. These heavy bags were placed on the back of the shoulders, standing on end, and then the laborers would run with them. Nothing puny about the Buganda! Near by a negro follower of Mohammed, with his face to Mecca, was saying his midday prayers, his constant bowing disturbing some little yellow and blue birds that were building nests in a tree which grew near the edge of the lake. What a place of color and romance — seminaked Buganda, a robed Mohammedan, brightly colored birds flying over blue waters, and beyond, riding at anchor. a modern lake steamer, the "Clement Hill"!

The ferry arrived, the two trucks were loaded aboard, and we started across the little bay which forms the extreme northern end of Victoria Nyanza. The boat sped along at the exorbitant rate of two knots per week; in fact, it moved so slowly I was unable to tell for sure in which direction we were going, but after a peaceful voyage, the opposite shore was reached and we hurried toward Kampala.

Entebbe is the British seat of government, while Kampala is the native capital of Uganda, beautifully situated among green hills and flower gardens, a place for poets to live and dream. Here lives the native king, Kabaka, who still holds his court and administers affairs to a certain extent.

Mr. Hill, who invited us to spend the night at his place, gave me a great deal of information concerning Uganda. There were less than two thousand white people in the protectorate, counting men, women, and children, but more than six thousand motor cars, which speaks volumes for the wonderful roads.

On the two highest hills sit rival cathedrals — one Church of England and the other Catholic. Both are beautiful and impressive buildings, though constructed by native labor. I made a visit to the Catholic cathedral, finding the interior marvelously done in hand-carved woodwork. It was hard to believe this entire structure had been built by the native Bugandas, for this edifice compared with many of the best in other parts of the world.

The Kabaka is an engaging potentate with modern ideas. I was told a story concerning him, showing how he applied the devices of the white man's civilization to the solution of problems arising out of his own native culture. In accordance with the customs of the Buganda, the king practiced polygamy, his position allowing him to add new members to his harem whenever his fancy dictated. In time his household became so plentifully stocked with wives that the place was overcrowded, so the Kabaka sought a way of diminishing his supply, without resorting either to divorce or to woman slaughter. He discussed it with his ministers and with a motor-car salesman, the result being that a few days later, the town was plastered with flaming posters, advertising an auction

sale, to be held at the Royal Palace, of surplus queens.
The event was attended by the entire native male population of Kampala and the surrounding district, for
those who didn't go to bid or buy went there to ogle
the wares and envy, or maybe commiserate, the
buyers. The auction was a huge success, for every
Buganda snob and toady was eager to boast of one
ex-queen among his wives. The bidding was lively
and high, and the king's money chest was enriched
by just the extent to which his harem was thinned out.
This method was a great improvement over the ancient
one of throwing the unwanted wives to the crocodiles.

Now we journeyed through Hoima and Masindi,
and a lovely blooming country where tropical flowers and shrubs blossomed everywhere and where
prosperous native plantations deployed their fertile
acres on each side of the perfect roads that wound in
and out among groves of pawpaws and bananas.

A drive through miles of deep, cool forests, where
elephant herds roam, brought us to the top of an
escarpment, and there far below us in the valley lay
Albert Nyanza, a sheet of blue water that reflected
back the rays of a sinking sun, for the day was near
its end. Beyond, in the hazy distance, was a barrier
of high mountains, from the sides of which smoke
columns were rising skyward from the fires of many
villages. There lived black men as far behind the
Buganda in civilization as he is behind the white man.
The mountains and the villages that clung to their
sides lay in that magic country, the Congo.

In the morning we crept down the serpentine trail
to the foot of the escarpment; then crossed the marshy
flat that was once part of the lake bed, to the little

settlement of Butiaba, which consists of a collection of huts huddled near the beach. The entire industry of the place is that of running, or assisting to run, the good ship "Samuel Baker," which carries the mails to the landings around the lake, and incidentally watches after the king's business in general.

The day was spent in arranging all the details for our crossing on the morrow. There was no end of red tape; it requiring as much fuss to cross Lake Albert as it does to cross the Atlantic, but if it cost as much in proportion to cross the Atlantic, Europe and America would be total strangers. Although transportation charges are high in this country, food supplies are more than reasonable. I bought some fresh fish from a native, paying two shillings for ten large fish, totaling about fifty pounds. They were fine and tasty. My only regret was that it would soon be impossible to get more of them. Chickens were also cheap, two shillings buying four of good size.

We returned to the rest house atop the escarpment to spend the night, and that evening, as I sat on the wide veranda, I gazed out over the flats below. As I watched the moonlight play on this beautiful lake, I reflected that it was not until after the outbreak of our own Civil War that this second reservoir of the Nile was known to civilization. During that period, Sir Samuel Baker, accompanied by his heroic wife, discovered this great inland sea, which he named Albert Nyanza.

The lake is hemmed in on its two long sides by mountains on the west and by the sheer walls of the escarpment on the east. It averages thirty miles in width and is about one hundred miles long. The

Victoria Nile, which starts at the Ripon Falls, empties into Albert Nyanza. From the bay in the north-eastern extremity of the lake, the true Nile, the storied river of antiquity, flows forth on its romantic journey — past village and modern city, through papyrus swamp and desert, flowing by the ruins of a bygone civilization and the monuments erected by departed kings, to mix its yellow flood with the blue waters of the Mediterranean. Thus meditating, I gazed toward the Congo mountains and wondered what lay beyond.

With ourselves and the equipment on board and the trucks in tow on a lighter, the "Samuel Baker" started across the twenty-seven miles of lake to Mahaji Port. Albert Nyanza is no mill pond; the waves rolled in long swells like those on a rough sea, causing the little boat to pitch and toss and making the lighter perform all sorts of strange antics. After four and one-half hours we reached Mahaji Port—one grass hut and a shaky pier covered with a black mass of human-ity constituting the entire town and population of this place.

During the crossing, Captain Fisher proved himself to be a fine fellow, willing to accommodate us in every reasonable way. Now he came to me, accompanied by a native official, with the information that a large bridge, spanning a deep canyon, had been wrecked by floods, and if we landed here it would be impossible to proceed into the back country. Upon asking this smiling Congo Negro when the bridge would be re-paired, he ambiguously replied, "In six months per-haps, or maybe in six weeks." This left no choice but to remain on board and travel down the Nile to the next landing.

Native laborers, the Buganda, loading grain into boats on Victoria Nyanza.

Alulu people who came to meet the boat at Mahaji Port.

While the crew was unloading a few goods and some cases of gasoline, I photographed the natives who were grouped on the pier. The most noticeable thing about this savage crowd was their nakedness. The men wore a scanty bit of cloth or skin, but most of the women were absolutely naked. In other parts of this dark continent I have gazed upon nude men by the hundreds, but this was the first time naked women had come under my observation. A few of them wore a small bunch of grass suspended from a string around the waist, and a half dozen had blossomed out in brightly colored calico. These people were members of the Alulu tribe, who, like their neighbors, the Lugwari, are opposed to their women wearing anything that hides the body. What a contrast to the Africa we had just left behind — this was the Belgian Congo!

Leaving Mahaji Port, we steamed past the mouth of the Victoria Nile where it empties into Albert Nyanza, then out of the lake into the Nile itself. As we paddled down the river in the darkness, some lights loomed ahead, and not long afterwards the "Samuel Baker" was tied alongside the river boat "Lugard," to which all of our goods were transferred. The latter was built for shallow water, only requiring two feet to keep it afloat. There is very little organization on these river steamers, the black men doing everything from piloting the boat to stoking the furnace. The white captain simply supervises and commands. Considering that these Negroes are only a few years removed from raw savages who know nothing of boats except how to row a dugout, it speaks well of their adaptability and lends encouragement to our belief in their ultimate progress.

Next morning thousands of the sacred ibis of Egypt flew about the boat and covered the trees along both shores like white blossoms. The country teemed with game. Families of hippopotami disported near the banks, while on the sandbars, crocodiles yawned in the sun. At near to noon my boy shouted "Tembu, bwana," and sure enough there were four elephants slowly walking along the water's edge on the eastern bank. They surveyed the passing boat for a few seconds, then with trunks flung high, wheeled about and ambled away through the high swamp grass.

This trip down the Nile was one of abounding interest. On the western side are many villages of the Lugwari and Alulu tribes, while the eastern shore is unpeopled. It is a closed area — closed to both white and black, for its swamps are deadly with sleeping sickness.

At the different stops along the river, to discharge cargo or take on wood for fuel, we were met by the entire population. These were a primitive people, both men and women wearing only what nature provided, but they seemed to be a happy lot, running aboard the boat with their loads of wood as if it were a great lark.

After leaving the wood station of Panyngoro, it only required two hours to steam to Pakwach, another fuel depot on the west bank. This place was twice the size of Mahaji Port, boasting of two grass huts! We were now a total of seven hundred four miles from Nairobi, the last fifty-four being by boat from Butiaba. While the naked men and women of this village were putting the wood on board, I took a look around and decided to land. This proved a ticklish job, for as each truck came off the lighter, it punched a hole through the pier floor, but this was nothing to what happened later, for we broke through every culvert on the road to Arua, one hundred twenty miles distant.

Before we were ready to leave, a sudden shower caused us to scurry for shelter and, while waiting for the rain to cease, the boat, with a salute of its whistle, drifted off down the Nile. After it had disappeared around a bend, I faced westward, where beyond the hills of Okollo stood Mount Emin Pasha. Once again I was gazing toward the Congo; once again wondering what fate awaited us there.

CHAPTER FOURTEEN

WHITE RHINOCEROSES

WHERE the River Nile flows as a sluggish stream between wide expanses of papyrus swamp, and the sun pours down a deadly heat, there still exist, in a small area, a few white rhinoceroses, the third largest of living land mammals.

After the shower at Pakwach, we headed inland. The trail we followed resembled a road, but we were the first to ever attempt its passage in motor trucks. Every culvert caved in, while most of the ground was so soft that we found it necessary to pull in low gear for many miles. Naked people ran out from the villages to gaze in wonder as we passed, for they had never seen a motor car before. Laughing and shouting, they would run after us like a lot of children, until the trucks outdistanced them. We stopped at Alui for lunch, finding here a boy who spoke Swahili. He gave us the cheerful news that many deep ravines were ahead — that some were bridged, but most were not. During the day, the second truck went through a culvert, breaking a rear spring, while hours of driving in low gear had burned out the clutch.

We camped the first night at Ngal, and hardly had the equipment been unloaded when a group of naked native girls arrived with water, firewood, eggs, and fowls. The camp was now plentifully supplied with meat, for I had made another fluke shot that afternoon,

Accidents like this occurred every hour or so on the trip from Pakwach to Arua.

Pulling the trucks over bamboo-covered culverts. The road looks smooth, but it was fresh earth and very soft.

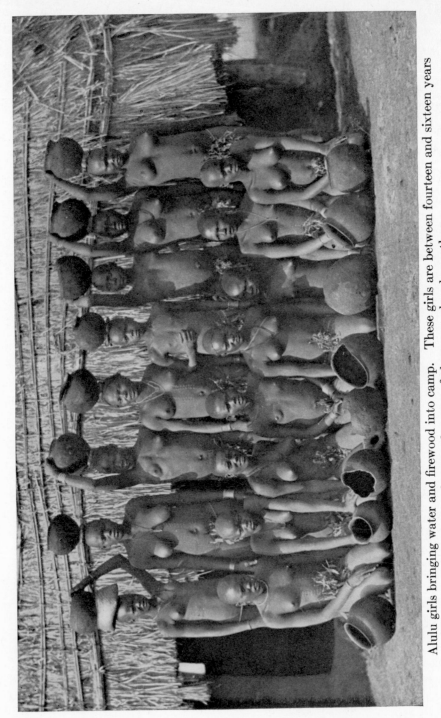

Alulu girls bringing water and firewood into camp. These girls are between fourteen and sixteen years of age and many of them are already mothers.

killing two oribi with one bullet. I had taken a careful bead on one animal, and the missile had passed through it and struck another which was standing beyond.

The next day proved to be one of the hardest of the expedition, for from sunrise to sunset our total mileage was ten and one-half. There were five bridges to traverse—not regular bridges as we think of them—but logs thrown across rivers, upheld by forked limbs and surfaced with bamboo.

We made an inspection of these primitive crossings as we came to them, finding it necessary to unload everything from the trucks and run them over empty. Luckily for us, as soon as the trucks stopped, a crowd of natives would appear almost at once, and these were put to work carrying the loads to the other side. The Alulu people are good workers, often running with their loads, seeming to enjoy it greatly. As I watched the women carry heavy burdens on their heads, I could not but wonder what they would think of the easy life led by the average civilized housewife, who sometimes complains if she has to get her husband an early breakfast!

Two of these bridges were more than fifty feet high and two hundred feet long, and, to lessen the chances of an accident, we hauled the trucks over with a long rope pulled by a hundred or more natives. Even then, it required plenty of nerve to sit at the wheel and guide the trucks, for the crude spans swayed like long snakes, while bamboo crosspieces snapped underneath.

After this arduous day, we were thankful to reach the village of Nebbi and make camp for the night. Here I sent for the Sultan, as I wanted to learn something about his people. He came at once and proved

17

to be a fine young man with strong features, a pleasant manner, and broad smile.

Gelasega was the name of this subchief who ruled over the Medaere, a subtribe whose territory extended from Ngal to Nebbi. He was the son of Sultan Amula, the paramount ruler of the Alulu, who holds his court at Okaro. We served him with tea, and then, as he spoke Swahili fluently, I was able to get first-hand information about this strange and little-known people.

The country of the Alulu covers that large area extending from the west bank of the River Nile into the high hills near Okollo, and I was assured that his people were very old, that they had lived in this country since the early time of man. What a history must be theirs! — a history, however, lost in the dust of ages, for try as he would, this young sultan could tell no tale of the past that rang true, so I found it necessary to confine myself to the present.

The marriage customs of different African tribes are always interesting, each tribe having some peculiar practice of its own. Among the Alulu, as among many other tribes, the woman is considered a valuable piece of property, a thing to be bargained over, to be sold and traded, to be used as a beast of burden, having no rights and few privileges.

Girls are married off by their fathers at from twelve to fourteen years of age, the girl having nothing to say in the matter. The father sells where he can get the best price. If he can sell to a rich man he may get as many as six oxen for her, while if he finds it necessary to sell to a poor man, the best he can expect is two oxen for the same girl. Cattle is the money of the country, the standard on which all value is based.

When the girl's father has agreed upon her purchase price, he kills a goat; the boy's father also kills a goat. Then a feast is prepared to which all the friends are invited, and thus the marriage is consummated with meat and a native beer called *mwembi*.

Each man has as many wives as he can afford to buy, for the more women he has, the more children he can raise, the girls to sell and the boys to work for him until their marriage, while the women, of course, in addition to bearing many children, do all the hard labor.

The father of a boy helps him to buy his first wife, which amounts to the same thing as a civilized father placing his son in business. He must earn the others for himself, and his success in life is measured by the number of wives he leaves to mourn his passing. When a husband dies, his wives, along with his cattle and other property, go to his eldest brother, who adds them to his list of assets. If the widows do not like their new husband, they can select some other man, who can get them by paying to the new owner their list price in cattle. Middle-aged and old widows bring a very small price, and sometimes the eldest brother who falls heir to an odd lot of old wives feels unkindly toward his late of kin.

When I asked this young chief about the custom of their women going naked, he replied that they had always gone so; that it was best for their bodies. A man was stronger and could take a chance of clothing breaking down his health; besides, there was only one man in a family to buy clothing for, but each man had many wives, and it would ruin him if he had to buy clothes for all of them!

We were traveling through a poor game country, although we encountered a few antelope, some kongoni, and wild pigs. According to our guide, there were large herds of elephants along the river and plenty of leopards and numerous lions in the highlands. The Alulu catch both lions and leopards in wooden traps; they also spear any of these cats that attack their stock. As we pushed farther toward the Congo, the contour of the country changed, small green hills, covered with short trees, taking the place of the flat tropical country adjacent to the river. Large groves of banana plants lined the streams, these proving to be the proper plantains which form one of the principal food supplies of these ancient people.

As we passed through the villages of Paida, Neapea, Zeio, Warr, Kango, and Logiri, the entire population turned out and cheered as the strange wagons roared by. This is Africa at its darkest — the Africa that the early explorers knew, unspoiled by the semicivilization that has arisen in so many parts, without, so far as my personal observations go, doing anything of real value for the black man.

At Arua I went to see the British official in charge of the district and his first question was as to the route we had come. When I replied "from Pakwach," he was more than surprised, and asked how many bridges we had wrecked! It seems that we were the first ever to land at Pakwach and motor to Arua, the road and bridges being only for foot safaris.

The government of Uganda and those who administer the affairs of the West Nile Province are not very keen to have anyone enter the district where the rare white rhino has its sanctuary. When they do give permission,

Alulu village in the hill country on the west bank of the Nile.

Uganda.   The bad boy of Africa, a bull buffalo.

At a rest camp during the journey from Pakwach to Arua.

A small Alulu boy takes his brother for a ride. Note his masterful haircut.

it is only with the understanding that under no circumstances will any of the beasts be harmed. Having assured them on this score, I was allowed to take my party out in search of the animal, in order that photographs might be obtained.

Forty-two miles by road brought us again to the Nile, and there we camped close to its shore. That night it rained like the flood, a real tropical storm, with huge flashes of lightning and deafening peals of thunder, the crashes of which rolled across the heavens with such tremendous roaring that the earth itself trembled.

Next morning pishi held up a glass of drinking water, alive with all sorts of grotesque creatures, for my inspection. I had been warned to insist upon the boiling of all water as a precaution against guinea worm and other parasites, but an interesting fact about the African cook is that he cannot be taught to boil water for drinking purposes. To him there is absolutely no sense in doing such a thing, but if you tell him to make tea, he boils the water thoroughly, because he knows that good tea cannot be made otherwise. For that reason, we never drank water in dangerous localities, consuming, instead, gallons and gallons of tea.

After breakfast, I went down to the river's edge to gaze upon the huge papyrus swamp that stretches from the opposite side to the distant horizon, a swamp that teems with poisonous reptiles and all that order of things that love the dark and the damp. Pythons of enormous size make this their home, but cross the river in search of small game. Hippos dwell on the edge, and many buffalo live not far away.

On our side of the Nile lives the white rhino — that rare and strange beast left over from the long ago, from the age when all the animals of the earth were weird of form and armed for battle. It was with a feeling that I had been transported back into the age of flying reptiles and saber-toothed tigers that I followed the lithe negro who strode in front of me, as the little party wound its way through the tall grass and over a landscape that fitted perfectly into my mental picture of the prehistoric earth.

No matter in what country you hunt rhino, it is always the same story of weary miles under a scorching sun, for all members of this family seem to pick the hardest and most trying country for their haunts. Mile after mile we walked, and soon I was dripping with perspiration; but just as I felt inclined to call a short halt, the boy ahead stopped short and pointed to a clump of small trees. Coming up to him, I made out two light-colored shapes standing in the shade. They moved slightly as I looked, thus proving that they were not ant hills, like the many "rhino" we had already seen. This cow and calf must have gotten a whiff of us, for they were very shy and gave us a hard half-hour's work in attempting to photograph them, the whole effort netting me one graflex negative and no motion pictures at all, or at least none worth bragging about.

When they shifted and got into the open, so that a good view was had of them, we appreciated for the first time the tremendous bulk of these animals. The cow loomed over the calf like an ocean liner over a tugboat, and the latter was large enough to attract attention in any company, even though it was only half grown. As Jones and I stalked them with cameras, rushing here and there to get into a position where a good picture could be taken, our two gun boys tried their best to keep close at hand, but twice when the cow lost her temper and snorted in our direction the boys made short work of getting into a high perch, leaving us sans guns and too tired to run.

The cow kept circling until she got our wind, then with a loud snort, kicked up her heels and made tracks too fast for us to follow. The calf also made tracks, sometimes getting in its mother's way, only to be pushed almost off its feet. Upon regaining its equilibrium it would then make a frantic start, soon overtaking its mother, and so they disappeared from sight.

Things had happened so fast, and I was so keen to get pictures, that I had little time to make notes of the animal itself, so we started in search of more white rhino, taking a long circle toward camp, which would carry us near the Nile. We came upon many water buck and some Uganda kob, but no rhino.

There was still about two hours of daylight left, so Jones, taking my heavy rifle and some boys with him, trekked along the Nile bank in the opposite direction from which we had just come. He found a place only a short distance away that was teeming with buck, while buffalo were plentiful. Wounding a buffalo bull, he started in pursuit, then had an experience which is interesting as proving how little is known about the distribution of some African animals. We had been assured by several men, who undoubtedly thought they knew the facts, that there were no common, or black, rhino in the district inhabited by the white members of the family.

The wounded buffalo ran over the brow of a small hill, with Jones following behind. As he neared the crest of the hummock, an ugly black snout appeared, and he raised his rifle to fire, thinking it to be the buffalo. He discovered his mistake just in time to save shooting a big black rhino bull who had heard him coming and was anxious to greet whatever came over the hill. Back tracking to windward of this beast, he gained a point of vantage and found that Mr. Rhino was guarding a female and a small calf. Here was a whole family of black rhinoceroses in a country supposed to be inhabited solely by the white representative of the species!

This is a wild and out-of-the-way country very seldom visited by white men, a district where primitive man still lives as he has for untold centuries, for the little contact he has had with the white race has changed him but slightly, and his ways of living not at all.

There is a young Scotchman who gets about this district in the interests of a large trading company, and as he happened along during our stay we had him for dinner one evening. He told us of an experience he had been through during the construction of his bungalow. The doors had not yet been hung, although otherwise the place was finished. He was sleeping in the bedroom and at his feet slept his only companion, a small dog. During the night he heard a slight noise and wakened just in time to catch a glimpse of a leopard as it bolted through the doorway with his dog in its mouth.

Leopards are bloodthirsty brutes anywhere, but seem to be very bad about here. I was shown a leopard skin, not yet dry, that had come off a large male killed by an officer at Arua, and was told that this spotted cat had attacked several native children. While the leopard is bad enough, he cannot compare with a lion that has turned man eater. Where game is plentiful there are very few cases of man-eating lions, but in a country like this where some districts are almost empty of game, they occasionally appear.

In a native village less than five miles from our camp, a lion had recently been killed after terrorizing the villagers for many months. This old lion started its career by killing a woman near the spring when she went for water. Having once tasted human flesh, it demanded more and laid in wait near the spring until another woman had been added to the list. The natives now avoided this place, but the man-eater was cunning and stalked the women as they worked in the sweet potato patches or in the maize fields, until it had killed and eaten eleven women. The men at last went to the white man for help. A trader came out from the post and managed to shoot the brute, but it will be a long time before the people of that village forget this terror of both daylight and dark.

Early in the morning we again went in search of the white rhinoceros, and this time were successful beyond all expectations. An hour's walk brought us to a place where some of the animals had wallowed that night; so, taking their spoor, we tracked them over hill and dale until I had just about reached the melting point. It was impossible to make out how many rhinoceroses were ahead of us, for the tracks would branch off and then join again, then all would walk almost in the same footprints. In far less mileage than we had cov-

ered on the previous occasion we came upon them.
Gathering the party together into a compact group,
the cameras were made ready for action, then with two
boys to carry the big movie outfit, one gun bearer for
any emergency that might arise, and Jones and I each
with a small camera, we crept slowly toward them.

Now both of us had stalked the black rhinoceros
and I had filmed more than one of these truculent
creatures, but this was a different animal, and the surprise and thrill that awaited us around the corner of a
small bush is impossible to describe.   There stood not
two but five huge beasts, one of which would tower
over a black rhinoceros like the Woolworth Building
over Trinity Church!   How many tons of flesh were
represented there I cannot state, but this mammoth
pachyderm gave me a good reason to look around to
see if the gun bearer were close at hand.   He was not!

The bull stood broadside on, a mountain of flesh
and bone, the profile of head and horns outlined
against the sky in such a way as to be more impressive
than if seen against a background of trees.   They had
no suspicion of our being there and went on feeding
and nosing about.   Placing the camera in position, I
began to grind away, and as I did, had the time to
make a few mental notes.   These rhino are not white,
but might appear so in certain light.   The actual color
is a light reddish brown.   The horns are very long and
quite slim, the front horn being the longer in all cases
— how long I would not care to say, for it would only
be a guess, but the record horn for a white rhinoceros
cow is over sixty-two inches.   Its muzzle was truncated
and had no prehensile tip, this being why it is sometimes referred to as the square-lipped rhinoceros.   The

skull has great length, and when the beast turned and faced me I could not but remark on the enormous width of its face, caused by the square mouth and flat front surface of the horn. When it walked, its head was carried low, and it seemed that the earth jarred just a bit.

The huge bull walked slowly to within thirty yards of me and then must have heard the clicking of the camera, for he moved away, to be followed by seven more! I filmed them all as they crossed the screen, one behind the other.

After this scene, we photographed the mammals for some three hours, from many different positions. In so doing, we took quite a few chances, for although their vision is poor and their hearing not very good, they have a marvelously keen scent, and as the wind was somewhat gusty and often veered about, it kept us busy keeping to their windward. Once the breeze suddenly changed and placed us in a rather uncomfortable position. We were almost surrounded by the eight rhinoceroses, when a whiff of air carried knowledge of our presence to a cow with calf. She turned on us and snorted, then made a short dash forward and things looked nasty for a while. Behind us, within forty yards, stood three of the group, two more were close at hand on our right, while the big bull was eying us from a distance of not more than fifty paces to our left. Had the cow charged, it would have been hard to decide which way to run!

We kept after a young bull, trying to get some real close-ups, until he got peeved at our persistence and charged. It came as a complete surprise, for we had by now got quite used to the rhinoceros and had lost all fear, so there was a mad scramble for a while. The beast had all the advantage, for in a hand-to-hand battle he would have won hands down, while we could not shoot, no matter if he did charge. As he rushed toward my four-thousand-dollar camera, I forgot all else and tried to attract his attention to myself, at the same time looking about for a suitable tree. He came about half way, then showed some hesitation, and, just at this point, Jones got hold of his gun and fired a shot into the air. The report frightened him and away he went, this time in the proper direction for a charging rhinoceros!

Well satisfied with the day and thankful that nobody had been hurt, we trekked back to our camp on the Nile. Going down to its bank for a swim and to watch the hippos disporting across the way, we discussed the white rhinoceros and its probable fate under any government other than that which now protects it. We agreed that it should continue to be protected; for although a formidable beast and well able to hold its own against any opponent in the animal kingdom, it would soon vanish under the gunfire of the modern hunter.

The white rhinoceros is a left-over from prehistoric times, a weird animal as well as a rare one, a ponderous beast still tramping through the torrid heat, amid the silent jungles that skirt the western shores of the ancient Nile.

Alulu mother. Her costume consists of a bunch of grass suspended by a
string. The baby's head is covered with a bowl.

An exceptional photograph of white rhinoceroses. In the center is a bull; the others are cows.

CHAPTER FIFTEEN

PYGMIES OF THE ITURI FOREST

FROM the Nile camp we motored to Arua and then made our official entrance into the Belgian Congo at Aru. The young Belgian in charge of the customs was very accommodating, causing us the smallest amount of inconvenience possible. After paying him several thousand francs, which he assured me would be returned at the opposite border, we motored over excellent roads, reaching Adranga at dusk. Here I found another customs officer, paying him a few thousand francs more on things the first man had overlooked.

Next morning Maniki rushed in to say that white men were beating the black men with whips, so I strolled out to see what it was all about. The Belgian officer was holding the regular Monday meeting and giving orders for the week's work. In the Congo they insist on able-bodied men doing a certain amount of labor. This is quite a contrast to the English method as practiced in Kenya, where most of the Negro men are a useless blot on the landscape, the native women being the beasts of burden who perform all the drudgery, while the men strut about aping the white man. In the Belgian Congo we saw few women at work, while most of the men were occupied with some task. The floggings to which Maniki drew my attention were administered with a hippo whip by a huge Negro soldier, at the orders of the officer, this method being used, in preference to fines, in punishment of trivial offenses. After each man had received several cruel strokes across his back, during which no sound was uttered, he would jump up, salute, and thank the Belgian officer.   During these proceedings, I told Maniki I thought a good whipping, on occasion, might inject a little pep into him and the rest of my boys.   He grinned broadly and said it was "baya sana"— very bad!

A few days of travel over an always changing countryside brought us to Gumbari.   The roadway for miles was banked by grass twelve feet high, then wound through long lines of banana, pawpaw, and mango trees.   Every village nestled near acres of pineapples and sweet potatoes.   We motored through the gold-mining district, finding Watsa a delightful place, boasting some modern buildings.   While crossing the Kibali River it commenced to rain, and we drove for several hours in a drenching downpour, reaching the Bomokandi River at nightfall.   Here we found enormous dugout canoes — the largest yet encountered — and were carried across to Gumbari, on a native ferry, where we were made comfortable in a government rest house.

Next day I called on the Belgian Administrator, who kindly loaned me an interpreter and guide, and also gave me permission to enter the Ituri Forest in search of pygmies.   As we neared the place where we were to leave the trucks and trek into the forest, a motor cycle came toward us, bearing two white men who greeted us in English.   They were Messrs. Leader and Johnson, Americans in charge of the near-by Assembly of God Mission.   We were glad to accept their invitation to spend the night at the station, and Mrs. Johnson prepared us the best meal we had eaten for many a day.

Early one morning a long line of Momvu porters slowly treaded their way to the tune of a doleful chant as we penetrated farther and farther into the dark depths of the great Ituri Forest.   My provost guard was heading the procession, while halfway down the line, as sole passenger in a Kipoi chair, I swung between the shoulders of four black giants, who repeatedly shouted to those ahead to hurry onward, saying, "Move faster, brothers, for has not the white master said that he wishes to reach the Ifi clearing before the day turns dark?"

That morning the local Momvu chief had supplied us with porters to carry ourselves and equipment into the forest, and now the long safari was under way over the lonely paths that wind for hundreds of miles through mysterious depths of tangled creepers and trees that forever hide the sun.

Often the trail was very narrow, while sometimes an overhead archway of palms and ferns was formed.   At such places these big Momvu men had to crouch until they were through the passage, for, although the foot-way was well worn, it had been worn by little feet belonging to a sprightly dwarf, to whose passing the vegetable tunnel offered no problem.

These cool byways are always wet, the leaves dripping moisture on to a boggy ground — a ground that has been damp for ages.   Creepers and moss cover the trees, while through the decaying matter that carpets the forest floor, ferns and flowers, toadstools and other fungoid growths, twist and turn, ever struggling upwards.

Many varieties of butterflies, big and little, and of all colors and designs, flew and fluttered in and about

the paths, while peeks into deep recesses that a stray
sun ray lit up, would disclose many more, and also
flowers and shrubs that were strange and handsome.

A journey into a forest such as this is a thing good
for the soul, for here in God's great cathedral of trees,
with bright shafts of sun flooding the glades and foot-
ways here and there, one is made to feel how little his
individual existence counts in the great plan of the
universe.

Just before we reached the clearing, a great commotion took place at the head of the line. We had come
to a place in the trail where millions of small red ants
had taken possession of the right of way, and when
the porters walked into them, they made a savage
attack on the bare legs of the men. A mad scramble
to get away from them gave me some hearty laughs,
then a wild ride as my bearers raced over the danger
zone. These ants are much feared by the natives, for
they will often come into the huts at night and drive
every living thing out. It is better to flee than to try
to combat their countless hordes.

At dusk we came to the clearing in the forest, a circular space about an acre in extent with a huge ant hill
some thirty feet high standing in the middle. Atop
this ant hill was a large hut of the bungalow type, and
here I made headquarters, while the main camp was
settled in a group of smaller huts on the edge of the
clearing.

From this perch I surveyed the scene below. All
around the fringe of the open space were food-bearing
trees — banana, pawpaw, mango — while many patches
of pineapples grew beneath. A few small fires were
blinking and winking, now that darkness was falling,

District chief Asanga, a typical pygmy of the Ituri Forest.

Ituri Forest Pygmies in Hoefler's Clearing, Belgian Congo. One hundred seven men, women, and children were called together by the drums of a few friendly Ifi.

and the early night birds mingled their odd cries with the chatter of some near-by monkeys.

Beyond the boundaries of the little clearing, and surrounding it like an ominous wall, stood the silent jungle, within whose mysterious depths strange people and strange animals lived and died, never knowing in all their lives anything but this world of trees. Overhead the clear sky was filled with stars, and just there, suspended over the tallest tree, hung the glorious Southern Cross.

Now up the hill came my guide, and trailing behind him were fifteen little men and women of the forest. They caught my fancy at once, for instead of the usual scowl of the Negro hereabouts, they had smiling faces and laughed in a way that was a treat to hear, while the tiny children, who looked at me with big wondering eyes, captivated me completely. They all stood around in a small circle and watched closely while I told the interpreter to explain our plans to them. After he had done so, they filed out with a nod to me and faded into the darkness toward the winking fires.

Soon from below was heard the first rumblings of the drums, to grow louder and still louder, until over the vast expanses of the forest it boomed and rolled, swelled to a mighty roar, and then fell to a deep whisper, telling in the pygmy code that white men had come into their country. Then all was silent and I heard in the far distance an answering sound, and then another, for such is the Ifi telegraph, the calling of the drums.

These drums are made from one solid piece of wood, hollowed out. Along the top, down the middle, is a long slit, the various sounds being produced by the

18

manner in which the drumsticks are used in relation to
this opening.

Hardly had the sun come over the horizon, when the
little men began to dance near the large hut which the
local Momvu use as a council house. We were using
it as sleeping quarters, and the sound of the drums
and tom-toms soon had us out of bed. This dance was
participated in by all members of the family, from the
oldest woman down to the smallest child. Even the
wee babies were there on their mothers' backs, and it
was a most amusing sight to watch their tiny heads
bob up and down as the mothers pranced and swung
to the rhythm of the music. I found these dwarf
people willing to do whatever they were asked. They
would run where others walked, but would soon tire of
everything except dancing, and after a little while
would say, "Our strength is gone, we must rest."

Before noontime, a hundred or more had come in
from the forest to join our camp. Their first act
was to construct themselves huts of banana leaves
and palm branches. This task required almost half an
hour's time. Men and women worked together, and
while the men cut the leaves the women wove them
into a beehive-shaped hut. Skins and other household
furnishings were placed inside, a fire was started outside the entrance, and behold, the new arrivals were at
home to callers!

Next they went to have a look at the strange men
with fair skins, for some of them had never before
seen a white man. Greetings were exchanged, and
then our friends would join the dance, or go in search
of old acquaintances, for gatherings such as this are
very rare.

I went to the hut atop the hill to do some work on the typewriter, and soon had a circle of them about me, a circle which stood there more than an hour without a single sound. To them the white man himself is strange enough, but his many things of magic are beyond comprehension; so, like children, they stood and gazed, wondering at the marvelous thing that made a clicking sound and strung odd-looking marks, one after another, over a blank white surface.

The Ituri Forest pygmy is not a Negro, nor has he much in common with the black men of Bantu stock who live near him. He is called the "tiki tiki" by the very few white men who know him, but to the many thousands of natives who live around the forest edge he is known as "Ifi." I wondered where this name originated until I heard their chants during the moon dances. During this wild dance they work themselves into a pitch of excitement by the weird chants that supplement the beating of the drums. Round and round they go, leaping, swaying, prancing, and all the time chanting a savage refrain, through which runs the oft-repeated words, "Ifi-ifi, O ha, ifi-ifi, mu'm ifi-ifi!" While in conference with their chiefs, I particularly inquired about the tribal name, and the pygmies themselves confirmed the information which had been given by the Momvu, that their true name was "Ifi."

In color, most of the Ifi are yellowish brown. Both men and women are well formed, the women being quite comely and the men muscular. Their features have a slight Oriental cast, and in some members of the tribe it was very pronounced. One man was almost the double of a Japanese I once knew in Los Angeles. In height they are shorter than the Bushmen of the Kalahari Desert, but in many other respects they are similar.

There seems to be a thread that weaves in and about through Africa, over the deserts, through the veldt, and into the forests, a thread of Bushman strain. At least I have found the Bushman type, the Bushman characteristics, in many parts of Africa through which I have traveled. Can it be that these forest dwellers are an offshoot of Bushman stock? They have a similar facial contour, the same kind of hair, and many habits and customs in common. It is possible that they were members of a Bushman clan who became separated from the main body of the tribes, who through the influence of wars and the invasion of their country by a more powerful people, were driven toward the great forest of the Congo, and in its mysterious recesses found safety.

However this may be, it is a fact that they are here in fair numbers, their district chief telling me by means of sticks laid on the ground that in all the forest lived about ten thousand of the Ifi tribesmen. They live in small clans of from twenty-five to fifty souls, over which a subchief rules. These subchiefs are under an overchief in the district, but whether or not they were all ruled by one paramount chief I was unable to find out.

They are a happy people and continue to multiply, for food is plentiful, whereas the Bushman seldom laughs, seeming to know that his clansmen are doomed to an early extinction, for in his country food is scarce. He has been driven into a district in which neither he nor anyone else could long survive.

There is a legend here among the Bantu people that, long before they entered the basin of the Congo, there

A pygmy subchief being carried on the shoulders of two men. A young girl, walking alongside, shades him with a large banana leaf.

The drums of the Ifi: the one suspended is a tom-tom used for dancing; the long drum at the left is used to send messages.

A man of the Momvu tribe, who has been adopted into the pygmy kingdom, assists at a ceremonial. This Momvu is less than six feet tall.

existed here a race of dwarfs, who were light brown in color, had crispy hair, and were known as the Batwa. Native tradition also says that these pygmies once lived near the present Lake Tanganyika, where we find today traces of an ancient Batwa kingdom antedating the arrival of the Bantu. The Batwa at that time had a tribal organization which resembled that in existence during the same time among the ancient Bushmen of South Africa. Some of these pygmy chiefs, like Asanga, whose portrait appears on page 333, can point to genealogies that run back two and three centuries.

Like the Bushmen, they are omnivorous, and, like many primitive peoples, are passionately fond of salt. The forest abounds in wild fruits and roots, while the animal life is fairly abundant. Being keen trackers and accomplished hunters, it is no great feat for them to keep the meat pot boiling. Not being fastidious about their food has its advantages also, for snakes, lizards, beetles, grubs, and in fact all suchlike are considered both tasty and nourishing.

In the killing of an elephant they show both courage and cunning, for this huge beast cannot easily be done to death by their puny weapons. They stalk him through the forest paths until he stops to sleep, and, as he dozes in some sunlit glade, creep within arm's length of his hind quarters, then sever the leg cords, thus making him helpless to run. A messenger is sent to the nearest village, the drums send out the glad tidings, and soon the hapless mammoth is surrounded by pygmies who spear him to death by heaving their weapons and then deftly recovering them from the elephant and using them again and again.

When the elephant is dead the whole clan gathers and scenes of wildest orgy take place. Holes are cut into his stomach and men crawl inside to get at the tidbits, such as the liver, heart, and kidneys. What a sight such a drama presents! Dwarfs of men, howling and yelling, driving pygmy spears into the giant of the animal kingdom until he crashes to earth among the dank ferns. Then the dance of triumph, the feast of meat, the savage revelries of primitive men. Not unlike the early history of our own race are the present-day lives of these pygmies.

The spears are small but well made, tipped with iron points and often decorated with ivory. Their bows measure twenty-eight inches of bowstring, both ends being decorated with monkey fur. The bow is made from a flexible wood and the string from a creeper. Arrow shafts are shaped from the center stem of the palm leaf, and the iron points from metal that they mine from the earth and smelt and pound into shape themselves. To make poison, they seek the akage tree, cut chunks from it, pound these into a pulp and squeeze the juice into a pot. The arrow points are placed in this sap and all are boiled together. It is a most deadly poison, and kills even the hardy buffalo within two hours' time.

While writing atop my ant hill in the clearing, it commenced to rain like the flood, while the lightning and thunder did their utmost to uphold the reputation earned by them in the tropics. Down below, the pygmies went scurrying about like busy ants, putting extra banana leaves on their hut roofs. The downpour ceased as quickly as it began, the sun shone brightly again, and then we had a ceremonial parade. The four pygmy chiefs were carried around the clearing in chairs swung upon the shoulders of two men.   Their subjects followed in wild disorder, shouting and chanting.   Young women shaded them with banana leaves, while others wiped their faces.   At the end of this procession walked the medicine man, performing a few crazy steps and later sprinkling water over the marchers when they assembled to the call of the drums.

I measured some of the men and women, finding that the women averaged two and one-half inches shorter than the men.   The tallest man measured fifty-seven inches and the shortest, fifty inches.   The average for the twelve of each sex measured was, for the men, four feet seven inches, and for the women, four feet four and one-half inches.   The tallest woman was fifty-six inches in height and the shortest fifty inches. Truly a small race.

The Momvu are a race of Bantu stock who, being men of unusually large stature, and living among dwarfs, have assumed a sort of overlordship toward the Ifi.   But nobody, not even the Belgian Government, levy tribute from this little folk, and the Momvu claim to rule over them amounts to a claim only, for the Ifi demonstrated this to us more than once.

A chief of the Momvu, by the name of Ongodi, made a visit to the clearing.   He came in state, being carried on the shoulders of his subjects in a huge chair.   I was standing near the hut door on top of the ant hill when this chief was deposited at the bottom.   As he arose from the chair, a royal retainer brushed the wrinkles from his coat tail, while another went ahead picking up sticks and other obstructions from the royal path. In haughty style he strode up to me and extended his hand in greeting. Now up came the prime minister and other members of the staff, all in a hand-shaking mood. I asked, in all the languages I knew, how the chief was feeling and how he was coming along in his kingship business. To each question he simply grunted; so I then told the interpreter to ask him and his retinue to have seats under a near-by banana tree, whence they could watch our methods in filming. The king started down the hill in grand style, but about halfway down tripped and spread his huge frame in the dust. The assembled Ifi went into hysterics over this. They rolled on the ground laughing and went running about slapping one another and guffawing, while some imitated his grand march and fall. All this time he and his court scowled, and some of the retainers shouted in angry tones at the fun makers.

Later we had a powwow in the large hut, during which he was referred to as the big chief. All the pygmy chiefs were present, and when they found that he spoke of them as under his rule, up they jumped, and, pointing their fingers at him, shouted that he was not their chief by any means, and had nothing to say about their affairs. In no uncertain tone they told him he might rule on the forest's edge, but that they still ruled in its depths, and if he did not think so, to come along sometime and find out. They are fiery little men, and in their element, the forest, a dangerous enemy.

Should foemen invade their domain, the pygmies wait along the paths and at the proper time let go a shower of poisoned arrows, then melt into the shadows, to reappear later and harass the survivors. No one knows the forest as they do, nor its many secret passages and byways.

During this meeting in the hut, one oɪ the women was suddenly seized with an attack of fits, flailing and tossing upon the floor until the others were thrown into a state of terrified commotion. None among the blacks stirred a hand to aid her, but all with one accord looked to me for help.

Fits were not in my list of ailments for treatment, nor could I recall one item in my medicine chest that might be effective in relieving the woman. In this state of uncertainty, I glanced about the room, my gaze falling upon a large bottle of vinegar that was always kept upon the table because Jones would not eat certain things without the assistance of this seasoning. Quickly filling a glass with this condiment, I handed it to one of my boys, telling him to pour it down the woman's throat. She swallowed it readily, ceased her flounderings at once, sat up, blinked several times, rolled her eyes ecstatically and stood up. With a pleased smile she surveyed the interior of the hut and after a little jabbering with a neighbor, inquired through the interpreter if I would let her have another glassful!

The Ifi medicine men have some interesting practices in connection with the use of herbs found in the forest. There is very little sickness among the pygmies, excepting that ringworm and other skin afflictions are much in evidence, but no matter what the bodily ill or hurt, the few herbs with which they are familiar must suffice. I asked the medicine man what was his procedure in the case of a snake bite. He replied he ran into the forest and obtained the root of a certain plant which he then burned, rubbing the ashes into the wound, which had previously been opened with a knife. When I inquired whether this treatment always cured the victim he quite frankly answered that some of the patients lived, but that most of them died, and added that such things as sickness and snake bites were an affair of God — that if God wanted people to live he would cure them; if not, they would die.

Now the district chief, Asanga, and his subchiefs, Akusu, Wavango, and Aimba, came to me and said that they were tired of life in the clearing and wanted to go back to the hunting trails. It had rained so much that our work was not yet completed, so by promising them presents I got their pledge to stay a few more days. It is hard to talk to them, for no one speaks their language but themselves. My interpreter spoke to them in a mixture of Ifi and Momvu which they understand. Some writer has claimed that they speak the same language as the Momvu, but in this clearing there were both Ifi and Momvu, and the Momvu insist that their language and that of the Ifi are entirely different.

However, we got along fairly well, and while I had them collected together I asked questions about their ways of living.

Their whole life is founded on a system which has no money or other medium of exchange, and this affects their social customs as well as all other matters. The old chief assured me that they do not want money, that they have no use for it, for they are happy now and want to stay as they are. The Momvu and other tribes living on the forest edge handle a few francs, and also use sheep and goats as a medium of exchange. The pygmies have no stock nor property of any kind, save their spears, bows, arrows, knives, drums, pipes, cooking pots, and a few skins. No man can store wealth, for there is none.

A man's family is his only source of boasting and pride, and these little men and women of the forest marry only for love!   The Negro tribes buy and sell wives as so many cattle, a woman being valuable for what work she can do and for the children she can bear to her lord and master, the children also being goods of value.   The girls are sold as wives and the boys do all the manual labor performed by the male.   The Ifi does no work, neither man nor woman, for his wants are simple, and the little that has to be done is more like play than work.

When a young man loves a girl and she loves him, they ask the father for permission to marry.   If he consents they go to the chief, who must also agree. He then marries them by giving one to the other after a long talk on the duties of a married couple.   They now live together for a while and if both are satisfied that their affection will endure, they report to the chief, who then seals the bond by some mystic rite, and the couple must live together as long as life lasts. I could find no polygamy among them.   The people are very moral, few being untrue to their mates.   If such a case does arise, however, the chief can sever the bonds and release the innocent party.   The culprit meets an untimely end, unless quick enough to fade into the jungle and keep away from the tribesmen.

One odd custom is that of the exchange of persons. If a man of one clan marries a girl of another, it is the custom for his clique to swap one of its male members for the girl, this being done in order to keep up the strength of each clan, as otherwise the one blessed with many girls would soon fade away, while that having the most boys would become too powerful.

The pygmies are very careful of their women, never parting with them to anyone outside of their own tribe, except in exchange for a rifle! The Belgians do not prohibit guns to the natives as do the British, and I often met naked savages walking along the paths carrying an old muzzle-loader. One pygmy subchief had such a weapon. It was a relic of many decades ago, being a large smoothbore with flintlock, without any flint. This gun had not been fired for many years, but the chief never went anywhere without it, a small boy proudly bearing it behind him on all occasions.

The pygmy men wear a covering of bark cloth, while the women get along with a girdle of leaves. The cloth is prepared by the wives, who strip the bark from a certain tree and, after soaking it in a stream, beat it out with ivory hammers. Judging by the appearance of some of this material, which I noticed on the men, it must wear very well. They never wash it and maybe the additions of grease and the curing properties of smoke from the camp fires preserve and toughen it.

The women sport two or three new dresses every day, or whenever their fancy dictates. Little groups go out forest shopping, presently returning with fresh leaves hung around their waists, suspended from a vine. After running around in the sun for a while, the leaves dry up and shrink, making another trip necessary to the dress section of this huge outdoor department store. Unless the climate changes a great deal, the pygmy women will never want for a plentiful supply of clothes, nor will their husband's dry-goods' bill ever be a cause for worry.

It was dusk. The chiefs, to whom I had been talking through my interpreter, had left, and going to the

Members of a pygmy family in front of an abandoned hut in Hoefler's Clearing.

349

The Ifi yell leader, who leads all the chants and dances.

The chief takes a smoke. The author was unable to find out what the Ifi smoke in these water pipes.

hut door, I looked out over the clearing and the darkening forest that had been my home for many days. Below, a baby's crying sent my thoughts to another land among the mountains, for this tiny baby cried just as do the babies of all climes and colors; its voice being the same as that of the baby next door at home — the one that the milkman awakens every morning.

When it grows older there will be no days at school, no dressing for company, no reason to keep clean. If it is a boy, he will simply learn to chant the tune of the clan, to swing to the rhythm of the dance, to read and send the messages of the drums, to hunt and hamstring the elephant, to fashion a bow and arrows, to make and throw a spear. If the baby is a girl, she will learn the latest style in which to place her girdle of leaves and will discuss with the other women the best leaves for different types of beauty and where to find them. She will watch the old women toast the green bananas and mix the right portion of ashes with the meat.

The intense blackness of the night, the awful stillness out in that ocean of trees, the dwarfs, and the winking little fires, all under a clear star-strewn sky, combined to carry me back over the bridge of time into that long ago when men with white skins wore loin cloths and trod the wilderness trails in search of food and shelter. I wondered if all the thousands of intervening years had brought the measure of happiness to some of us that these people enjoy, for they do enjoy life every day, dancing and chanting, visiting one another, hunting when necessary. This is their life, simple in all its elements, from the day of birth until death claims their pygmy bodies.

Engrossed with such thoughts as these, I strolled down to my dark-room tent at the edge of the forest. As I stood at its entrance in the darkness, a husband and wife crawled out from beneath their shelter of leaves. He ignited a torch of dry banana stalk at the little fire, and bearing the blazing brand on high, while she carried a small water jar, they strode past me on the trail that leads to nowhere.

Slowly they walked down the path, the burning torch dimly lighting the way, shadows flickering as the firebrand threw grotesque shapes against the dark trees. As they grew dim in the distance, I shouted them a farewell, but they did not hear. Soon the light blinked out. My pygmy friends were gone, engulfed in the silent jungle, tiny shadows in a primal wilderness.

CHAPTER SIXTEEN

HEART OF THE CONGO

IT rained a great part of the time during our stay in the Ituri forest. The very atmosphere was saturated with moisture, everything becoming so water-soaked that it soon doubled its weight. My films gave me a great deal of worry, for I feared that all this material which I had worked so hard to secure would be ruined by the dampness and heat.

Nearly the entire pygmy population of the clearing followed us to the edge of the forest, where they surged around the trucks. Jones was tinkering with the motors, from which we had long ago removed the mufflers, and when he would push down on an accelerator, the unearthly racket caused great excitement among the dwarfs. They would shout and laugh and crowd around until Jones tooted the horn. This always sent them scurrying away pell-mell, only to return shortly and make signs for him to do it again.

We took the four chiefs for a buggy ride, and while Jones sped around the corners and up and down gullies, I watched their actions. As they crouched in the back of the car, holding on to the sideboards for dear life, expressions of pleasure, fear, horror, and other emotions passed over their faces. This experience impressed them immensely, but the speed was too great to please them and they were glad to be deposited safely back on earth once more. Their admiring subjects immediately surrounded them, to ask about their sensations while riding in the white man's "thunder wagon."

After presenting the chiefs and the rest of the tribesmen with gifts of salt, cloth, and trinkets, and trading them out of a few bows and arrows, we paid a brief visit to our friends at the Mission, then proceeded to Faradje, where we received the first mail since leaving Nairobi. At this small post no one was able to change my large English notes, so we had to make a ninety-mile round trip to Aba for that purpose. Aba is on the main road to Rejaf and proved to be a trading center and white settlement of some importance due to its proximity to the rich Nile country of the lower Sudan and the fact that it benefits by regular steamer communications on the mighty river.

There are a great many chimpanzees in this district. The young Belgian officer who invited us to his house for refreshments had one of these apes for a pet and spent most of the evening telling us what a wonderfully smart animal it was.

Upon returning to Faradje, I was told it would be impossible to continue westward on the main road to Dungu, our informant saying it would be necessary to make a short detour. After traveling about one hundred fifty miles, during which we crossed three large rivers, the N'zoro, the Kibali, and the Yebu, which were swiftly running muddy torrents due to the heavy rains, we commenced to wonder exactly what was meant by "a short detour." We negotiated these crossings with considerable difficulty, between rivers plowing for miles through soft mud, but eventually reached the remote village of Shifowando.

Here the local sultan paid us a visit, bringing as presents two scrawny fowls and ten aged eggs, for which he expected much salt and whatever else he could talk us out of. Some of the women at this village were wearing elephant-hair bracelets, and both Jones and Austin tried their ability as traders, the results showing that Jones made the best deals, not only on the bracelets but on other items. He even succeeded in trading the chief an old coat for a pair of elephant tusks!

During the middle of the night a loud commotion awoke the countryside, and above the shouting could be heard the voice of Ali, our cook, who always assumed leadership when no white man was present. A swarming army of safari ants had entered the bandas where the boys were sleeping. They were now jumping around in a panic, brushing ants off one another and shaking them out of their clothes. These savage insects often drive the inhabitants of an entire village from their huts. The dreaded jiggers were also here in abundance, and for many days afterwards our boys were busy picking them out of their toes. These tiny bugs burrow beneath the skin, where they lay their eggs, causing a fester which becomes very painful. Unless this sac is removed before it hatches, a dangerous infection will result. The natives become quite expert at locating and removing these egg sacs.

The following morning we drove through a veritable garden spot; a country abounding with tropical and semitropical fruits. We found our old friends the pawpaw, banana, and pineapple on every hand, while castor beans, tobacco, cotton, sago, and sweet potatoes were constantly in evidence. Late in the afternoon

19

we motored through a district containing many elephant
herds. For miles we strained our eyes and ears, expecting to encounter them at every turn, for the whole
countryside spoke eloquently of their presence. At
one place they had crossed the road just ahead of us,
leaving a path resembling an earthquake's destruction.
Trees were thrown about in grand confusion, while the
ground was plowed up in all directions.

We arrived at Wanda just ahead of a thunderstorm
and, finding no huts available for our use, we made
record time in putting up the tents. This task was
barely completed when the storm broke with tremendous fury and continued to drench the district
throughout the entire night. We were soon swimming
in red mud and everything became damp and clammy.
A heavy rain may be enjoyed while sitting in a comfortable room looking through a window, but in the
jungles it loses most of its poetry. To make our
misery at this camp complete, Austin was stricken
with a bad attack of fever.

For many years the Belgian government has maintained a training station for elephants at Wanda.
From the wild herds that roam in the surrounding
forests, they capture young animals and these are
brought to the post for a course in discipline. They
are then sold to plantations or to the missions. The
African animal is quite different from the Indian
species, a much harder beast to domesticate, never
becoming entirely docile. Until the Belgians undertook this work, it was thought impossible to train the
African elephant. They have succeeded to a certain
extent, but the results obtained are small considering
the amount of effort and time expended, and it is not

likely that this animal will ever become a great aid to mankind, comparable to his Indian cousin.

My object in coming here was to hire, if possible, guides and porters to take us among the wild herds for the purpose of securing motion-picture scenes. Our prospects of success were shattered when I learned from the Belgian officer that all the available man power was engaged in some sort of governmental work. Without porters it would be difficult to operate and, not being interested in photographing tame elephants, we packed up and left immediately the storm was over.

When the rain clouds had cleared away, the fiery sun appeared, causing the moisture to arise in wisps of steam from the soaked ground. It was oppressively hot, but the cooling breeze generated by the moving trucks afforded some relief as we journeyed from Wanda to Api through a land of plenty.

When we had passed beyond the district where the Belgians have brought the natives under their absolute control, we found lazy groups lying about in the villages. A man can build himself a comfortable cluster of huts in less than a month and there live, rent free, for the balance of his days. Building sites are gratis to all comers, it only being necessary to clear the jungle away, while all needed materials are ready at hand, without any expense whatsoever. The method of construction is quite simple; sticks are placed in the ground to form a circle, while others are bent to make a conical roof. The whole frame is then lathed with bamboo and covered with grass. After the huts and stockade have been completed, a few fowls and some dogs are added to the scene, whereupon the man lies down to spend the balance of his life resting.

There was a boom going on in one district, and along our route for miles the natives were clearing the forest and building new huts. I wondered what price business sites were bringing at the corner of Elephant Trail Avenue and Leopard Path Boulevard and how many centuries would have to come and go before the streets would be paved!

Immediately after passing one of these new country homes, something leaped from the tall grass into the jungle road. As it ran down the path in front of me, I recognized it to be one of the rarest of animals, a black leopard. Before I could get a rifle to my shoulder the cat jumped back into the dense fifteen-foot-high grass, where it was hopeless to follow.

The Belgians have instilled respect for the white race into the black men of the Congo. As we sped by natives walking on the road, they would stand to attention and salute. I shall never forget the grotesque figure of one old man with an ancient musket. This gray-headed giant was clothed in tatters and wore a forlorn hat that must have been as aged as the muzzle-loader which he carried. When the truck approached, he wheeled around and presented arms in the most approved fashion, the combination of man, clothes, and musket making a pathetic but ludicrous picture.

The sound of the approaching trucks brought men, women, and children running to the road from all directions. Then they would line up to salute as the motors went roaring by. We were continually crossing rivers, none of the larger streams being bridged. At some of them we found native ferries, but as we penetrated farther into the country our difficulties in traveling steadily increased.

Building a hut in Belgian Congo.

One of the government ferries in Belgian Congo.

Elephants in the forest north of Api, near the Uere River. Although there are many thousands of elephants in the Belgian Congo, they are shy and hard to approach.

Among the things that the traveler in this part of
Africa will never forget are the tiny gnats and sand
flies that pester you night and day, leaving white
blisters that itch for hours.   Instead of enjoying a
refreshing sleep, the nights are spent in scratching
bites and fighting mosquitoes.   During the daytime
we would forget these annoyances while speeding among
the ferns which filled the spaces beneath towering
trees that hemmed in the narrow roadway.   We
journeyed through the cool, unending forest, where
the songs of birds, the call of monkeys, the lazy drone
of insects, and the multitudes of brightly colored
butterflies added color and sound to the allurement of
a pristine paradise.

The Belgian Congo is forty-four times as large as
the motherland and is rich in natural resources.   I
found her transplanted sons to be industrious, but
working under serious handicaps.   There is a lack of
sufficient capital and also a shortsighted policy which
discourages development by foreign nationals.

Upon arrival at Api, we found conditions to be much
the same as those at Wanda.   The wild elephants were
two days' foot safari away, and there were no porters
to carry our equipment.   Regardless of this situation,
I decided to try for elephant pictures in this district,
so camp was made.   Now Jones became seriously ill,
the symptoms indicating sleeping sickness, making it
necessary that I drive one hundred seventeen miles to
the mission station at Buta, where I placed him under
the care of the Sisters.

After arranging things for Jones, I made a tour around
the town, which I found to be quite an unusual place.
While stopped in front of a store, a young Belgian came

up to tell me in broken English about a large quantity of gasoline and Mobiloil which the Vacuum Oil Company had sent there for the expedition. These supplies had come up the Congo River to Bangui and across country to Buta.

Returning to Api, I went immediately to the officer in charge to see if it were possible to arrange for porters. It was not! During our conversation I learned something about their work with the elephants. They have been capturing young animals from the wild herds in this district since 1900. The fourteen half-grown elephants at this station were taken out every morning for training, then driven to the river each evening, and, after a good scrubbing, were returned to their feed grounds, there to be chained for the night. While walking among these tethered animals, which seemed as gentle as those found in a circus, we discussed the widely circulated story, accepted by many as a fact, that African elephants were untamable. These were certainly the African species, for this was the heart of the Dark Continent and within a few miles of their birthplace! The officer's information was interesting but of no great help in assisting me to get the pictures I sought.

Realizing that nothing could be accomplished by depending on the authorities for help, I scouted around until successful in securing a guide. Then, with my own boys acting as porters and carrying a limited amount of equipment, I hiked off into the jungle. After some of the most arduous work of the expedition, I was able to secure a few motion-picture scenes and some still photographs of the mammoth pachyderms that roam through the Congo forests.

On May twenty-first we motored to Buta. En route I made my fifth crossing of the Uele, a rapidly flowing tropical river. It required nearly an hour's paddling and poling by a score of natives to make the trip. On this occasion they missed the landing by several hundred yards and had a hard struggle against the strong current which flows near the bank before they were able to tie the rickety ferry to the crude wharf. While the trucks were being taken ashore, I bought some beautifully decorated ivory from a native who had just arrived from the bush. Some of these black men have been brought up by the Fathers at the Mission, who have taught them numerous crafts, one being wood and ivory carving.

Our fears that Jones had been stricken with the dread malady of sleeping sickness proved unfounded, for upon driving up to the hospital building we found him to be quite well. They had treated him so splendidly he hated to leave, but it was necessary that our journey be continued immediately, so, after restocking our food supplies and loading on as much gasoline as it was possible to carry, we again headed westward. No one could tell us for a certainty how far it was to Bangui, nor the condition of the road, providing there was a road.

As we sped toward Bangassou we constantly encountered natives walking along the paths with huge nets slung over their shoulders. Whenever we reached a large river, I would scan it in search of fishermen using these enormous seines but never found any in use. One day the mystery was solved, for, during a stop for lunch, we heard distant shouting, and, upon going to investigate, found one of these nets strung across a pathway. Shortly some men arrived carrying spears and bows and arrows. Hanging from a pole, carried between two of them, was a small antelope. The people in this district trap most of their animal food by placing snares across the game trails and driving whatever they can into them.

After two hundred fifty miles through deep forest, we arrived at the Bomu River, to find that the streams were getting wider and the ferries smaller. It was dusk, and as we stood on the Belgian side gazing toward the French Congo beyond this river — which is here wider than the Ohio at Cincinnati — we were wondering how long it would take to build a raft large enough to float the trucks across, when some natives came into view poling a crude affair made of three dugouts with rough planks secured on them. It did not give an impression of being exactly safe, but was better than nothing; so we took a chance and sailed. Several trips landed the expedition at Bangassou and there we met some lonesome Frenchmen who treated us to wine and a very fine dinner. They were surprised to find that we had come all the way from the east coast by motor and assured us that nobody else had ever done so.

After an enjoyable evening with the Frenchmen, three of us went to retrieve one of the trucks which had slipped off a narrow bridge into a deep gully. In order to get it out, we needed a heavy plank, so strolled down to the ferry landing to borrow one. While we were struggling up the bank with this huge timber, a man rushed out from a near-by bungalow, waving his arms and shouting to us in a mixture of French and whatever the native language is. Joe tried to match gestures with this human windmill, while Jones and I assisted the boys with the plank. Joe finally succeeded in convincing the zealous patriot that we had no intention of crippling the ferry service, nor of stealing the government wharf!

On the way to Fouroumbala we crossed numerous rivers and decided that if the ferries became any smaller we would pick one up and take it along with us. The great Congo forest dwindled away and we entered an open country dotted with small hills, finding Fouroumbala to be beautifully situated near a large river that wound among grass-covered miniature mountains.

On May twenty-seventh we reached Chief Bamba's village. We were now in a wild country of rolling hills with dense woods of scrubby trees every few miles. In the open spaces stood huge ant hills, about twenty feet high, covered with soft green grass.

The natives in this country were of a primitive type. At one place disease was rampant. It was a district of imbeciles, cripples, old men at twenty, and child mothers. Nearly every man and woman was afflicted with goiter, elephantiasis, or some other horrible distortion. Old people stumbled along in pitiable attitudes, their limbs warped out of shape by some malady. These savages wear little or nothing, lie about in the shade, and seem to have no occupation. Their huts are odd, being shaped like inverted funnels and are made of grass.

For days the so-called road had been lined with straggling groves of rubber trees. These people manage to eke out an existence from the small pittances received for the crude rubber. In addition to what few supplies they purchase from the traders, their diet consists of fowls, goats, and yams.

We had been living on an exclusive chicken and egg menu for a long time, so when the first opportunity presented itself I bought a goat, paying its owner more money than he had ever seen before — twenty francs — less than eighty cents!

Toward noon one day we passed an old man and a young woman. The man was carrying a spear while the woman followed behind with a heavy basket on her head. After going a short distance, one of the trucks stopped on account of a gasoline pipe breaking, so we spent a little time there making repairs and having lunch. While the boys were placing the cook's boxes back on the truck, the graybeard and the young girl came walking along. She was carrying the same basket on her head, and also the man's spear, while he had a small bundle wrapped in leaves, cradled in his arms. As he neared us a broad grin overspread his ebon face and at the same time he gently swung his burden to and fro. Stepping up I lifted the leaves, to find beneath a newborn babe. The mother had given it birth since we had passed them a short time before and was now continuing the interrupted journey, while its father, or her father as the case may be, carried the infant.

We had noticed for several days the abundance of children; they were everywhere, of all sizes and both sexes. There is surely no race suicide in the French Congo and the question naturally arises of what will develop in regard to this population in the years to come. The white man prevents tribal warfare and his doctors lessen the death rate. If this condition continues for a few decades, the Dark Continent will be swarming with a black horde.

We were now climbing into a higher altitude, and the nights were somewhat cooler, for which everyone was thankful. Upon leaving the forest behind, we thought our itching and scratching days were past, for the gnats and sand flies had disappeared. Now a small grass fly took their place, doing very well at the task of keeping a person miserable. These pesky insects are so minute that the human eye can hardly detect them, and, being so tiny, the mosquito nets were no barrier. The torture we endured from these winged tormentors confirms my opinion that this will never become a popular tourist route.

Nature balances all things; so, to compensate for these villains of the insect world, she has liberally supplied this tropical land with gorgeous butterflies, with huge, showy moths, with dragon flies that dazzle the eyes, and with multitudes of other harmless and splendid creations.

One evening we camped near a large village which was inclosed by a stockade. The chief sent messengers inviting us to visit the royal hut. Upon arrival, we found him and the other members of the court having a beer-drinking contest, and they insisted upon our sampling the product, which tasted like a mixture of poor vinegar and worse cider. Within the inclosure were grouped the huts belonging to the chief's many wives. These women were all young and must have been selected with great care from the entire tribe, for they were much better looking and seemed a great deal cleaner than any we had previously seen in this district.

During the conversation I casually glanced at my watch, whereupon the chief hurriedly issued some orders. Presently a man came running back with a

large silver watch almost as big as an alarm clock.
When this was given to the king, he placed it in a
pouch suspended from his waist.   At frequent intervals thereafter he would reverently lift this contrivance
forth and gaze upon its handless countenance.   Per-
ceiving that none of us paid any particular attention
to this, he finally passed it to the prime minister, who
gravely placed it to his ear and listened for a few
dramatic moments.   Then with an attitude of supreme
importance he wound up the watch and handed it back
to His Majesty, who, after glancing about the circle
to see if all had been duly impressed, placed it back
into his pocket.   I now requested permission to inspect
this relic, finding it to be nothing but an empty case
with a stem-winder that made a noise like a coffee
grinder!

Later in the evening, with his full court and all
his wives in attendance, the king came to our camp
to listen to the Victrola.   He carefully explained to the
assemblage the phenomenon of the white man's magic
sound box, and to everything he said there was a
regular Hollywood chorus of "yeses" — this boy was
some chief!

Several days' travel brought us to Bangui on the
beautiful Ubangi River, the principal tributary of the
mighty Congo.   This town is a large trading center,
being in touch with the outside world by means of
water transport, and here I had the first opportunity
in a long time to mail letters and films.   Because of
the polyglot mixture of races, white, black, and Arab,
we found it to be an interesting place.   The shops were
glorified five-and-ten-cent stores, where the savage
from the bush, after walking many miles through the

Enormous dugout canoes at Bangui. A comparison with the steamboat "Paris" gives an idea of their size.

Another view of an elephant herd in the Belgian Congo forests.

The grass huts which looked like inverted funnels.

Near Fouroumbala, French Congo.   Notice the covered dugout canoes and
the luxuriant tropical vegetation.

hot sun, spent his few francs on pieces of gaudy cloth,
or on more useful articles, such as enameled pots, pans,
and cups.

Representatives of the Vacuum Oil Company gave
us a royal reception, and I was glad to learn that my
supplies of gasoline and Mobiloil had arrived, for now
we could proceed westward to our next depot. A
young Frenchman invited us to dinner, during which
Joe and Austin got into a heated argument over who
was the best farmer, a Norwegian or a German. The
discussion ended in a tussle, Jones and I having ring-
side seats. Nothing serious happened, except that
they failed to settle the momentous question at issue
— a disappointment from which Jones and I required
several days to recover.

Next day the boat came in with a cargo of gasoline,
dried fish, cement, iron roofing, and wine, and reloaded
with palm oil, palm kernels, and ivory. This small
wood-burning side-paddler makes two trips a month
to connect with the larger boat that plies the Congo.
It presented a unique picture with its piles of wood
covering the decks, with chickens and goats chasing
one another through the passageways, and with bananas
and freshly washed clothes hanging from every possible
protrusion. The neat French captain stood on the
bridge nervously twisting his mustache as he watched
a black man cooking his food on a small fire beneath
the gangplank, and another who was doing some mend-
ing on a portable sewing machine which rested against
the smokestack.

Information proved hard to get here, for most travel
is by water and little is known concerning the roads,
or rather paths, that lead out of the place. We were

told it would be impossible to proceed to Fort Archambault by motor, and that if we did reach that post, there we would surely find the end of the road.

We had heard such predictions before; so, after replenishing our food and gasoline supplies, we shook many hands and acknowledged many *bon voyages*, then, on June first, headed toward Lake Chad.

We stopped at Bogangolo and were delayed at Kabo while some repairs were made to the trucks. We plowed through miles of deep sand and followed faint serpentine trails among heat-stunted trees, but finally managed to locate Fort Archambault, a French military post, which here lies baking in the sun, on the fiery edge of the great, grim desert.

CHAPTER SEVENTEEN

THE STRANGE VILLAGE
OF KIYA BE

FORT ARCHAMBAULT is noted mostly for heat. From near its portals the desert sweeps to the horizon — an ocean of sand, empty and silent except for the gentle murmur of caressing winds. The crocodile-and-snake-infested River Chari, which is here shallow but very wide, flows slowly around the north end of the post, and its other sides are hemmed in by native villages, built within inclosures of grass matting. Back of these frail stockades, as beyond the river, lies the mystery that is Africa.

It is a French administration point and military headquarters set deep in the very heart of Equatorial Africa. There is a large parade ground where black troops step and march to commands in French, while interested wives and concubines sit under shady trees, smoking pipes, laughing and jesting, and sometimes fighting. A few squat buildings of red brick and white plaster, where dirty half-castes barter and sell in the interests of their lords and masters, who are sometimes their fathers as well, are clustered near the barracks.

Cool and neat bungalows nestle in wonderful gardens behind brick walls that hide them from easy view. There are wide sandy avenues lined with rows of flamboyant trees and another species which I named the

Rhino Horn Tree, because of the short protrusions
resembling miniature horns which covered the trunks,
reminding me of the weapons sported by the great
pachyderms of the thorn thickets.

The kindly French Commandant gave us a comfortable bungalow in which to live. It was surrounded by
a garden containing many rare and wonderful tropical
trees. A high wall inclosed this entire establishment,
which had been the Commandant's residence until a
short time previously, when a new and more pretentious place was provided.

Across the avenue stood the large native hospital
where a young Russian doctor, now serving under the
French flag, did his best to check the avalanche of
disease that ever flowed toward his gates. On the day
following our occupancy of the bungalow, I was seated
on the broad veranda pounding on my trusty typewriter when I noticed four husky black men, bearing
a crudely made litter, enter the doorway to the hospital. Behind them walked other boys carrying on
top of their heads a white man's kit. Calling to our
pishi, Ali, whose knowledge of Arabic was now serving
us well, I strolled over and watched as the ebon male
nurses lifted from the litter what had once been a
robust Frenchman, but who was now only folds of
yellowish skin over protruding bones. An intense
black beard and deep-sunken eyes gave this man an
unearthly appearance, but the suffering that his thin
body and burning eyes bespoke is impossible to describe. The doctor injected quinine; then, although
very weak from the fever, the Frenchman attempted
to tell us of his adventures, but the Russian would
not allow it.

Belgian Congo. The lady with the envied profile.

Some tribes on the Congo bind the heads of their children.

A primitive woman of the French Congo. Her entire kitchen equipment is shown in the photograph.

Dugout canoes on the River Chari, near Fort Archambault.

The author visits the chief of the Wasara, a tribe of giants living in the French Congo near the Sara River. The scars on the faces of these men are charms.

Two days later, I paid a visit to this man and found him much improved. In very good English he told me of joining two other white men who were seeking wild-animal pictures. One of them was an ex-officer of the former Kaiser, who had fled Germany after the World War and here sought an outlet for his adventurous spirit, and the other was a young German photographer. They had entered the bush from near the village of Kabo, intending to explore the country between the River Ko and the Bahr Sara, where they hoped to find the rare giant eland.

When this work had been completed, they planned to make their way by native dugout canoes down the Bahr Sara to its junction with the Chari, and then, entering the Bahr Salamat a short distance to the north, pole their way upstream to the kraal of Ke, and from there trek overland to the strange village of Kiya Be.

Things had progressed well enough until fever took charge; then the young photographer died, and after his burial the two remaining members had quarreled and separated, the Frenchman making his way toward Fort Archambault. En route he went down with a bad attack of fever, spending several days at an unmarked village until the chief built the litter and sent some of his men with him to the post.

I asked him about this singular place of Kiya Be and what he knew of its queer inhabitants. He had talked to a French officer who led a detachment of Senegalese troops to the village some years past in an attempt to enforce the French prohibition against the horrible disfigurement practiced by the Sara Kyabe women. He described them as resembling broadbilled ducks, having lips as large as dinner plates.

20

One of my objects in coming this way was to film, if possible, these grotesque beak-faced women, so I went to the Commandant to gain his permission and assistance. He told me what he knew about them and estimated the village of Kiya Be to lie about sixty-five miles beyond the river. He cautioned me that it was desert country, that no wheeled vehicle had ever made the journey there, for the sand was deep and water scarce; but when I told him I was very eager to visit the place, he called a messenger and sent orders to a near-by chief, commanding that canoes be lashed together into a raft, so that our trucks could be transported across the Chari.

I left the Commandant's office to find Ali talking in Arabic to a tall man of the desert, who used his hands in an expressive way to emphasize his words. As Ali and I walked toward our bungalow, he confided to me that, according to the Arab, the country was very bad, the people were bad, the food was bad, the water was bad, everything was bad! I replied that I didn't expect the food to improve as long as he did the cooking and was willing to take a chance on everything else.

In spite of Ali Ramazan's deficiencies as a cook, he was my most valuable black man, always willing to undertake any task assigned to him. As his name indicates, he was a follower of the Prophet of Islam, but none of us considered Ali a true believer, for, although he would never eat the flesh of any animal, unless he himself had cut its throat, while saying the prescribed words, still not one of us had ever found him praying, either with his face toward Mecca, or any other direction.

Two days after our friendly chat on the way to the bungalow, his long thin body was sprawled half buried in mud and water, while he struggled to chop away some planks that prevented us from getting the truck out of the river in which it was partly submerged. We had been working here for hours under the rays of a red-hot sun in a vain attempt to get the truck back on hard ground. Jones and I were exhausted, but Ali kept chopping away, while we watched with rifles ready for the slinking crocodiles that craved this thin morsel from the flock of Mohammed.

The Chari River was crossed without any great amount of difficulty. The ferry was worse than crude; so we had loaded one truck as lightly as possible, carrying just the absolute necessities, and had left the other in the fort. Miles of plowing through deep sand had then brought us to a narrow tributary where it looked as though we should have to turn back. Some scouting around, however, located a few dugout canoes which were rigged up into what we thought a safe conveyance. We boarded the rickety affair all right and safely crossed the channel, but when I attempted to drive up the other bank, the planks leading from the ferry to the shore broke, allowing the rear of the truck to fall. The wheels were suspended in air and for a second it appeared as if the whole outfit would slide into the water, but the end of the body caught on the ferry, and, while it hung precariously in this position, we hurriedly ran a steel cable from the front bumper to a large tree. I then dispatched our guide for help, and he returned in about an hour with forty natives, but in spite of all their tugging on a big rope, the truck would not budge.

Jones then discovered that the body was wedged
tightly by the broken planks, and it took hours to remove these. When Ali finally emerged from beneath
the truck with the chopping task completed, I told the
guide to round up our black army. He began shouting
at them as if they were miles away instead of right
under his nose, for it seems to be the approved thing
in this country to shout at the top of your voice whenever possible. With forty black giants and giantesses
lined along the ninety-foot rope, I gave a signal and
they a mighty pull, shifting the truck forward about
three feet, whereupon Jones took up the slack on the
cable. By this slow method we managed to get the
rear wheels on solid earth once again.

So ended the episode of the sunken ferry, excepting
that a gasoline feed pipe was torn away, which kept
us in this inferno of heat for another hour or so. When
we did get under way again, it surely was a relief to
feel the cool breeze in our faces as we drove along.
Speed soon became impossible, however, for we now
entered the desert, and as the sand became deeper we
shifted down a gear at a time until there was none
lower, then pulled along for hours at a snail's pace, with
hardly enough power to spare to climb a molehill.

We were constantly stopping to put in gasoline and
water. With that fiery orb hanging over our heads,
and the heat from the sand coming up to meet us, it
seemed at times as though the melting point had been
reached, both for the motor and for ourselves. We
passed near many villages surrounded by walls of
grass matting. Inside the inclosures were cone-shaped
huts and small grain-storage huts, all arranged facing
toward the center. Special stockades of strong wood-

work were observed in each village. These were to contain the live stock at night, for although lions are scarce about here, those that do exist become very bold, while the leopards are both numerous and destructive. Hardly a night passes but some unfortunate goat or sheep falls a victim to these spotted cats.

These people are real raw savages, knowing little of the white man and nothing of the world beyond the River Chari. As we passed, the entire population of the villages would come out to gaze in wonder at the fearsome and snorting animal. The men would salute and stand awkwardly as if uncertain whether to prostrate themselves before this strange thing or to run. The women were absolutely naked and stood there quite unabashed, with astonishment written all over their faces. Children are the same the world over, and these boys and girls yelled in glee, shouted and waved, while some of the bolder ones ran alongside the truck until they were called back by frightened mothers.

Among these natives I noticed individuals who were very tall, some that had fine features with thin lips. The younger women especially were not only possessors of wonderful bodies, but many of them had a bearing and classical features of which any prize beauty of the white race might well be proud.

Unfortunately most of these people of both sexes had disfigured their faces. The skin had been cut and earth worked underneath until it caused odd-shaped blisters. There were regular designs, those of the men differing from those of the women, while the figures of the younger generation seemed to follow a more elaborate pattern than that found among the older people.

Along this trail of sand and dancing heat waves, we encountered these villages of primitive life, where we would stop for a cooling drink of water drawn from deep wells and kept in earthen jars. Then we would again plow along in low gear, deeper and deeper into the silence of the endless waste.

This was not yet the true desert, for we were some of the time in groves of stunted trees, where often a buck would start up at our approach, while always thousands of guinea fowl ran noisily from us, or with a mighty whirring of wings take to the air for a short flight. My shotgun came in handy here and it was not long until we had plenty of these game birds stuck away in the cook's box. Ali asked me if I preferred fried kanga — guinea fowl — for breakfast, or would I have it curried? I told him I would much rather have it shredded and served with sugar and cream!

It was many hours after sunset when our guide finally pointed to a cluster of fires that blinked afar and stated that there was the village of Kiya Be. With the aid of the headlights and a lantern our boys made us comfortable in a large hut, while the cook busied himself getting something ready for us to eat. Black bodies are hard to see on a black night, but our sense of smell told us that we were encircled by a curious group, and shortly the noise made it evident that the crowd was growing. As we sat down to eat they closed right in upon us. This proximity was not very appetizing, but it would not have been wise to order them away.

After the meal, the chief arrived with his lesser chiefs, whereupon I called Ali to find if his knowledge of Arabic would help us. It did, for the chief himself

talked Arabic, as did some of his men.   Greetings
were exchanged, and then I told them of our friendly
mission, simply that we wished to visit with them for
a few days, watch them dance, and talk to the women
who carried the disks in their lips.

It was of no use to explain we wanted to photograph
them, for they know nothing of pictures, and without
doubt if they had been shown a reproduction of themselves, it would have caused trouble.   When dealing
with primitive people who have no knowledge of
photography, I always remember what nearly happened
to me on the island of Zanzibar, when a huge Negro
tried to cleave me in two pieces with a big banana
knife, because he said I had stolen his spirit from his
body to carry away with me.   It was only because of
quick action on the part of my boys that I was able
to save my own body to carry away.

During the conversation I learned from the chief
of what had happened to the German of whom the
Frenchman spoke.   He had been killed by crocodiles
while bathing in the river near the village of Balbedjia.
A horseman had brought the news two days before.
Crocodiles were very bad in all these streams and had
killed many people, said the chief.

After the morning sun had peeped over the horizon
we had a chance to survey our surroundings, finding
that Kiya Be was really a cluster of several villages,
with one very large inclosure in the center.   This odd
place was a fort.   The square was constructed of
double rows of matting, through which no arrow or
spear could penetrate.   Inside the wall stood a large
building of red earth of about two-and-a-half stories
high, with two towers joined together by a passageway.

In both turrets were loopholes that looked like eyes, while the top of each was covered with a plaited grass roof that resembled nothing so much as a Chinese hat. Within the walls were also many small food-storage huts and a well of clear water.

Never before had any of us found such a queer place, with such a strange medley of people. There walked a tall man of over seven feet, naked except for a string of leopard claws about his neck. There stood medium-sized men wearing loin cloths and armed with long spears, while others wore the long flowing robes of the Arab. Naked women and children strolled about, or carried bundles or jars on their heads, while sheep, goats, dogs, and a few beautiful horses mixed with the scene. Men and women sat or stood beneath the scattered trees, or walked slowly from one shady spot to another through the white heat.

An oppressive silence hung over this village, where things seemed to move like shapes in a dream. The whole setting gave me a creepy feeling, while the burning, blistering heat made it easy to imagine that this was the region of the damned, especially when a line of old women — dried up and bent — slowly passed in parade before us. They were the disk women, strange creatures that looked like nothing belonging on this earth.

It is hard to describe these women except to say that they are repulsive and yet command your sympathy. Both the upper and the lower lip are distended to a seemingly impossible size. The lower is usually the larger, some of them being a good eight inches across the wooden plate around which the flesh of the lip is stretched, so that from the side they look like a broad-

Village of Kiya Be, French Congo. Scene inside the outer wall, showing a group of lip-women and younger girls around the native orchestra.

Women of the Sara Kyabe. The practice of distending the lips originated in an attempt to prevent the slave hunters from taking the women, their good looks making them too attractive to the slave traders.

French Congo. Two marvels of Kiya Be. These women look like nothing on earth and are repulsive to say the least, but it is only when the disks are removed that the real savagery of the thing is apparent, for once the lips are exposed, the view is most disgusting. Some of the disks worn by these women are a good eight inches across. The weight of the disks makes the wearers walk in a stooping posture and prevents them from talking or eating well.

En route to the village of Kiya Be the party nearly lost this truck which fell into the channel.

This youth tried to swap his pet hyena and marabou stork for a wife.

388

billed duck.   One thing is sure; they look much better with the disks in place than without them, for when the saucers are removed and the distorted face exposed to view, then the real savagery of the practice is fully apparent.

Using Ali as an interpreter, I found that the neighboring tribes who scarred their faces did so in early childhood when they were taken through the rites of devil worship.   With them it was a religion and had not been brought about by any necessity, but the Sara Kyabe commenced the practice of inserting disks in the lips of their women as part of a plan to save the tribe from extermination.   Now that the need has passed, they continue this disfigurement because it has become an old-established custom, and is now considered a mark of prestige.   No woman can hope to attain any prominence unless she sports a pair of saucer-lips, and the larger her adornments, the higher her social standing.   It is a case where beauty much adorned is beauty adorned the least, for without these disks the Sara Kyabe are the finest looking black women in their part of Africa, and behind this fact lies the reason for all the woes of the clan.   In the days of slave raiding, when Arab bands swept out of the desert in their quest for "black ivory," they never failed to call upon the Sara Kyabe, because, on account of their exceptional beauty, these women brought the highest prices on the slave markets.   The product eventually became so scarce that even the girl babies were taken to be brought up by the Arab women until old enough to sell.   In the raids upon their villages, many of the men were slain, so between this killing of the defenders and the stealing of women,

the tribe was nearly wiped out.   How long this reign
of terror continued is impossible to say, but finally
the tribe built this central fort, around which the many
scattered villages were collected.   When the marauders
came out of the sands, the people would retire within
its protecting walls where they were able to withstand
the Arab assaults.   But further to discourage the
slave hunters of their desire for Sara Kyabe women,
they instituted the practice of disfigurement.

Although slavery still exists in Africa, there are no
more slave raids, and the French government is doing
its utmost to stamp out this custom of the disks, as
well as the devil worship among the neighboring tribes.
The undertaking is a gigantic one, but, after all, it is
only one of the millions of problems which the white
man must overcome if he wishes to conquer the vast
continent of Africa.

These black women all smoke some sort of pipe, but
to watch the disked ones try to enjoy a smoke would
cause a wooden Indian to laugh.   Not only is it hard
for them to handle a pipe, but impossible for them to
talk or eat naturally.   They are always slobbering,
and walk with their heads down as if in shame; the
weight of the disks, of course, causing this.   Their
facial expression is that of a dumb animal which has
been wounded and wonders what it is all about.

We were plentifully supplied, during our stay, with
chickens and eggs, these folk proving in many ways
to be more hospitable than most.   This may have
been due to the fact of their few contacts with out-
siders, many of them never before having looked upon
white faces.   My experience indicates that the raw
savage found in the bush is quite a nice fellow, seldom

causing trouble, but that those found near the towns have taken on all of the white man's vices and none of his virtues, with a result that is far from pleasing.

On the early morning of June seventh we started to retrace our wheel tracks to Fort Archambault, leaving the village just after dawn, before the heat waves had commenced their dance. The difficulties of the return journey were not great, but we experienced one near catastrophe when we underestimated the number of dugout canoes needed to support the loaded truck. Upon pushing our rustic ferry away from the bank, it began to fill with water, requiring some quick work on our part to prevent the outfit from sinking with all on board. It seemed funny afterwards, but at the time was anything else, for all the valuable equipment of the expedition would probably have been lost.

My last remembrance of the strange village of Kiya Be was of a group of disked women, with heads bent low, plodding slowly through the dazzling heat toward the queer fort that stared so grimly through its port-hole eyes into the vastness and ominous silence of the great Sahara.

CHAPTER EIGHTEEN

PLATEAU OF THE PAGANS

AFTER several days of heartbreaking toil, during which time the expedition experienced its worst hours in Africa, we arrived at Bousso. Here, in a large comfortable hut that overlooked the broad River Chari, with a cool breeze blowing away the insect pests and bringing relief from the stifling heat, I could relax for a while; but in retrospect I endured again those memorable days of struggle beneath the scorching rays of a fierce sun as we had gradually fought our way here from Fort Archambault. We were now four thousand one hundred sixty-three miles from our starting point at Mombasa, but still some thirteen hundred miles from Lagos, and I wondered what fate awaited us along the road to the Slave Coast.

At Fort Archambault the Commandant had arranged some scenes for our camera. We photographed natives spinning and weaving cloth and others who gave us primitive syncopation on crude instruments— a sample of original and pure jazz. The orchestra consisted of drums, a contrivance resembling a marimba, and several flutes, each pitched in a different key. We filmed a young swain of the village in his attempts to trade a pet hyena and a marabou stork for a lovely bride, and we paid a visit to the location where over two thousand men were clearing the jungle and preparing the ground for a landing field.

We had found a few of the Wasara giants, members of a tribe where every man towers nearly seven feet in height. My original plan was to visit their villages along the Sara River, but lack of time prevented; so I contented myself by gathering at one point those who were scattered among the other natives around the fort. They proved to be an interesting people, practicing devil worship similar to the tribes adjacent to the Sara Kyabe and scarring their faces in a [like fashion.

During our hundred-mile trek from Fort Archambault to Miltou, the trucks had barely moved mile after weary mile through deep sand. We had become lost in blind ends to the paths, and had followed the river, hoping to arrive at some landmark, only to get bogged down in a reeking fever swamp where the mosquitoes nearly ate us alive.

One night, while attempting to reach a village, we repeatedly ran into deep mudholes. After one particularly bad stretch of marsh, we had attained hard ground and thought that all would be fair sailing for a while, but had only gone a few hundred yards when both trucks became mired good and fast. Worn out by hours of continuous toil, we sought rest by camping on the spot. Immediately black clouds of mosquitoes swarmed in to greet us, and during the night their singing outside the net kept me awake. The buzzing of their billions of wings made a sound resembling a distant waterfall. While listening to this fearful refrain, I heard lions roar and hyenas howl, and wondered what they would look like running around in little cages made of netting. I felt sorry for the lions — and sympathy for the mosquitoes that bit the hyenas!

We started the day's work by digging the trucks from the mudholes, then alternated our time between building corduroy roads over morasses and pulling through the sandy stretches between. This blistering day of struggle netted us fifty-eight miles forward, bringing us to the native village opposite Bousso before nightfall.

Game had been scarce for a long time, and my four black boys were constantly complaining about the food, saying they wanted meat and posho, although they knew that posho was unobtainable in this country. They were homesick and became both lazy and sulky. This trek was no picnic; in fact, quite a different sort of safari than one into the game fields of East Africa, where work is comparatively easy and game plentiful.

While camp was being made, Jones and I sallied forth to look for much-needed meat, not only to silence the grumblings of the boys, but to satisfy our own longing for a change of diet. In a little valley near the village we discovered a few small herds of antelope, and, after a long, laborious stalk, each secured a buck. There was joy and feasting in camp that evening.

In the middle of the night I was awakened by an unusual noise, and walking to the trucks, I turned on a spotlight to investigate. Its beam disclosed three lions standing within twenty feet of our beds! There were no firearms on the trucks and I did not feel like returning toward the lions in order to reach the rifle leaning against my cot. Neither did I think it wise to disturb my sleeping companions, knowing that lions are liable to attack a suddenly moving object.

Noticing that the bright light annoyed them, I continued to direct it into their big yellow eyes until, becoming provoked at my attentions, they trotted away. In the morning I learned from the local chief that these three cats were professional man-eaters who had been prowling around the villages of the district for many months.

We had been advised to follow this side of the river, but when three days of work in the deadly heat, with insects almost driving us mad, only carried us forward six miles, we decided to try the other side. After digging out of one mudhole, only to fall into another, the third night had found us nearly buried in a quagmire, with miles of swamp stretching ahead of us. Our enforced camp was in a veritable pesthole where clouds of bloodthirsty mosquitoes, assisted by armies of ravenous gnats that flew right through the nets, made the night miserable. In the morning we were covered with white blisters that burned and itched. As we jumped about in a vain attempt to keep the merciless insects away while we swallowed our breakfast, it was unanimously agreed that here was the very fringe of hell itself.

Joe and I scouted ahead to see if the road was passable, finding it was not. The swamp extended as far as we could see from the highest eminence. During our absence, Jones had managed to get the trucks on to dry ground, only to discover that one of them had developed a loss of power, due to a short circuit which he could not locate. Leaving him and Austin behind, Pedley and I returned to the village, where we left our truck, and, securing a canoe, crossed the river to Bousso.

There were no white men at this remote post, but
a native in charge who spoke French. When he
proudly informed us there was a telegraph line running to Fort Lamy, I immediately prepared a telegram to the governor, inquiring about the best way
to get through. When I proffered it for sending,
however, this man shrugged his shoulders and said the
wire would not work; that he didn't know why, but
he did know that his ticker had ceased to tick a long
time ago!

Joe and I gained some information about the terrain on this side of the river, coming to the conclusion
that our only hope lay in attempting to reach Fort
Lamy via Massenya. This made it necessary to transport the trucks across the river, so our ex-telegrapher
sent messengers forth with instructions to bring in a
small army of helpers and enough dugout canoes to
construct a raft. He then led us to a hut perched
high on the river bank, and now, two clean-looking
black boys, dressed in spotless white, brought us a
real treat in the way of a meal, consisting of two kinds
of green vegetables, excellently seasoned meat, and a
gallon jar of fresh sweet milk. Everything was well
served, and we learned that both these boys had been
trained in the household of the governor at Fort
Lamy. During this repast a sudden thundershower
cooled the atmosphere, but enjoyment of it was tempered by the knowledge that every drop of rain made
our progress westward more difficult.

At daylight, while crossing the river on the way to
the trucks, I shot a huge crocodile. When the bullet
struck, he jumped for deep water, but died before
reaching it. These reptiles are exceptionally savage

Crossing the River Chari, at Bousso, on a raft of dugout canoes.

The native orchestra which rendered original and pure jazz.

Camel caravan leaving the village of Mai Ache.   This gives a striking example
of ancient versus modern transportation.

A view of Fort Lamy from the River Chari.   The party's stay was cut
short by the approach of heavy rains.

in this region, taking a large toll from the black population every year. The natives will not even place their hands in the water, only bathing in the very shallow pools near the shore while others stand on guard. The crocodile undoubtedly causes at least as many deaths as any other African killer. A game warden in Tanganyika shot a large crocodile, and, having its stomach cut open, made a list of the contents, his record of items being as follows: three spinal columns, fourteen arm and leg bones, eleven brass arm rings, three coiled-wire armlets, a glass-bead necklace, a few stones of various sizes, a length of fiber cord and a quantity of undigested porcupine quills.

With our small army marching ahead of the truck, we proceeded to the relief of Jones and Austin at Camp Miserable. Upon arrival, we loaded the greater part of the equipment on the heads of these porters and the balance into our truck, and retreated from the Battle of the Swamp. Jones sat grimly at the wheel as his truck back-fired its way to the village, and, hearing this uneartly commotion, the entire population rushed out like New Yorkers running to get a view of passing fire apparatus. Strange to say, however, all this rumpus failed to frighten several herds of antelope and a flock of spur-winged geese which we passed near the swamp. I shot one of the geese with my 7 mm., it proving to be a huge bird of greenish color, with red spots on its head. At each wing elbow protruded a cruel hook similar to the spur on a bantam rooster.

The crossing of the river presented a real problem, and we only averted calamity by a small margin. We

21

made three trips, one with the equipment and one each with an empty truck. I sailed with the last load, amusing myself on the slow journey by shooting at crocodile heads. These reptiles swim along near the surface, with their knobby eyes protruding, and after a little practice, I was able to sink one with a single shot. Every time a bullet struck, the boys shouted with glee, for each of them had probably lost some near relative to these flesh eaters of the Chari.

After leaving Bousso, we found the country to be mostly sand, but managed to creep along, trekking over a landscape as wild and far away from the world as any man could wish to find. The heavy pulling caused the trucks to heat up until they would start firing ahead of time and stop. During these bitter days I was thankful we had brought a plentiful supply of good lubricating oil, for a burned-out bearing or scored cylinder at this time would have been a calamity, the consequences of which no one could foretell. The dwindling supply of gasoline worried me, for we had not anticipated pulling for days at a time in low gear, and, even if we should reach Fort Lamy, I had no means of knowing whether gasoline would be available there or not, my next depot being Maidugari.

One evening we camped near a small village, and after dinner I paced up and down in front of the huts until Joe threatened to hog-tie me. There was plenty to worry about, and I found it easier to think after the sun went down, being especially good at this while walking under the stars. I tried to plan a way to bring the work to a successful close and get out of the country as quickly as possible. My three companions were commencing to get along like a bunch of strange dogs, while the black boys continued their complaints about the food and the fact that we were always moving westward, and I was not feeling exceptionally fit myself. The morale of the crew was hard to keep at par, not due to any particular fault of theirs, but because no human being could go through all we had endured without feeling the strain both physically and mentally.

In addition to these things, I knew that another battle awaited me across the Atlantic. There was no way of knowing how the movie-going public would react to my completed picture. I only knew they were fickle in selecting entertainment. If I could have looked into the future and have known I was to meet Mr. Walter A. Futter, a motion picture producer of New York and Hollywood, this phase of the problem would have given me small concern, for his genius was to manifest itself in the compiling of my material. He was destined to be the first to see its dramatic and thrilling screen possibilities, and by using his remarkable knowledge of showmanship, he was to rearrange a few sequences in such a way as to mold the whole into a sensational film, without the building of thrills in any way lessening its educational value.

We had a difficult time getting started next morning, the trucks having sunk into the deep sand, but finally got them rolling, and after a few miles in low gear, ran on to hard ground, where once again we sailed merrily onward in high. We were traveling over dried-up swamp land, now an excellent road, but one which would become a bottomless morass with the first heavy rain. While speeding along, the leading truck suddenly pitched into a soft spot up to the chassis.

In trying to pull it out with a rope, the other truck dug below the hard surface, becoming hopelessly mired. So it went, day after day, alternating mud and sand, hope and despair, seemingly without end.

While crossing one dazzling expanse of desert, we saw what we thought to be a mirage. It appeared as if an automobile were approaching, but we didn't believe it. Some time later, however, we found a parked car in which a black boy reclined. He told us in French that two white masters were in a near-by hut having their midday meal; so, without further ado, we joined them. One proved to be a French captain of aviation, who, with a doctor companion, was making a tour of survey. He didn't say what for and we weren't particularly interested, because, as Joe remarked, if they were contemplating a paved highway, it would be constructed too late to do us any good. I suspect, however, his visit had something to do with airplane landing fields, for the intention of the French government is to establish regular air lines here, the only logical way to solve the transportation problems of this far-flung empire. Our meeting was one of mutual advantage, for after lunch and a glass of wine, during which we swapped information, they were able to follow our wheel tracks toward Bousso, while we used theirs as a guide to Fort Lamy, and the fact that these tracks marked the way gave us renewed courage.

Toward evening, as we rounded a curve into a little vale, a large leopard sprang out of the short grass, but was gone before anyone had a chance to fire a shot. He was stalking a herd of hartebeest or a group of water buck which were standing near by. For days

His Excellency, the Governor at Fort Lamy, bidding the author good-by after playing the hospitable host.

The baby elephant found at a small village in the French Congo. The chief asked $25 for him.

The Emir of Dikoa himself.

View of the truck mired in the swamp from which it was rescued by the Emir of Dikoa.

we had been passing through clouds of guinea fowl, but now they were becoming so thick as to constitute a nuisance.   At dinner that night, Austin outlined a plan he had perfected for a guinea-fowl canning factory.   Jones wanted to know where he would get the cans and other necessary items, and suggested that swarms of the birds be driven with airplanes to factories along the seacoast.

Late one afternoon we were surprised to find ourselves approaching a large settlement, which proved to be the town of Massenya, boasting five Frenchmen and one Frenchwoman.   We had dinner that night with the administrator and breakfast the next morning with a young doctor and his wife, the first white couple we had seen since leaving the mission on the edge of the Ituri Forest.

Trouble rode with us all the way from Massenya to Fort Lamy, but a few things of interest varied the monotony of our struggles over desert sands and through swamps.   We came to a village where the Emir tried to sell us a baby elephant, the price being reasonable enough — about twenty-five dollars — but we were hundreds of miles from the coast and had no way of supplying it with the proper food.   We passed through Mai Ache, the farthermost outpost of the camel patrol, an Arabian style village, teeming with horses and camels, all adorned with brightly-colored trappings.

Jones had ridden with me as a passenger for a while and told me of his seafaring life; that this was his first land cruise, and I had suggested the title for a book — "An Able Seaman's Cruise across Africa in the Good Ship 'Constant Grief'."   Later Pedley told me of his former close association with Lord Kitchener — of how he had carried a precious dispatch, sealed in a small silver tube placed in his eardrum, through enemy lines. The locale was India — it was a dangerous mission — the fate of an army depended upon him — his hairbreadth escapes were many! He fought his way through regiments single-handed, but finally delivered the message which ultimately gave the control of India to England. He received many medals for this — the one he showed me attesting to his ability as an expert marksman.

So the hours melted into days, each of which presented its problems and hardships, but always we moved forward. We hurriedly left one village in the midst of our evening meal, when loud peals of thunder warned us that we might be stranded there for weary months. We raced ahead of a storm which threatened to bar our way, and by sheer good luck rolled into the outskirts of Fort Lamy, less than an hour before it deluged the countryside.

In the morning I went to pay my respects to Lieutenant Governor Buhot-Launay, finding him to be a pleasant French gentleman. Knowing that we were coming, he had hoped we could remain for some time and visit Lake Chad, where there were many interesting things to picture, but now he advised against staying any longer than necessary, because the heavy rains would soon transform the surrounding country into a vast shallow lake, making it impossible for us to reach the coast. Even one good rain would make the way impassable, not only for motor trucks but for horses and camels, thus marooning us until the next dry season; so the Governor said it was either a case of moving *tout de suite* or remaining as his guests for three months or more.

This would not have been a hardship if the dinner he tendered us that night were a criterion. It was a regular banquet, with champagne and several other kinds of wine. We marveled at the ability of these Frenchmen to have such excellent food in these out-of-the-way places, and I doubt if any member of my party will ever forget this dinnner, or how very kind the Governor and his aides were to us at Fort Lamy.

I might add that we all attended this banquet in our safari outfits, I being the worst tramp of the lot, for most of my clothes were in Nairobi and my safari kit had been reduced to practically nothing. What I wore was sadly in need of washing, but we had been moving so fast lately — or rather had been putting in so much of our time trying to move, that there had been no opportunity to have washing done, and, strange to say, I had not seen a barber shop for over three thousand miles!

Next day, as a guest of the Governor, I was driven to all the interesting places in and around Fort Lamy. This district would hardly appeal to tourists, nor will it ever become a popular summer resort, for this was the beginning of the cool season, with the thermometer indicating ninety-six degrees Fahrenheit. In May, before the rains lowered the temperature from one hundred thirty degrees or more, the Governor said that woodwork exposed to the sun felt like red-hot iron.

The town is divided into three sections, one part being the Arab quarters, one the Negro location, while the white officials and traders live grouped along the river. The native market was crowded with humans and swarming with flies. Dirty Negroes, men and women, squatted around little heaps of millet, dried fish, peanuts, and other native viands, while miscellaneous bottles holding mysterious mixtures were displayed for sale. The hut-wives were wending their way among these stall-keepers, arguing and making as much fuss over a penny's worth of dried shark as a civilized woman would do over her Christmas turkey.

There were three general stores, and to these I went searching for supplies. Everything is transported into this place by camelback or in ox wagons, so I discovered that prices were slightly higher than at home; flour being twenty cents a pound and sugar forty cents for the same amount. I found one ten-gallon drum of gasoline, which, after considerable bargaining, I was able to buy for the reasonable sum of twenty-two dollars! The Governor supplemented this with a loan of thirty gallons from the government store, which I was to return by camelback from Maidugari.

At two o'clock on the next afternoon, the trucks were placed aboard a ferry which His Excellency had kindly provided, and when we had bidden him and his staff good-by, the motor boat pulled us toward the western bank. On the way across, the Frenchman who was guiding the boat pointed to the sky, and, speaking rapidly in his native tongue, delivered an oration containing many "toot sweets." He was right — we would have to hurry, for black clouds and flashes of lightning threatened us from three directions. We decided to drive all night in order to cross the dangerous ground between us and Maidugari.

For the first fifty miles we kept ahead of the storm, but after dark the trucks began slipping and sliding around. It was evident that a heavy rain had fallen just ahead of us, so we stopped to put on chains, then continued onward until the second truck sank into a sand pit in the bottom of a river bed. It required three hours to dig out of this place, during which time some passing natives informed us there was a large village two days' foot safari westward. In high hopes of reaching this place by morning we again started, but after traveling about fifteen miles through sticky mud, my truck dropped into a deep hole. It was possible to spin all wheels by hand and two hours of strenuous labor failed to help matters; so once again, between midnight and dawn, we lay down to sleep in a cheerful swamp, where we found a large colony of mosquitoes, every member of which was at home. We had recently armed ourselves with a supply of citronella oil, which the trader guaranteed would keep a mosquito at his proper distance, but we must have secured the wrong brand, for their songs of glee had never been so jubilant as upon this occasion.

The mosquitoes made sleep impossible, so before daylight, Joe set out on foot to summon help. Some hours later, as I was walking around in an attempt to evade the mosquitoes and reflecting with considerable bitterness on the vicissitudes that had beset our trucks for the last few weeks, I heard the strains of martial music swelling on the morning air. Presently came the occasional neigh of a horse, then the sound of hoofs on the trail, and soon the throbbing of drums and the shrilling of fifes — or whatever they were — making a sound resembling the skirl of Scottish pipes.

As the tumult increased, I beheld a cavalcade approaching, under the leadership of Joe. It was our relief from the village of Dikoa and I am sure not even the beleaguered British at Lucknow received their rescuers with greater joy.

Right handsomely had the Emir of the village responded to our appeal for assistance. He had called out the army — and the navy — and himself rode at its head. Mounted and afoot, the relief expedition marched, the Emir astride a beautiful black horse, caparisoned in trappings of gold and silver. The dusky monarch himself was attired in flowing robes of purple-and-blue silk, elaborately gold-braided and hung with jewels. He was a colorful, indeed gorgeous, figure, but quite matter-of-fact regarding the business at hand. At a word from him, the army halted, the natives surrounded the bogged truck, and, while the band tooted away for dear life, the husky blacks lifted the truck bodily and placed it on dry land.

Amid wild shouts and good-natured banter we were escorted to the village, a pretentious place of ornate mud houses of Arabian architecture. A high wall encircled the town and we halted at the main gate, where the Emir rode up to me and gravely shook hands. I bade good-by to this African potentate with a real feeling of gratitude.

For a few miles after leaving the village, we motored over sand which had been hardened by the rains, but twenty miles before reaching Maidugari, we arrived at the edge of what looked like a lake, into which the wheel tracks disappeared. After a consultation we came to the conclusion that the road must run through this pond, and nothing remained but to try our luck. If

the trucks sank here it would be their last sinking
spell and we would have to swim from then on.   This
proved to be an occasion where things appeared worse
than they really were, because the ground beneath the
water was hard sand and held the weight of the trucks
very nicely.   The pond averaged about a foot in
depth and, as we sped along, the trucks threw water
like a racing motor boat.

For days we had been in a district teeming with
wild ducks, geese, and other species of waterfowl.
Every pond, no matter how small, was thickly covered
with them, and we could always look into the sky and
see wedged-shaped flocks in flight.   It was indeed a
paradise for the bird shooter, but would be quite difficult for the week-end sportsman to reach.

When passing through the drier parts of the region,
we encountered a few antelope, resembling Thompson's
gazelles, and numerous troops of monkeys; one a
large, black-faced species and the other a brick-red,
medium-sized animal, and, after leaving Dikoa, we
observed many thousands of the beautiful golden-
crested cranes.

After hours of splashing through this shallow lake,
we gradually ascended to higher ground, and shortly
thereafter stopped in front of a large house in Maidugari.   We selected this place for our first call because
from a tall flagpole in front, the Union Jack fluttered
to the breeze.   It was the home of the English Resident, who administered this section of Nigeria.

When my homesick black boys looked upon the
British flag, grins spread from one ear to the other,
for they thought we had completely encircled the
globe and had arrived back in Kenya Colony!   They

were further assured when two blacks dressed in the familiar kanzu came out and greeted me in Swahili. However, when these boys explained that they had served in a Nigerian regiment which fought in the East African campaign of the late war, and told how long it had taken them to get there and back, my boys were nearly heartbroken.

The Resident greeted our party in a most friendly manner, and upon learning we had driven all the way from Mombasa, heartily congratulated us on accomplishing the feat, then insisted that we have sundowners and dinner with him. It seemed we were alternating our nights by sleeping in swamps between banquets, and I wondered how long it would be until the next swamp night.

The Vacuum Oil Company had our supplies awaiting us, and, after arranging with their agent for the return of the borrowed gasoline to Fort Lamy, we restocked and headed westward toward Jos. Ill luck still attended us and trouble with the clutch on one truck delayed the expedition for two days, but in spite of this and the fact that Jones was unable to shift gears on his truck, we managed to move forward, thankful that the road was smooth and free of mudholes.

After passing through Putuskum and Bauchi we climbed upwards, gradually gaining altitude until we had reached the sky-land of Nigeria, a region lying between three and four thousand feet above sea level, the far-famed Plateau of the Pagans.

Dismal Camp, between Jos and Rahamma.

The tin mine near Jos, where Jones borrowed a lathe.

A scene in the native market in Jos. Here, amid flies and filth, a mixed population haggles over their household supplies.

One of the trucks mired in a swamp.

CHAPTER NINETEEN

FAREWELL TO AFRICA

MY three days in the hospital at Jos allowed me an opportunity to think over past adventures and to plan the last leg of the journey to Lagos. The expedition had reached the town on June twenty-fifth and I had entered the hospital on July third. Jones was at a tin mine trying to manufacture a truck axle from discarded scraps and Joe and Austin were marooned at Dismal Camp.

Jos is romantically situated among high hills on the Pagan Plateau. It is the center of a large tin-mining area and a seat of government for northern Nigeria. It maintains a sizeable white population and boasts of many good stores and supply houses. A branch railroad connects it with the main line that runs from Kano to Lagos.

Nigeria is the land of the Hausa, the Fulani, the Pagan, and numerous other tribes ranging from pure negroid to those in which Berber blood predominates. Here Great Britain is engaged in the tremendous task of supervising nineteen million blacks in their struggle toward civilization. The entire white population of Nigeria, a territory comprising three hundred thirty-five thousand seven hundred square miles, is less than six thousand, which includes not only British officials but individuals engaged in private enterprises of all sorts. The government policy is "Nigeria for the black

415

man — let him work out his own destiny under the supervision of as few white men as practical." We found the natives employed in every kind of industry and profession, and they seemed to get things done somehow.

The plateau is the home of the Pagan and his rights in the land are protected by the British government, it not being possible for any outsider, white or black, to purchase land. Even in the town of Jos, the buildings are standing on sites which have been leased and cannot be bought. The Fulani and Hausamen were brought into this part of Nigeria by the white man, and now have a firm footing as traders and work-men, clerks and servants. The Borroroje, or Bush Fulani, has become the cattle and stock owner of the highlands, while the better class, the Filanen-Gidda and the Hausamen, are to be found in towns and settlements acting as servants and performing all those multitudes of tasks below the white executive.

One striking thing in West Africa is the attitude of the natives toward the white man, for, although you find them acting as station masters on the railroad, as postmasters, and holding other responsible positions, with some of them assuming an attitude of equality with the whites, the great majority look upon the European as a superior being. They refer to him as "the lion" and, when he approaches, fall upon their knees, bowing their heads in the dust as he passes. It is their form of salute and no polished Fulani or Hausaman considers it good manners to stand in the presence of a white man, always remaining on his knees during the course of a conversation, only arising when you indicate that the talk is finished. He will never turn his back, but retreats from your presence facing you, bowing as he goes.

We had been entertained the first night by several Englishmen connected with the tin mines and the next evening had dinner with Mr. and Mrs. Walker of the government staff. It was due to Mr. Walker's efforts that we were installed in the old hospital, a ramshackle building, but a palace compared to other places where we had camped. During dinner and afterwards, we had discussed America and Nigeria. Although the usual term of service for a man on the West Coast is eighteen months, followed by a four-to-six-months leave at home, I was interested in the information that stringent regulations were in force concerning the entry of white women and children into Nigeria. It seems that young children cannot enter the country at all and women are not allowed to remain more than a few months. Although many wives accompany their husbands from England to stay for the allotted time, still it means that the man must be separated from his family for the greater part of his life. The salaries are high, but the drain on a person's health is great, and those who spend many years on the West Coast are short-lived after their return home.

During our stay in Jos, pishi made daily trips to the native market, where I am afraid the civilized housewife would find very little to attract her, for, like all of these primitive bartering places, flies and filth were much in evidence. On one occasion I had accompanied pishi and, upon entering a long shed to buy meat, we were pounced upon by all the butchers in the market, each telling me that the other fellow's meat was no good, but that his was very fine food for white men.

Guinea-fowl eggs were on sale forty for a shilling, while the lowly potato was almost worth its weight in gold. Native viands seemed cheap enough and there was a great variety. Many of the Hausamen and Fulani are quite wealthy and these buy European food, even purchasing regulated amounts of wine and other liquors.

The few white women in Jos occasionally visit this market, where it is more than likely they will meet a group of primitive Pagans from the country, neither man nor woman of which will be wearing a stitch of clothing. These naked people, who are found throughout the plateau region, conduct themselves in such manner that no one has ever insisted upon their wearing clothing.

We found that the gum and tobacco addicts of civilization were running a poor second to the marathon masticators of Nigeria. The chewing of kola nuts is a universal habit here, men, women, and children spending their pennies for this fruit which is offered for sale on every hand. The effect of this constant facial exercise is seemingly harmless, although as a spectacle it is no prettier than that afforded by rows of gum and tobacco chewers in the subway train. The kola nut stains the mouth and teeth a deep red, thus destroying the principal beauty of the black man—his double row of gleaming white ivories. For many decades the kola nut has kept the jaws of the native Nigerian busy. It is his favorite indoor and outdoor sport.

The roadside beauty parlors indicated progress. Beneath a shady tree, with a group of children watching proceedings, the operator could be seen fixing her

An outdoor beauty parlor near Jos.

The author bidding old Maniki, his faithful gun bearer, good-by.

The band of the first battalion.

The rank and file of the Nigerian Regiment is composed mostly of Hausa tribesmen. These men make excellent soldiers and have an enviable record.

customer's kinks into a Nigerian wind-blown bob, or maybe rubbing the lady's face with sheep fat to give its black surface a high luster. We could not help admiring the effect, nor will we ever forget our olfactory sensations when approaching close to these sheep-dipped beauties. The practice of anointing the body is usual among African tribes, some of them using animal fats and others fish oil, but most of them employing vegetable oils which they themselves extract.

We soon learned that the natives in this part of Africa were entirely different from any encountered before, speaking a pidgin English which was very amusing, some of their expressions being remarkable. As prevaricators, they easily take the world's championship. At one of the garages I met a boy as black as the ace of spades, posing under the name of "Ford." Upon asking if he were any relation to the famous maker of a well-known car, he replied, "Yes, him my brother!" When I inquired if Mr. Ford knew about the relationship he said, "He write me, I write him, every week. Letter come top-side yesterday!" As my trucks were just about to breathe their swan song, and I was contemplating buying another truck to finish the journey to the coast, I asked this boy if he would use his influence in getting me a reduction. He answered, "Ford truck, him good, way past sardines, me write 'em tonight."

My announced intention of continuing the trek to Lagos by motor had received very little encouragement, practically everyone saying it was hopeless because of the many tributaries of the Niger which were now in flood. Past observations had taught me that most obstacles were mental; so I did not let

22

these doleful tales lessen my enthusiasm to complete the journey by truck. I had found that no matter what questions you asked the black man in Africa, he gave you the answers which he hoped would please you. The Europeans we had met in the Congos had seemingly adopted this same custom, the result being that many of their flattering but incorrect reports led us into difficulties which could have been avoided. However, our subsequent experiences in Nigeria proved that when an Englishman gave you information, it was usually accurate.

Jones had repaired the trucks as best he could under the circumstances. We had added a new supply of steel cable and blocks and tackle to our equipment, and early on the morning of June thirtieth left for Rahamma. It had been raining practically all the time of our stay in Jos, but we had hoped to reach this place before nightfall, as our information indicated it was only forty miles distant. We covered the first ten miles easily, but then the fun commenced. The floods had demolished all the bush bridges, and every mile or so it was necessary to erect a new one. About noontime I stopped at a small stream through which we would have to build a bridge of stones. As this would require several hours, I ordered pishi to prepare lunch and then Joe and I started construction work while waiting for the other truck to catch up. When more than an hour passed without it putting in its appearance, we went back to see what was wrong. Upon approaching it, we found Jones and Austin crouched under the rear end with the differential housing open. In reply to my query, Jones said that the wheels refused to revolve, for the simple reason that a rear axle was broken. This, of course, was a minor matter; all we had to do was send for a new one — to Detroit, Michigan! We towed the truck to the stream and established ourselves at what was later named Dismal Camp.

Because some bright individual at the factory had failed to include a wheel puller in the tool kit, it took the balance of the day to remove the broken axle. It was twisted apart, near the gear, and we found, upon inspection, that it had been holding together by a mere thread for a long time.

Next day Jones and I returned to Jos in the other truck, finding that a heavy rain had preceded us, totally wrecking our crude bridges. After toiling for the entire day to negotiate the intervening twenty-seven miles, we had reached the town at dusk. Upon arrival, I cabled my wife, for she had not heard from me for nearly four months, nor I from her. My message said that I was very well, and so I was that evening, but the next morning they carried me to the hospital, with my second bad attack of fever.

Now, after three days, Jones reported that he had fashioned an axle on the lathe at the tin mine; so, although still weak, I accompanied him to Dismal Camp next morning. The balance of the day was spent in refitting the axle and then we found the clutch was broken, making it impossible to change gears. We returned to Jos once more to repair the clutch, and, upon attempting to reach Dismal Camp again, encountered another heavy storm which deluged the plateau, making our last journey long and difficult.

Then came days of misery, of heartbreaking toil; futile hours spent in pouring rain, fighting through oceans of mud; nights of wretchedness beneath dripping skies, sleeping in wet clothes under soggy blankets; days when we worked like mad to get through to Rahamma, expecting to find it around every turn in the trail or over the top of each hill. Storms and floods engulfed us, converting the roads into roaring torrents, the country into an endless sea.

One evening, as darkness neared and the water deepened, Jones was driving ahead while I attempted to follow in his tracks. Without warning, my truck fell into a deep hole near which he had passed. We were in the lowest part of a swamp, with water standing from three inches to two feet deep all over the place. It was soon inky black, and, as further progress was out of the question, I took a gasoline lantern and went in search of a site on which to erect the tent. I often think of this incident, of how I went around with this light in one hand and a stick in the other, measuring the depth of the water, seeking a shallow spot for camp. After searching for an hour in the rain, I found the driest location to be four inches under water, so here we pitched our tent.

We were all wet to the skin and shivering with cold; it was difficult to get a fire started; mosquitoes buzzed around in glee; then, to add to our contentment, we found that the tent was now leaking like a sieve! Sitting on the edge of our cots, with our feet dangling in the flood, we feasted on cold beans and herring, then, removing our boots, crawled beneath wet blankets, where, due to exhaustion, we soon dropped off to sleep.

Next morning we gazed on a cheerless world, for, although the rain had stopped, the sun failed to shine. In the gloomy swamp we slushed around in the mud and water trying to extricate the truck, but without the assistance of fifteen natives who chanced by, we never could have budged it. We had only moved forward a few hundred yards when another rear axle twisted in two, and for the first time on the expedition I was somewhat discouraged. There was nothing to do but leave the crippled truck and attempt to reach Rahamma in the other, which we finally succeeded in doing after a trek that proved to be anything but a pleasure jaunt.

We found the framework of a bridge spanning the river near Rahamma, but without any flooring yet in place. Here I put Joe in charge of the equipment, while Jones and I returned to the other truck. It took us two and one-half days to transport the balance of our goods and tow the disabled truck to the bridge. Meantime Joe had moved us into some large dry huts maintained as rest houses by the government; but we found that the white construction foreman had failed to keep his promise of placing planks across the structure so that we could pass, his excuse being that it was a holiday and the natives refused to work. The truth of the matter was that he had become paralyzed drunk on gin, entirely forgetting to give the native workmen the necessary orders. When the planks were finally provided and the trucks pushed across, we placed the crippled one on a railroad flat car, and, putting Maniki in charge, I dispatched it to Zaria. With the balance of the equipment packed on the remaining truck, we prepared to push through to Kaduna.

On the evening before our departure we were guests of a British officer formerly of the Indian army. He served us with a dish found only in this part of the

world, a "groundnut stew," which consists of a conglomeration of everything in the kitchen, boiled in a
thick soup of peanuts. This concoction is seasoned
with a triple concentrated extract of tobasco sauce and
served piping hot. If the unsuspecting victim sur-
vives the first spoonful, he is considered properly
initiated into the Order of True Nigerians, but the
final diploma of merit cannot be issued until he has
eaten also a "palm-oil chop." This latter mixture can
be approached only in an asbestos suit, and the approved method is to eat this blood purifier on Sunday
afternoon and then, after washing it down with several
glasses of pink gin, go to bed. If all members of the
party are still alive on Monday morning, the "chop"
is considered a huge success.

During the evening Joe told this man of his former
close association with Lord Kitchener and about the
message-in-the-eardrum adventure. The story varied
a great deal from the way he had told it to me, for the
locale was now Persia rather than India, and instead
of an entire army's fate depending on his success, it
was only a regiment or so, and the prize won for England was not India but the Suez Canal! After Joe
had spoken his piece, our host told about some of his
experiences with the Nigerian black men.

It seems the West African native uses his head,
literally if not figuratively, and this officer told of his
frustrated efforts to introduce modern methods among
his black laborers. He had imported some wheelbarrows, and after showing the workmen how they
should be used, felt that he had speeded things up
considerably. Returning later where the men were
excavating, he found them filling the wheelbarrows

with earth all right, but instead of wheeling the load, they placed the barrow and its contents atop their heads and carried it to the dumping place!

On another occasion it became necessary to transport a heavy flywheel for some distance through the jungle. At considerable trouble and expense he had built a four-wheel cart, upon which was loaded the flywheel. Giving instructions to his headman to have this pulled out to a certain location, he proceeded to his headquarters shack. Several days passed without any sign of the blacks and the much needed flywheel, so he went out to look for them, and, after a few hours travel on horseback, beheld what looked like a huge serpent crawling through the bush and upon closer approach he heard the chanting of many men. Coming up to this strange human centipede, he found a whole army of black men bearing upon their heads a cross-work of poles, and on top of this reposed the four-wheeled cart, with the wheels tied to keep it from rolling, and inside the cart was the flywheel!

An Irishman then related how he had sent his house boy after some postage stamps. The boy was gone a long time, as usual, but eventually reappeared, carrying on top of his head a large flat stone weighing about fifty pounds. When asked where the stamps were, he pointed to the stone, saying, "There they be, Master," and calmly lifting this slab of granite, he put it on the floor, with the explanation that the wind kept blowing the stamps off his head, so he had placed the rock there to hold them down!

These things seem foolish to a white man, but their explanation lies in the fact that these Negroes have no pockets, and disdaining to carry anything in their hands, place everything on top of their heads, no matter how small or how big.

Next morning I asked the local weather prophet if he thought we would have a storm that day, to which he replied in pidgin English, "I find 'em, I see 'em, I no look 'em," meaning, of course, that he could not see any storm clouds or other indications of bad weather.

When I went to the railway station to inquire about the transportation of my truck, I found the black man in charge talking over the telephone in Hausa, interspersed with English words. His conversation sounded something like this, "Oh, hello, you there? Blxonkt hubnok fipnoter gullentaken, thanks much, wegoxlop fomergot, call me later, cherrio!"

In one corner of the room a black telegrapher was sending and receiving messages in English, although he could not read or write the language. These men learn the code equivalent of each letter in the English alphabet, being able to send and receive perfectly, although the sense of the message remains a mystery to them.

Hausa is more or less a universal language in Nigeria, but there are many other languages and dialects spoken. In Bauchi Province alone more than sixty-four different tongues are in use. Arabic forms the base for several dialects, but the most picturesque expressions are those uttered in pidgin English. The native Nigerian considers sardines the finest treat obtainable, while kerosene is a wonderful thing because it gives off light; therefore anything excellent is "good past sardines," while anything wonderful is "very good, way past kerosene."

As we again headed westward, we left Joe waving good-by from the rest house, for on the morning of our departure he had come to me with the information that he had secured a good job locally and wished to remain in Rahamma.

At the slow rate we were progressing, I figured it would take another six months to complete the journey to Lagos. There seemed to be a jinx attached to the expedition, and every time an obstacle was overcome, two more sprang up to take its place. The heavy strain was beginning to tell on all of us and, the first night out from Rahamma, Jones was striken with fever. We had arrived at a camp in the bush, the headquarters of an Englishman who was supervising road work. He invited us to stay in his hut, which we were glad to do as it had commenced to rain heavily. During the night Jones took a turn for the worse, making it impossible for us to move on the next day.

On the second morning the sky was badly overcast. Meanwhile I had arranged for Jones to remain at this camp until he felt able to proceed by train to Kaduna via Zaria. I intended to push on with the truck at once, for every hour of delay invited additional misfortune. After all preparations had been made to start, Jones decided to go along with us. We then had to wait two hours while he shaved and otherwise prepared himself for the trail, for if anything happened to him he intended to look his best.

Shortly after leaving this camp, the truck sank into a deep pit of mud and slime, so I dispatched a boy to bring assistance. With the help of forty natives, who responded to our appeal, we managed to get under

way again in five hours, but three miles farther on we
stuck again, and, as darkness was approaching, we
camped on the spot.

Lightning flashed and distant peals of thunder rolled
across the heavens; dark clouds scudded between us
and the moon, and a group of hyenas sang a sorrowful
serenade, their melancholy howling adding a dismal
note to the dreary pitter-patter of the rain. Jones
was very sick during the night and his condition added
to my anxiety; for if the rain should prove a heavy one,
our chances of getting through to the hospital at
Kaduna would be meager.

Only a light shower fell, however, and the morning
dawned clear and bright. The trail was still hard
but almost impossible to follow on account of the high
grass which had overgrown it, making it often appear
as if we had strayed on to the wrong path. It was
providential that the storm of the previous night had
passed around us, for otherwise we would never have
reached Kaduna, the ground over which we sped so
easily needing only one heavy rain to make it an impassable quagmire.

After placing Jones and one of my black boys in
the hospital, I scouted around seeking road information, becoming acquainted with Lieutenant Colonel
Percy Battye, an officer of the Welsh Guards, now
commanding the First Battalion, Nigerian Regiment,
Royal West African Frontier Force. This famous
band of black troops was formed by General Lugard
more than thirty years ago. The four battalions
comprising the regiment are distributed throughout
Nigeria; headquarters being Kaduna, Kano, Calabar,
and Ibadan.

This regiment conquered the German Cameroons during the late war, and then were sent to East Africa for further service. It is remarkable how well these black men are trained. They love the army because of its bright uniforms and glamour, and the fact that it sets them apart from other members of the community. They present a striking and colorful picture in their red tunics, and although bare-footed, this fact seems in no way to detract from their appearance. Most of the men in the ranks are from the Hausa tribes, and the official language of the regiment is Hausa. All natives love music, and this battalion had a band of which they could well be proud. Not a member of the organization could read a note or play an instrument three years previously, but now rendered many difficult military airs with a masterful finish. The Colonel arranged for a parade of the battalion, during which they "trooped the colors," a very impressive ceremony.

After this, we were entertained at mess by the Colonel and his officers, and he told me about an elephant hunt which nearly cost him his life. He had gone out with a friend and, after following the elephant all morning, came upon it at noontime. They tossed a coin to determine which should have the privilege of collecting the ivory, the Colonel winning the toss. After stalking close to the animal he found it was a cow with poor tusks; so, deciding not to molest the elephant, he turned to go, and in doing so tripped over some vines and fell. The cow heard this and charged him. He managed to twist his rifle toward her and, firing when she was twenty feet away, put a heavy bullet through her heart and spine. The huge animal tumbled almost at his feet, pushing several small trees to the ground which pinned him where he lay. It took forty men some time to cut down the trees and pry him loose from this prison, and, although seriously hurt, he was thankful to be alive.

During our days in Kaduna awaiting Jones' recovery, I spent the time in collecting information about the roads to Lagos, and in making a trip to Zaria. After sending a few dozen wires and talking to everyone available, I came to the conclusion that it would be absolutely impossible to motor from Kaduna to Jebba, which lies on the western side of the Niger River. The rains had been almost continuous in the district for some time and the many tributaries of the Niger were of flood proportions and these had to be crossed. The crude bridges had all been washed away and the lowlands were deep under water. It looked like a hopeless task, especially as I had only one truck left and no way of knowing how long it would hold together. Considering these things, and the fact that the members of the expedition were in bad shape physically, I concluded the best method would be to transport everything by rail from Kaduna to Jebba.

Removing an axle from the truck, I proceeded by train to Zaria, there to install it in the disabled truck, which I later drove back to Kaduna. Someone with a genius for writing comic operas should make this railroad journey to Zaria. The station masters are black, as are the conductors and everyone else. There are three classes of passengers: first, second, and third. First class is for whites only, and, as I was the only light-complexioned passenger, they had to haul a special coach for my benefit.

The station was in a great hubbub, the platform swarming with dark humanity. Officious black men in gold-braided uniforms pushed through the common herd, which milled about in a happy but aimless manner. A big black mammy with a six-foot tier of baskets atop her head and a squalling youngster strapped on her back, elbowed her way toward a third-class coach, stopping en route to pay her compliments to an undersized Son of Ham who rudely got in front of her.

Through this clamorous throng, men in flowing robes of bright silks strode toward second-class coaches, followed by seminaked servants carrying their baggage. In this class also rode the black mistresses of white men, and women considered good enough by their native masters to be separated from the rabble.

Most of the coaches were for the accommodation of that tumultuous mob which rushed pell-mell for seats when the guard threw the doors open. After this scramble was over, the station master's first assistant flunkey appeared with a large bell which he swung mightily to and fro, this being the warning that if all present were in favor of the move, the train could proceed. No dissenting votes being heard, the station master expanded his chest like a pouter pigeon and gave a majestic sweep of his arm, and thereupon the train guard blew a shrill whistle. Upon hearing this the engine driver tooted his siren and we were off — for ten miles!

When the dusky conductor came in to get my ticket he asked where I was from, to which I replied, "Mombasa." He wanted to know if it was near Lagos. I tried to explain its location, but he failed to comprehend. However, his ignorance was no greater than that of a white police officer, whom I later met in Lagos. This representative of law and order could not understand how we had arrived in Nigeria without coming through some seaport. When I told him we had entered the country via Maidugari, he wanted to know why the port officials there had failed to make us comply with the immigration regulations.

Our average speed to Riga Chikun was twelve miles an hour, although I believe the train could make better time. Upon our arrival there and also at Birnin Yaro and Farin Rua, we were greeted by the entire population. The train crew mingled with their numerous friends on the platforms, while the station masters, in their rear-admiral's uniforms, paraded for the benefit of the assembled throng. As Zaria is only about forty miles from Kaduna, we finally arrived, and there I went to the house of a friend, Mr. Bostock.

Zaria is a walled city similar to Kano, but I had little time to go sight-seeing; in fact, my zest for such things was at low ebb; besides, most of my visit there was spent in playing host to a bug which took up its quarters in my left ear. After driving thousands of miles through the heart of Bugland in the Congos without any untoward incident, a green and yellow Nigerian insect with fuzzy legs had to choose my ear for its final resting place. While going through its horrible death struggles, it felt the size of a humming bird, but when the doctor finally dislodged it, after two days, we found my visitor to be only a medium-sized bug.

Upon my return to Kaduna we placed both trucks on flat cars and that evening boarded the train for

Jebba, where we arrived the next afternoon. Near the eastern span of the bridge that here crosses the coffee-colored Niger, stands a monument to Mungo Park and his companion who were lost in the Garafiri Rapids a short distance upstream. Up the river towers the famous Ju Ju Rock, which at one time was a place of sacrifice. In the olden days — not so long ago at that — it was a custom at a certain season of the year for the witch doctors to take a young girl to the place of killing and there beat her to death against the rock. Her cries were supposed to pacify the gods of the river and prevent harm coming to the rock, which, in its turn, sheltered the island on which they lived in the middle of the stream, safe from the attacks of fierce surrounding tribes.

Later I attempted to visit this rock, but no reward I could offer would induce the local boatmen to take me there. They said the place was the home of evil spirits and frightful animals. Superstitious tales built up over a long period of time has made of this harmless rock a fearsome place, a haunted region, which is cautiously avoided by all the natives in the district.

It was interesting to know that, although the Niger has its source almost at the Atlantic's edge, it is one of the longest rivers in the world. It rises in French Guinea, back of a small range of mountains which is visible from the Atlantic port of Freetown, Sierra Leone. From there the river flows northeast to Timbuktu in the French Sudan, then, making a huge bend, runs in a general east of south direction until reaching Lokoja, where it turns directly south to pour out of many mouths into the Gulf of Guinea.

On the morning of July twenty-ninth, we left Jebba in my truck, the "Maudie H," for Lagos, leaving Jones behind with "Jacqueline H." My plan was to return him an axle from Lagos which he would install in the disabled truck and then follow. Our route lay through Ilorin, where I replenished my gasoline and Mobiloil supplies at a Vacuum Oil depot. Then we proceeded to Ogbomosho, where the night was spent in an excellent rest house, close to which was an American mission and hospital. One of the doctors, hailing from Virginia, came over to pay us a visit, and we talked far into the night about "the States."

Starting early next morning, we drove hard all day, passing many villages, such as Oyo, and through Ibadan, the largest native town in Nigeria. From there to Abeokuta and onward to Lagos, we traveled a district reminding me of our own Southland. There were savanna lands fringed by lagoons, and we crossed miles of country similar to that about New Orleans. The principal occupation of the natives is the growing of cocoa for export, although, because of the dense population, it is also necessary to raise great quantities of yams, peanuts, and Guinea corn for domestic use.

Late on the afternoon of July 30, 1929, we crept slowly over the narrow bridge that connects Lagos Island with the mainland, and thus completed the first trans-African journey, from East to West, by motor truck through Central Equatorial Africa. The distance from the East Coast was five thousand five hundred forty-five miles, excluding side trips, but we had traversed thirteen thousand two hundred eighty-two miles of veldt, swamp, jungle, mountain, and desert since leaving Mombasa.

Storm over the Niger River. The domelike rock in the distance is the famous Ju Ju Rock.

The end of the trail. One of the trucks on the beach at Lagos, where the Atlantic rolls against the western shores of Africa.

438

Lagos, at last! How thankful I was to know that our land journey was ended; that from here onward someone else would be captain of the ship. Lagos is the chief port of Nigeria, situated on an island lying in the large lagoon formed by the Ogun and other small rivers. It does a large export and import trade, the United States furnishing most of the motor vehicles, kerosene and gasoline, soft lumber, flour, cube sugar, lanterns, canned fish, and canned foods. The exports include palm kernels, palm oil, tin ore, cocoa beans, peanuts, hides and skins, mahogany logs, and raw rubber.

The European section of the city is very beautiful, the more pretentious houses being surrounded by immense grounds containing a great variety of trees and flowering shrubs. The odor from the multitudes of blossoms is something a visitor will not soon forget. Government House faces the channel which leads to the sea and the breezes from the Atlantic temper its spacious corridors. Here I was invited to luncheon by His Excellency, Sir Graeme Thomson, Governor of Nigeria, both he and his gracious wife wishing to congratulate me on the successful completion of our long journey.

The native population consists of a conglomeration of races. You meet those who are still primitive and likeable, but, in contrast to these, there is the black man who apes European ways and has convinced himself that he is a superior being to the white man. Between these two extremes is that large and happy class of natives which forms the backbone of Nigeria, and upon whose shoulders rests, in a great measure, the future progress of this potentially rich country. Most of the natives are supremely happy, having almost attained a heaven on earth, in a country where nature provides lavishly and where their well being is supervised by capable Englishmen who see to it that they always walk forward and never backward.

To me, one of the most interesting things in Lagos was the local newspaper. Its unintentional humor supplied me with many a laugh, the advertisements being especially ludicrous. One man offered for sale: "Biscuits and flour, raincoats and chocolate, Mountain Dew whisky, motor oils and London gin, trunks and fire extinguishers, and other classes of goods! There were others, but the advertisement of a local undertaker topped them all. It was headed in large type:

FRIENDS! COUNTRYMEN!!
FELLOW-CITIZENS!!!

Your Serious Attention Please?
Why!
Why worry!!
Why worry as to how to arrange for Coffin, Veil, Glove, Socks, Shrouds, Hearse, Wreath and Cemetery space or Vault etc. etc. for the burial of your dead!!!

These can be easily supplied within a moment's notice and at very moderate and reasonable price at

Messrs.
A. BANK. ANTHONY & SONS
Sympathetic Undertakers.
Sympathetic to both the living and the dead!!

We were given quarters in the government rest house, which faces the race track. Jones arrived a few days later, and when the party was all together again there was much to talk about and plenty to do. One of the outstanding features of the expedition was the fact that, during all these thousands of miles of trekking through thorn thickets, over rocky hills and across desert sands, we had not had one single puncture or flat tire on either truck, a great tribute to the sturdiness of General Cord Tires, and a record which I doubt ever will be surpassed.

I spent three weeks of intensive effort preparing for our departure. There were passport regulations to attend to, both for ourselves and the boys; items of equipment to be shipped to America, and other odds and ends to be taken care of. It was necessary to arrange for the transportation of my four black boys back to their homes in Nairobi. This I did through the agent for the Woermann Line, who routed them from Lagos to the Canary Islands. They remained three weeks in Las Palmas awaiting the "Adolph Woermann," the same ship that had brought the expedition to Africa, and she carried them direct to Mombasa, where they arrived seventy-six days after leaving Lagos. All this time the intense heat and the fever in my system were sapping my strength and when I finally stepped on board the ship, I seemed to be walking in a daze from which I did not entirely recover until we had been several days at sea.

Before leaving, I took the trucks down to the beach where the white-capped breakers were rolling high upon the sands. It was the end of the trail for them, but their drivers would soon be aboard the white mail ship steaming for what the coasters called "home," sailing back to the noise and hustle, to the unending strife and struggle of the white man's civilization.

As the ship passed the last point of land that juts out into the narrow channel, a company of native soldiers, resplendent in their scarlet jackets, stood at attention, while the buglers sounded the Nigerian farewell. For many of those who heard the notes echo over the water, it would indeed be their last view of that enchanting continent, but as for me, would I never again hear the roar of the surf nor watch the tall palms bend to the breezes of the Slave Coast? I wonder!

A GLOSSARY OF NATIVE AFRICAN WORDS AND EXPRESSIONS

Most of the words occurring in this glossary are Swahili, the language in general use in East Africa. Swahili is a member of the Bantu family of languages and has been influenced to some extent by accretions from Arabic, Hindustani, Persian, and Portuguese. It has a written language and literature of considerable antiquity.

The vowel sounds are remarkable for their purity, are never slurred or combined into diphthongs, nor are they affected to any marked degree by the presence of certain consonants.

a should be pronounced somewhat as in English "far": marked ä.

e as the pure sound in "eh!" (very short): marked ĕ.

i as "ee" in "feet": marked ē.

o as "o" in "go": marked ō (o represents also another sound somewhat as "oe" in "toe," pronounced shortly and without the second half of the English sound).

u as "oo" in "moon": marked o͞o.

The other marks used in this glossary are listed in the following key:

râre, căt, hẽr, mīne, begĭn, côrd, dôg, bûrn, cŭt, ou as in "mound."

A

Ali Ramazan (ä'lē räm'ä-zän), *Arabic*—man's name. Name of the expedition's cook.

B

banda (bän'dä), *Swahili*—hut.

bango (bän'gō), *Swahili*—wart hog.

baraza (bä-rä'zä), *Swahili*—originally "veranda," but now corrupted to mean any large meeting where discussion takes place, from the fact that the natives became accustomed to gathering around the white man's veranda, from the shade of which he dispensed justice.

bardo kidogo (bär'dō kē-dō'gō), *Swahili*—not just yet; after a bit; wait awhile.

baya sana (by'ä sä'nä), *Swahili* —very bad!

Benogie (bĕn-ô'gē), *Ikoma*—name of a small river.

Blangetti (blän-gĕ'tē), *Swahili*—name of a river.

boma (bō'mä), *Swahili*—a thorn inclosure.

bwana (bwän'ä), *Swahili*—master.

Bwana Chai (bwä'nä chĭ), (exception to the rule as given in key, *ai* as English *ī*), *Swahili*—Master Tea.

C

chai (chĭ), (see note above), *Swahili*—tea.

chakula (chu[as in *chuck*]-kōō'-lä), *Swahili*—food.

chakula tiari (chu-kōō'lä [as above] tī-är'ē), *Swahili*—food is ready.

D

dhow (dou'd), *Arabic*—a small sailing vessel.

donga (dŏn'gä), *Swahili*—a grass-filled ravine.

dik-dik (dĭk=dĭk), smallest of the antelopes.

duka (dō'kä), *Swahili*—shop or store.

E

El Moran (l mōr'ăn), *Masai*—warrior.

F

faru (fâr'ōō), *Swahili*—rhinoceros.

Filanen-Gidda (fĭl-ä'nē-ĭn=gĕd'-dä), tribal name.

Filani (fĭl-ä'nē), tribal name.

fisi (fē'sē), *Swahili*—hyena.

fundi (fōōn'dĕ), *Swahili*—skilled workman.

G

gerenuk (gĕr'ä-nōōk), *Somali*—Waller's gazelle.

ghee (ghē), *Hindu*—animal oil.

Gurmeti (gōōr'mĕ-tē), *Swahili*—name of a small river.

H

Hausa (hou'zä), *Hausa*—tribal name.

I

Ifi (ē'fē), *Ifi*—tribal name of pygmies.

Ikoma (ĭ'kō-mä), *Ikoma*—tribal name.

impalla (ĭm-pä'lä), a species of antelope.

Ituri (ē-tŭ'rē), name of forest.

J

jambo (jäm'bō), *Swahili*—a greeting.

Juma (jōō'mä), *Swahili*—a boy's name.

K

kabaka (kä-bä'kä), *Buganda*—ruler.

Kahindi (kä-hĭn'dē), *Swahili*—a boy's name.

kala (käl-lä'), *Swahili*—jackal.

kanga (kän'gä), *Swahili*—guinea fowl.

Kano (kär'nō), name of town.

kanzu (kän'zōō), *Swahili*—flowing white tunic.

karongo (kä-rông'gō), *Swahili*—roan antelope.

kiboko (kē-bō'kō), *Swahili*—hippopotamus.

kidogo (kē-dō'gō), *Swahili*—little; few.

Kilimafeza (kĭl-ä'mä-fĕ-zä), name of mine.

Kilimanjaro (kĭl-ä'mĕn-jä-rō), name of mountain.

Kilindini (kĭl-ĭn'dē-nē), *Swahili*—deep water.

Kio Muren (kē-ō' mōō'răn), *Nandi*—long warrior.

kipande (kē-pän'dē), *Swahili*—card; native's registration certificate.

kipoi (kē'poy), native chair or litter.

Kitchamuli (kĭtch-ä'mōō-lē), name of man.

Kiya Be (kī-ä' bē), name of village.

kongoni (kŏn-gō'nē), *Swahili*—Coke's hartebeest.

kraal (krôl), *South African Dutch*—a stockade.

kuku (kōō'kōō), *Swahili*—chicken.

kuru (kōō'rōō), *Swahili*—water buck.

kutua (kōō-tōō'ä), *Nandi*—lion headdress.

kwanga (kä-wän'gä), *Swahili*—hyrax.

L

Legumukum (lĕg-ä-mōō'kŭm), *N'jemps*—name of district.

long (lông), *Nandi*—shield.

M

Maniki (män-ē'kē), *Wakamba*—name of man.

manyatta (män-yät'tä), *Masai*—thorn-inclosed village.

Masai (mä'sī), *Masai*—name of tribe.

mbogo (m-bō'gō), *Swahili*—a buffalo.

menge (mĕng'gē), *Swahili* — many.

m'kuba (mä-kōō'bä), *Swahili*— big.

Mombasa (mōm-bäs'ä), *Swahili* —name of town.

Momvu (mōm'vōō), *Momvu*— name of tribe.

Moshi (mō'shē), *Swahili* — Smoke: name of a town.

mpofu (m-pō'fōō), *Swahili*— eland.

Musoma (muh-sōō'mä), name of town.

mazuri sana (mōō-zōō'rē sän'ä), —good; very good.

Mvita (mä-vē'tä), *Swahili*— Town of War: name of town.

mwembi (mä-wĕm'bä), *Alulu*— beer.

N

nagana (nă-gä'nă), *South African native name*—a disease transmitted by tsetse fly to live stock.

Nairobi (nī-rō'bē), name of town.

Nandi (năn'dē), *Nandi*—name of tribe.

n'dower (n'dou-ĕr), *Swahili*— medicine.

Ngetuny Siiya (n-ghē'tōō-nē sē'-yä), *Nandi*—Lion's Claw: man's name.

n'goma m'kuba (n'gō-mä mä-kōō'bä), *Swahili*—big dance.

ngotit (n'gōt-ĭt), *Nandi*—spear.

N'jemps kidogo (n'gĕmps kē-dō'gō), *N'jemps-Swahili*— Little N'jemps: name of tribe.

nyanza (nī-ăn'zä), lake.

nyumbu (n-yäm'bōō), *Swahili*— wildebeest.

O

Olaitorio (ō-lē-tōr'ē-ō), *Nandi* —subchief's name.

Onyango (ō-yän'gō), boy's name.

P

paa (pô), *Swahili*—small antelope.

pishi (pē'shē), *Swahili*—cook.

posho (pō'shō), *Swahili*—rations.

punda (pōōn'dä), *Swahili*—donkey.

punda milia (pōōn'dä mä-lē'ä), *Swahili*—zebra.

S

safari (sŭf'fär-ē), *Swahili*—journey; caravan.

Sara Kyabe (sä-rä' kī-ä'bē), name of a tribe.

Serengetti (sĕr-ĕn-gĕt'ē), name of plains in Tanganyika.

Serra Nyiro (sĕr-rä' när'rō), name of a river.

shamba (shäm'bä), *Swahili*— farm; cultivated fields.

shauri (shou'ē-rē), *Swahili*— palaver; council plan; advice.

shenzi (shĕn'zē), *Swahili*—a raw savage.

shoroa (shō-rō′ä), *Swahili*—oryx.

Sienna (sē′ăn-ä), name of district.

simba (sĭm′bä), *Swahili*—lion.

sombe (sōm′bē), *Nandi*—ostrich-feather headdress.

suara (sōō-ä′rä), *Swahili*—Grant's gazelle.

Swahili (swä′hē-lē), *Swahili*—name of a tribe.

swala (swä′lä), *Swahili*—impalla.

swalla (swä′lä), *Swahili* —Thompson's gazelle.

T

Tanganyika (tăn-gän-yē′kä), name of territory.

taya (täy′yä), *Swahili*—oribi.

tembu (tĕm′bōō), *Swahili*—elephant.

tiari (tī-ä′rē), *Swahili*—ready.

Tiki-tiki (tĭk′ē=tĭk′ē), local name for pygmies.

tohe (tō′hĕ), *Swahili*—reedbuck.

topi (tō′pē), species of antelope.

toto (tō′tō), *Swahili*—small boy; baby animal.

Tsavo (sô′vō), name of a river.

tui (chōō′ē), *Swahili*—leopard.

twiga (twēg′ä), *Swahili*—giraffe.

twiga menge (twē′gä mĕng′gē), *Swahili*—many giraffes.

V

veldt (vĕlt), *South African Dutch* —plains or parklike country.

W

Wakamba (wä-kăm′bä), *Wakamba*—name of a tribe.

Wasara (wä′sä-rä), *Wasara*—name of a tribe.

A LIST OF THE PRINCIPAL ANIMALS
MENTIONED IN THE TEXT

A

Abbott's duiker (see duiker)
African buffalo (see buffalo)
African elephant (see elephant)
African lion (see lion)
antelope, roan (*Hippotragus equinus*)............Swahili: *karongo*
One of the largest and most beautiful of the antelopes.
Easily recognizable by its grizzled roan or rufous coat. This
much sought trophy weighs slightly over six hundred pounds.
It is nowhere abundant.

B

Beisa oryx (see oryx)
black rhinoceros (see rhinoceros)
blue duiker (see duiker)
buffalo, African (*Syncirus caffer*) ....Swahili: *mbogo*
There are several races of African buffaloes, ranging from
the great black beast of the Cape to the small red buffalo
found in the Congo. Distinctive features of the typical race
are the enormous helmetlike horns and the shortness of the
face. These animals are among the most ferocious and
vindictive of beasts. Height at shoulder, about five feet.

C

cheetah (*Acinonyx jubatus*)
The cheetah, although resembling a cat, has some things in
common with the dog, its claws not being retractile. This
animal is trained to hunt like a dog and is sometimes called
the hunting leopard. It is considered the fastest of all run-
ners up to four hundred yards. Also found in India and
Persia.

common duiker (see duiker)
common jackal (see jackal)
common water buck (see water buck)
common zebra (see zebra)

D

Defassa water buck (see water buck)
dik-dik (*Rhynchotragus species*) .Swahili: *paa*
These are the smallest of the antelopes. There are many species, the Kenya Colony dik-diks weighing about seven pounds when fully grown.
duiker, Abbott's (*Cephalophus spadix*) . . . . .Swahili: *paa*
duiker, blue (*Cephalophus monticola*) . . . . .Swahili: *paa*
duiker, common (*Cephalophus grimmi*) . . . . .Swahili: *paa*
The duiker family consists of an extensive group of mostly small antelopes confined to Africa. The word "duiker" means "diver" and the animal was so named because of its peculiar method of running. The horns are generally present in both sexes. Some of the larger members weigh about thirty pounds.

E

eland (*Taurotragus oryx*) . . . . .Swahili: *mpofu*
The eland is the largest of all antelopes, a full-grown bull standing as high as six feet at the shoulders. In spite of the great size of these animals, they are exceedingly graceful and often leap over one another while running.
elephant, African (*Elephas africanus*) . . . . .Swahili: *tembu*
The African elephant is distinguishable from the Indian elephant by its greater size and larger ears. They are still abundant in many regions of Central Africa. There is an authentic record of an African elephant which was eleven feet three inches in height and there probably have been larger animals.

F

fringe-eared oryx (see oryx)

G

gazelle, Grant's (*Gazella granti*)................Swahili: *suara*
Next to the tommies, the Grant and subspecies, *G. robertsi*
and others, are the most abundant of the East African small-
game animals. They are considerably larger than the tommie,
standing about thirty-four inches at the shoulder, the male
weighing about one hundred sixty pounds.

gazelle, Thompson's (*Gazella thomsoni*), familiarly known as
"tommie"................................Swahili: *swalla*
The Thompson's gazelle is, without doubt, the most abundant of the smaller game animals in East Africa. They are
fine eating. The males weigh about sixty pounds and the
does about half of that.

gerenuk or **Waller's gazelle** (*Lithocranius walleri*)..Somali: *gerenuk*
This animal is easily recognizable by the great length of its
neck and slender legs. It is in the habit of raising itself on
its hind legs when browsing. Found only in restricted areas.
Height at shoulder, about forty inches; weight, about one
hundred fifteen pounds.

giraffe (*Giraffa camelopardalis*)..................Swahili: *twiga*
There are several local races of the giraffe. The okapi
(*Okapia johnstoni*) belongs to the giraffe family, but, unlike
the larger animal, which prefers parklike country, the okapi
lives in the equatorial forests.

gnu (see wildebeest)

H

hippopotamus (*H. amphibius*)..................Swahili: *kiboko*
A full-grown bull of this semiaquatic animal measures
about four feet ten inches at the shoulder, has a total length
of about fourteen feet, and weighs more than three tons.
Their tusks at one time had great commercial value, being
used in the manufacture of artificial teeth.

hyena (*Crocuta crocuta*)..........................Swahili: *fisi*
The spotted hyena, which abounds throughout East Africa,
is the largest of the three species. They are classified as
Carnivora and, although allied in some respects to the cats,
differ a great deal in the structure of the skull. They have

more teeth than the cats and their claws are nonretractile. Weight, about one hundred seventy-five pounds.

hyrax (*Procavia species*) .... Swahili: *kwanga*
The hyrax, although a very small animal about the size of a rabbit, belongs to the same order, and is classified with, the elephant. They are widely distributed throughout Africa, Arabia, and Syria, some twenty species of them existing. Their weird cry, especially the cry of the tree hyrax, has thrilled many a tenderfoot during his first nights under the African stars.

I

impalla (*Aepyceros melampus*) .... Swahili: *swala*
The impalla is the most graceful of all antelopes. These animals are capable of leaping long distances. The males carry beautiful horns. In the typical species, the height at the shoulder is from about thirty-four to thirty-eight inches, and the weight of the adult animal is from about one hundred thirty to one hundred sixty pounds.

J

jackal, common (*Canis aurens*) .... Swahili: *kala*
There are several species of jackals, including the beautiful silver-backed jackal found in certain districts of Tanganyika. Widely distributed throughout Africa and Asia.

K

kongoni (*Alcelaphus cokei*) .... Swahili: *kongoni*
The natives apply the word "kongoni" to all members of the hartebeest family, but Coke's hartebeest is the one usually meant by hunters when referred to as "kongoni." Color, uniform bright fawn; weight, about three hundred pounds.

L

leopard (*Felis pardus*) .... Swahili: *tui*
The leopard is probably the most widely distributed of all the cats. He ranges through Africa, the Caucasus, Asia

Minor and throughout Asia generally. He is called by many,
names in many languages, but in every part of his vast range
he is known as a bloodthirsty killer. There are records of
leopards weighing as much as one hundred sixty pounds.

lion, African (*Felis leo*)..........................Swahili: *simba*
At one time the lion was widely distributed over certain
parts of Asia. The species is found not only throughout
Africa, but in Mesopotamia, Persia, and a small area in
India. The Indian species(*Felis leo gujratensis*) is distinguished
by its small tawny mane. In Africa this animal has been
classified into a number of geographical races, some now
extinct. The Barbary lion (*Felis leo barbara*) was at one time
common in North Africa and probably still exists in the
Mediterranean littoral. From Senegal a species known as
Felis leo senegalensis extends toward and probably into the
Sudan. In Uganda lives *Felis leo nyanza*. The Kenya
Colony and Tanganyika lion is sometimes referred to as the
Masai lion (*Felis leo massaicus*). In Somaliland there is a
smaller lion (*Felis leo somaliensis*). There is also a *Felis
leo bleyenberghi* in the Belgian Congo and a *Felis leo kamptzi*
in the Cameroons. Freshly killed lions have been weighed,
tipping the scales at five hundred pounds, and although
there may have been specimens weighing more, this is
doubtful, most full-grown beasts probably attaining a weight
of between four and five hundred pounds.

M

mountain reedbuck (see reedbuck)

O

oribi (*Ourebia species*)............................Swahili: *taya*
This small antelope is widely distributed throughout Africa.
Its flesh is very fine eating.

oryx, Beisa (*O. beisa*)............................Swahili: *shoroa*
oryx, fringe-eared (*O. callotis*)..................Swahili: *shoroa*
There are several species of this beautiful antelope, all of
which bear the long, straight horns, with the exception of
Oryx algazel, whose recurving scimitar-shaped horns and

whitish coloring make it a very distinct species. The oryx is supposed to be the unicorn of antiquity. Height, four feet or more at the shoulder; weight, about four hundred fifty pounds.

Q

quagga zebra (see zebra)

R

reedbuck, mountain (*Redunca fulvorufula*)..........Swahili: *tohe*
reedbuck, Ward's (*Redunca wardi*)................Swahili: *tohe*
 The mountain reedbuck is considerably smaller than the Ward's. There are several species widely distributed.
rhinoceros, black (*R. bicornis*)....................Swahili: *faru*
 The black rhinoceros is distinguishable from the white species more because of the prehensile tip to the upper lip than because of any difference in color. It also differs in the form of horns and ears and in the position of the eyes. It is smaller than the white rhino, but even at that a fair-sized beast.
rhinoceros, white (*R. simus cottoni*)................Swahili: *faru*
 At one time this huge beast, the third largest of land mammals, was abundant, especially in the district between the Zambezi and Orange rivers, but has now been exterminated except where rigidly protected. It is the northern species which inhabits the west bank of the Nile River.
roan antelope (see antelope)

T

Thompson's gazelle (see gazelle)
tommie (see gazelle, Thompson's)
topi (*Damaliscus korrigum jimela*)
 Resembles the hartebeest, but is much richer in color, with lyre-shaped horns. Weight, about three hundred pounds

W

Waller's gazelle (see gerenuk)
Ward's reedbuck (see reedbuck)

wart hog (*Phacochœrus œthiopicus*)...............Swahili: *bango*
These members of the pig family are plentifully distributed throughout Africa and are, without doubt, the ugliest of its citizens. Weight, two hundred pounds or a little more; height at shoulder, about thirty inches.

water buck, common (*Kobus ellipsiprymnus*).......Swahili: *kuru*

water buck, Defassa (*Kobus defassa*)..............Swahili: *kuru*
The water bucks and their small allies, the kobs, are widely distributed throughout Africa. There are several species of water buck, all of them being medium-sized antelope, the larger specimens weighing about four hundred pounds.

white-bearded gnu (see wildebeest)

white rhinoceros (see rhinoceros)

wildebeest or **white-bearded gnu** (*C. taurinus albojubatus*)
Swahili: *nyumbu*
This race of wildebeest is common in East Africa. It resembles the American bison while running. Weight, about five hundred fifty pounds.

Z

zebra, common or **quagga** (*Equus quagga*)...Swahili: *punda milia*
The zebra is widely distributed throughout Africa and, although he forms the principal food supply for the *Carnivora* and every man's hand seems to be against him, he still roams the veldt in countless numbers.

24

INDEX

Illustrations are indicated by italic page numbers and map references by *M*.

windmills, 13.
wine at Malaga, 15, 16.
witch doctor, 3.
World War, 9, 18, 33, 44, 377.
Wyoming, 241.

yams, 365, 436.
Yebu, 354.

Zambezi, 3.

Zanzibar, 25, 26, 33; adventure with native of, 383; Sultan of, 23, 25.
Zaria, 425, 432, 434.
zebra, 36, 40, 53, 63, 64, 90, 114, 117, 118, 124, 137, 138, 169, 227, 249, 251, 252, 254, 259, 260, 264, 284, 291, 292; baby, 249, *265*; chief food of Ikoma, 65.
Zeio, 316.
Zulu, 3.